Intersections
Readings in Sociology

General Editors

Ralph B. McNeal, Jr.
University of Connecticut

Kathleen A. Tiemann
University of North Dakota

A Customized Sociology Reader
Compiled by:

Kirsten H. Olsen

Anoka-Ramsey Community College

Department of Sociology

SOC 1111: General Sociology

Director of Database Publishing: Michael Payne
Sponsoring Editor: Robin J. Lazrus
Development Editor: Catherine O'Keefe
Editorial Assistant: Ana Díaz-Caneja
Marketing Manager: Kathleen Kourian
Operations Manager: Eric M. Kenney
Production Project Manager: Jennifer M. Berry
Rights Editor: Francesca Marcantonio
Cover Designer: Renée Sartell

Cover Art: "Apartments in Buenos Aires, Argentina," by Glen Allison, courtesy of PhotoDisc. "Figures," courtesy of Eugenie Lewalski Berg.

Printed in the United States of America

Please visit our website at *www.pearsoncustom.com*
Attention bookstores: For permission to return any unsold stock, contact Pearson Custom Publishing at 1-800-777-6872.

ISBN-13: 978-0-536-37030-3 ISBN-10: 0-536-37030-3

Intersections is now part of the Intersections Collection.

PEARSON CUSTOM PUBLISHING
75 Arlington St., Suite 300
Boston, MA 02116

Preface

The fascination of sociology lies in the fact that its perspectives make us see in a new light the very world in which we have lived all our lives...

Peter Berger

Pearson Custom Publishing and General Editors Ralph B. McNeal, Jr. and Kathleen A. Tiemann are proud to bring you *Intersections: Readings in Sociology*.

Our highest goal in the creation of *Intersections* is that it does, in fact, assist you in capturing that 'fascination of sociology' Peter Berger refers to above and which so many of us, as teachers, want to impart on our students. A traditional way of doing this has been to expose the students to central sociological ideas and examples of sociology in action through a book of readings. While *Intersections* is a reader, it is anything but traditional due to the way it is being provided to you.

With *Intersections*, we have endeavored to provide you with a rich and diverse archive of high quality readings in such a way that both professors and students will have easy and cost-effective access to the minds and ideas that illuminate and help explain some of the central ideas and issues of sociology. Within *Intersections* you will find over 380 readings and 19 topical introductions—both of which will be updated and expanded on a regular basis—from which you can choose only those readings and introductions that are germane to your particular course. No longer will you and your students have to be dependent on the standard large and expensive 'one-size-fits-all' college reader, which often includes more material than will be covered in the course, yet often also lacks those particular pieces that are viewed as essential by individual instructors. In addition, a classification system for each selection provides helpful information on how the selections might be organized to allow the various perspectives on the course to be pursued. Although the primary course for which *Intersections* was developed is the introductory sociology course, the size and quality of the database may also make it a good resource for a variety of other courses such as marriage and family and gender studies.

However it is used, it is our ultimate hope that you will find *Intersections* to be an essential source of readings in sociology—a source noted for its depth, breadth, and flexibility—that meets the highest scholarly and pedagogical standards.

Acknowledgements

A project of this scope cannot be undertaken without the assistance and advice of our colleagues. We wish to thank the following people who helped us tremendously in the development of *Intersections*.

Andrew Scott Ziner (Cedar Crest College) wrote introductions for two sections: "Aging" and "Health & Medicine"; Charles M. Brown (Ohio University) wrote introductions for the "Religion" section; David A. Merrill (University of Wisconsin) wrote introductions for both "Politics & the Military" and the "Work & the Economy" section; and, lastly, Donald Branson (University of Connecticut) wrote an introduction for our readings on the environment ("Population, Communities and the Environment.")

In addition, the project idea and execution was reviewed several times as it was being developed, and each of the following provided valuable feedback and suggestions which strengthened the project: Victor Agadjanian, *Arizona State University*; Kathleen Almquist, *Mesa Community College*; Robert Althauser, *Indiana University*; Andrea Baker, *Ohio University of Lancaster;* Felix M. Berardo, *University of Florida*; Dennis F. Berg, *California State University, Fullerton*; Karen Bourg, *Nashville State Community College*; David L. Brunsma, *University of Alabama, Huntsville*; Russ Buenteo, *University of South Florida*; Thomas Calhoun, *University of Nebraska*; Allison R. Camelot, *California State University, Fullerton*; Lori Campbell, *Ohio State University and Ohio Wesleyan University*; Ralph Cherry, *Purdue University, Calumet*; Ione Y. DeOllos, *Ball State University*; Michael Dreiling, *University of Oregon*; Gregory Elliott, *Brown University*; Morten G. Ender, *United States Military Academy*; Polly A. Fassinger, *Concordia College*; Charles Faupel, *Auburn University*; Celestino Fernandez, *University of Arizona*; Theresa J. Fish, *Lake Superior College;* Lisa Frehill, *New Mexico State University*; Robert Futrell, *University of Nevada, Las Vegas*; Susan G. Greenwood, *University of Maine*; James Hawdon, *Clemson University*; Laura Hecht, *California State University*, Bakersfield; Shirley A. Hill, *University of Kansas*; Amy Holzgang, *Cerritos College;* Robert B. Lee, *Foothill College*; Diane Levy, *University of North Carolina, Wilmington*; Michael Lewis, *Christopher Newport University;* Philip Luck, *Georgia State University*; Kristy McNamara, *Furman University*; Phyllis Myers, *Normandale Community College*; Carrie Uihlein Nilles, *Marshall University*; Milagros Peña, *University of Florida*; Brea L. Perry, *Indiana University;* Karl Pfeiffer, *University of Alaska*; Mary F. Radosh, *Western Illinois University*; Terry Reuther, *Anoka-Ramsey Community College*; John Reynolds, *Florida State University*; Randi Rosenblum, *Hunter College*; Michael T. Ryan, *Dodge City Community College;* Constance L. Shehan, *University of Florida*; Jim Spickard, *University of Redlands*; Sue Spivey, *James Madison University*; John Stolte, *Northern Illinois University*; Peter Taylor, *Colorado State University*; Celeste Watkins, *Northwestern University*; L. Susan Williams, *Kansas State University*; R. Dean Wright, *Drake University*; Mary Lou Wylie, *James Madison University*; Andrew Scott Ziner, *Cedar Crest College*.

Contents

GLOBAL INEQUALITY

RACIAL AND ETHNIC INEQUALITY

STRATIFICATION BY GENDER AND AGE

THE FAMILY AND INTIMITATE RELATIONSHIPS

RELIGION AND EDUCATION

POPULATION, COMMUNITIES, AND HEALTH

GLOBALIZATION, THE ENVIRONMENT, AND SOCIAL CHANGE

Invitation to Sociology

PETER L. BERGER

In this classic essay, Peter Berger gives us a peek at the kinds of people who become sociologists and the things that interest them. He argues that the "fascination of sociology lies in the fact that its perspective makes us see in a new light the very world in which we have lived all our lives." While looking at familiar things in an unfamiliar way is exciting, it can also make us uncomfortable, because it calls into question our previous understandings of the world. Berger's "Invitation to Sociology" reflects a well-known sociologist's passion for the discipline.

... The sociologist . . . is a person intensively, endlessly, shamelessly interested in the doings of men. His natural habitat is all the human gathering places of the world, wherever men come together. The sociologist may be interested in many other things. But his consuming interest remains in the world of men, their institutions, their history, their passions. And since he is interested in men, nothing that men do can be altogether tedious for him. He will naturally be interested in the events that engage men's ultimate beliefs, their moments of tragedy and grandeur and ecstasy. But he will also be fascinated by the commonplace, the everyday. He will know reverence, but this reverence will not prevent him from wanting to see and to understand. He may sometimes feel revulsion or contempt. But this also will not deter him from wanting to have his questions answered. The sociologist, in his quest for understanding, moves through the world of men without respect for the usual lines of demarcation. Nobility and

---

"Invitation to Sociology," by Peter L. Berger, reprinted from *Invitation to Sociology*, 1963, Anchor Books/Doubleday & Company, Inc. pp.1-24. www.randomhouse.com

degradation, power and obscurity, intelligence and folly—these are equally *interesting* to him, however unequal they may be in his personal values or tastes. Thus his questions may lead him to all possible levels of society, the best and the least known places, the most respected and the most despised. And, if he is a good sociologist, he will find himself in all these places because his own questions have so taken possession of him that he has little choice but to seek for answers.

. . . We could say that the sociologist, but for the grace of his academic title, is the man who must listen to gossip despite himself, who is tempted to look through keyholes, to read other people's mail, to open closed cabinets. Before some otherwise unoccupied psychologist sets out now to construct an aptitude test for sociologists on the basis of sublimated voyeurism, let us quickly say that we are speaking merely by way of analogy. Perhaps some little boys consumed with curiosity to watch their maiden aunts in the bathroom later become inveterate sociologists. This is quite uninteresting. What interests us is the curiosity that grips any sociologist in front of a closed door behind which there are human voices. If he is a good sociologist, he will want to open that door, to understand these voices. Behind each closed door he will anticipate some new facet of human life not yet perceived and understood.

The sociologist will occupy himself with matters that others regard as too sacred or as too distasteful for dispassionate investigation. He will find rewarding the company of priests or of prostitutes, depending not on his personal preferences but on the questions he happens to be asking at the moment. He will also concern himself with matters that others may find much too boring. He will be interested in the human interaction that goes with warfare or with great intellectual discoveries, but also in the relations between people employed in a restaurant or between a group of little girls playing with their dolls. His main focus of attention is not the ultimate significance of what men do, but the action in itself, as another example of the infinite richness of human conduct. . . .

In these journeys through the world of men the sociologist will inevitably encounter other professional Peeping Toms. Sometimes these will resent his presence, feeling that he is poaching on their preserves. In some places the sociologist will meet up with the economist, in others with the political scientist, in yet others with the psychologist or the ethnologist. Yet chances are that the questions that have brought him to these same places are different from the ones that propelled his fellow-trespassers. The sociologist's questions always remain essentially the same: "What are people doing with each other here?" "What are their relationships to each other?" "How are these relationships organized in institutions?" "What are the collective ideas that move men and institutions?" In trying to answer these questions in specific instances, the sociologist will, of course, have to deal with economic or political matters, but he will do so in a way rather different from that of the economist or the political scientist. The scene that he contemplates is the same human scene that these other scientists concern themselves with. But the sociologist's angle of vision is different. When this is understood, it becomes clear that it makes little sense to try to stake out a special enclave within which the sociologist will carry on business in his own right. . . . There is, however, one traveler whose path the sociologist will cross more often than anyone else's on his journeys. This is the historian. Indeed, as soon as the sociologist turns from the present to the past, his preoccupations are very hard indeed to distinguish from those of the historian. However, we shall leave this relationship to the later part of our considerations. Suffice it to say here that the sociological journey will be much impoverished unless it is punctuated frequently by conversation with that other particular traveler.

Any intellectual activity derives excitement from the moment it becomes a trail of discovery. In some fields of learning this is the discovery of worlds previously unthought and unthinkable. . . . The excitement of sociology is usually of a different sort. Sometimes, it is true, the sociologist penetrates into worlds that had previously been quite unknown to him—for instance, the world of crime, or the world of some bizarre religious sect, or the world fashioned by the exclusive concerns of some group such as medical specialists or military leaders or advertising executives. However, much of the time the sociologist moves in sectors of experience that are familiar to him and to most people in his society. He investigates communities, institutions and activities that one can read about every day in the newspapers. Yet there is another excitement of discovery beckoning in his investigations. It is not the excitement of coming upon the totally unfamiliar, but rather the excitement of finding the familiar becoming transformed in its meaning. The fascination of sociology lies in the fact that its perspective makes us see in a new light the very world in which we have lived all our lives. This also constitutes a transformation of consciousness. Moreover, this transformation is more relevant existentially than that of many other intellectual disciplines, because it is more difficult to segregate in some special compartment of the mind. The astronomer does not live in the remote galaxies, and the nuclear physicist can, outside his laboratory, eat and laugh and marry and vote without thinking about the insides of the atom. The geologist looks at rocks only at appropriate times, and the linguist speaks English with his wife. The sociologist lives in society, on the job and off it. His own life, inevitably, is part of his subject matter. Men being what they are, sociologists too manage to segregate their professional insights from their everyday affairs. But it is a rather difficult feat to perform in good faith.

The sociologist moves in the common world of men, close to what most of them would call real. The categories he employs in his analyses are only refinements of the categories by which other men live—power, class, status, race, ethnicity. As a result, there is a deceptive simplicity and obviousness about some sociological investigations. One reads them, nods at the familiar scene, remarks that one has heard all this before and don't people have better things to do than to waste their time on truisms—until one is suddenly brought up against an insight that radically questions everything one had previously assumed about this familiar scene. This is the point at which one begins to sense the excitement of sociology.

Let us take a specific example. Imagine a sociology class in a Southern college where almost all the students are white Southerners. Imagine a lecture on the subject of the racial system of the South. The lecturer is talking here of matters that have been familiar to his students from the time of their infancy. Indeed, it may be that they are much more familiar with the minutiae of this system than he is. They are quite bored as a result. It seems to them that he is only using more pretentious words to describe what they already know. Thus he may use the term "caste," only commonly used now by American sociologists to describe the Southern racial system. But in explaining the term he shifts to traditional Hindu society, to make it clearer. He then goes on to analyze the magical beliefs inherent in caste tabus, the social dynamics of commensalism and connubium, the economic interests concealed within the system, the way in which religious beliefs relate to the tabus, the effects of the caste system upon the industrial development of the society and vice versa—all in India. But suddenly India is not very far away at all. The lecture then goes back to its Southern theme. The familiar now seems not quite so familiar any more. Questions are raised that are new, perhaps raised angrily, but raised all the same. And at least some of the students have begun to understand that there are functions involved in this business of race that they have not read about in the newspapers (at least not those in their hometowns) and that their parents have not told them—partly, at least, because neither the newspapers nor the parents knew about them.

It can be said that the first wisdom of sociology is this—things are not what they seem. This too is a deceptively simple statement. It ceases to be simple after a while. Social reality turns out to have many layers of meaning. The discovery of each new layer changes the perception of the whole.

Anthropologists use the term "culture shock" to describe the impact of a totally new culture upon a newcomer. In an extreme instance such shock will be experienced by the Western explorer who is told, halfway through dinner, that he is eating the nice old lady he had been chatting with the previous day—a shock with predictable physiological if not moral consequences. Most explorers no longer encounter cannibalism in their travels today. However, the first encounters with polygamy or with puberty rites or even with the way some nations drive their automobiles can be quite a shock to an American visitor. With the shock may go not only disapproval or disgust but a sense of excitement that things can *really* be that different from what they are at home. To some extent, at least, this is the excitement of any first travel abroad. The experience of sociological discovery could be described as "culture shock" minus geographical displacement. In other words, the sociologist travels at home—with shocking results. He is unlikely to find that he is eating a nice old lady for dinner. But the discovery, for instance, that his own church has considerable money invested in the missile industry or that a few blocks from his home there are people who engage in cultic orgies may not be drastically different in emotional impact. Yet we would not want to imply that sociological discoveries are always or even usually outrageous to moral sentiment. Not at all. What they have in common with exploration in distant lands, however, is the sudden illumination of new and unsuspected facets of human existence in society. . . .

People who like to avoid shocking discoveries, who prefer to believe that society is just what they were taught in Sunday School, who like the safety of the rules and the maxims of what Alfred Schuetz has called the "world-taken-for-granted," should stay away from sociology. People who feel no temptation before closed doors, who have no curiosity about human beings, who are content to admire scenery without wondering about the people who live in those houses on the other side of that river, should probably also stay away from sociology. They will find it unpleasant or, at any rate, unrewarding. People who are interested in human beings only if they can change, convert or reform them should also be warned, for they will find sociology much less useful than they hoped. And people whose interest is mainly in their own conceptual constructions will do just as well to turn to the study of little white mice. Sociology will be satisfying, in the long run, only to those who can think of nothing more entrancing than to watch men and to understand things human.

. . . To be sure, sociology is an individual pastime in the sense that it interests some men and bores others. Some like to observe human beings, others to experiment with mice. The world is big enough to hold all kinds and there is no logical priority for one interest as against another. But the word "pastime" is weak in describing what we mean. Sociology is more like a passion. The sociological perspective is more like a demon that possesses one, that drives one compellingly, again and again, to the questions that are its own. An introduction to sociology is, therefore, an invitation to a very special kind of passion. . . .

Questions

1. According to Berger, what is the role of curiosity in sociological studies?
2. What do sociologists study?
3. Why did Berger argue that sociology can be dangerous? If sociology can be viewed as dangerous, to what extent might sociologists also be viewed as dangerous?
4. What does Berger mean when he says that "things are not what they seem. . . . Social reality turns out to have many layers of meaning. The discovery of each new layer changes the perception of the whole." Provide an example to illustrate Berger's statement.

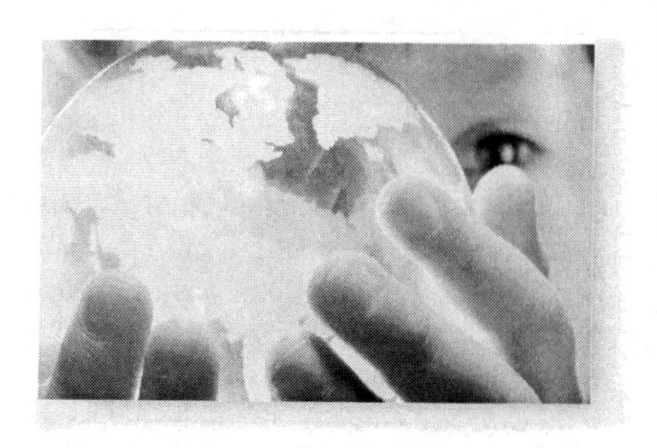

Sociological Perspectives

KATHLEEN A. TIEMANN, GENERAL EDITOR

"The fascination of sociology lies in the fact that its perspective makes us see in a new light the very world in which we have lived all our lives" (Berger, 1963, p. 21).

As the above quotation by Peter Berger suggests, sociology is the study of the everyday world that most people take for granted. Sociologists learn to view the world differently than the average casual observer does. They are curious about everyday life and have an urgent need to understand the forces behind human behavior.

For example, consider the circumstances under which people might help others. Let's say it's ten o'clock at night on a crowded New York City street. Suddenly, a woman screams, "Help! He's got my purse!" You might think that since there are a lot of people around, some of them will help the woman. You might also think that the more people who are around, the less likely it is that a would-be criminal will commit a crime. Surprisingly, however, research done by

John M. Darley and Bibb Latané (1968) showed that these assumptions are actually incorrect. Through a series of experiments, Darley and Latané demonstrated that an individual in need is *less* likely to receive help when many people are around. The reason for this is simple: Bystanders expect that someone else will offer help, so they feel no personal obligation to take action.

Another example is the progress our society has made in overcoming traditional gender-role stereotypes. Many of us would assert that women are no longer seen only as "decorative" objects by men, and that men are no longer measured solely by the size of their wallets by women. Sociologist Simon Davis examined this issue in a study he conducted in 1990. He asked: Do single people today still seek mates that meet traditional stereotypes; i.e., men as "success objects" and women as "sex objects"? To find out, he analyzed the personal ads that appeared in the *Vancouver Sun* newspaper. Surprisingly, he found that despite increased flexibility in gender roles for men and women alike, those who submitted ads to the personals still sought partners who met stereotypical gender-role descriptions.

These and other research results (Darley & Latané, 1968; Davis, 1990) run counter to our common-sense explanations of how the world works. This is why sociology can be both exciting and somewhat unsettling. To make sense of our social world, sociologist C. Wright Mills (1959) argued that social-science researchers (and students) must develop a quality of mind that he called the sociological imagination. As he explained, this frame of mind provides a unique vantage point from which we can view and understand social phenomena. Our sociological imagination helps us grasp how social, historical, cultural, economic, and political factors guide the choices we make, how we perceive and make sense of our world, and how we live our lives. It also reveals that phenomena we interpret as personal troubles may actually stem from larger public issues that affect many people.

Three Perspectives

That said, how do sociologists actually study human social interaction? Unlike casual observers, sociologists design and conduct systematic studies guided by theoretical frameworks. These frameworks not only help them determine what kinds of phenomena to study, they also influence the focus of studies.

The three primary theoretical perspectives that sociologists use are: the structural functionalist perspective, the conflict perspective, and the symbolic interactionist perspective. Each provides a different vantage point from which to understand our social world. Although different in certain key respects, the *structural functionalist perspective* and the *conflict perspective* are macro-theories; that is, they look at society from the viewpoint of social structures. Hence, both of these perspectives allow us to analyze whole societies and social institutions. More specifically, structural functionalists focus on how the various parts of a social system work together so as to support that system's order and stability. In contrast, the conflict perspective sees social order and stability as the results of domination of weaker societal members by more powerful members. From the conflict perspective, while these sorts of social arrangements may create stability, they also spawn division, hostility, and inequality.

In stark contrast to these macro-level orientations, the *symbolic interactionist perspective* is a micro-theory. It lets us concentrate on the more personal, individual aspects of social life. Instead of concentrating on societies and institutions, symbolic interactionists focus on phenomena such as face-to-face interactions and the meanings we give them. Taken together, the three theoretical orientations help us gain a rich, multifaceted understanding of social life.

Sociology in Action: Quantitative and Qualitative Research

Sociologists conduct research on a wide mix of diverse topics. The research method they select hinges on the question they want to answer and the theoretical perspective that has generated the question. Some sociological research is best described as quantitative. That is, the researcher analyzes only those things that he or she can count or otherwise measure.

For example, a quantitative approach made sense for the research done by sociologists Scott J. South and Glenna Spitze (1994). South and Spitze were interested in the amount of time men and women spent on male-typed tasks (mowing the lawn, fixing things), female-typed tasks (cleaning the house, doing laundry), and gender-neutral tasks (paying bills, running errands) around the house. The two researchers learned that, while both male and female study participants spent more time on female-typed tasks, the amount of time they spent on housework and the types of tasks they did depended on their living arrangement. Specifically, never-married men who live with their parents seem to spend more time doing female-typed tasks than doing male-typed or gender-neutral tasks. Such men in this study averaged 15 hours of housework per week. Their female counterparts (that is, never-married women living with their parents) contributed an additional four hours per week. For men, it seems that living at home is a "good deal" because it minimizes the time they spend on household activities. For women, the "best deal" in terms of housework is apparently living with parents, and the "worst deal" is being married. In this research project, married women averaged 36 hours of housework per week, compared to their husbands' 18 hours.

Not all sociological research is quantitative, however. Much of it is qualitative. To grasp the difference between these terms, imagine researching how many *times* someone does something, versus exploring *how* someone does something. Daniel Chambliss (1989) illustrated the contributions of both quantitative and qualitative research when he investigated the differences in athletic performance between Olympic-caliber swimmers and other swimmers. While it may seem easy to explain performance differences by arguing that Olympic-level swimmers are more talented or gifted than other athletes, Chambliss was not satisfied with this common-sense explanation. Instead, he drew on six years of observations he had made of swimmers of diverse levels of ability. He noted that the number of hours practiced (a quantitative measure) between the groups was similar, but that the *way* in which the swimmers practiced (a qualitative difference) was enormous. Specifically, during practice sessions, the technique, discipline, and attitude of the best swimmers differed qualitatively from those of lesser swimmers. For example, Olympic swimmers arrived at practice on time and demonstrated a professional attitude. While at practice, they made every turn, every dive, and every stroke as if they were participating in a live competition. The result was a qualitative difference in performance between the two groups.

The research by South and Spitze (1994), Chambliss (1998) and other sociologists typically focuses on normal, everyday activities. However, sociologists sometimes conduct research under unique, challenging and even dangerous situations. For example, Alice Fothergill (2003) undertook a qualitative, longitudinal study to discover how beliefs about poverty and welfare are affected in the context of a natural disaster. To do so, she interviewed 40 women who survived one of the worst floods in US history. Among other things, Fothergill wondered how women from different social classes would respond to the stigma associated with accepting charity. Contrary to what you might have guessed, she discovered that the upper-middle-class and the lower-class women in the study actually had less trouble coping with the stigma of charity than the working-class and middle-class women. This raised an interesting question: What factors made it possible for these women to accept charity without feeling stigmatized? Fothergill argued that the upper-class women were insulated from this stigma because of their social class and resources. Because the lower-class women had already experienced poverty and understood the structural reasons for it, they did not experience a severe drop in social standing nor did they experience a significant change in their stigmatization. Moreover, Fothergill reveals how these women's experiences as flood victims not only helped them become more sympathetic to other natural disaster victims, but to those who became poor due to the loss of their job or health problems.

A Code of Ethics

Because sociologists study human social behavior, they must take extreme care not to harm their research participants. To help them in this goal, the American Sociological Association (the professional organization for American sociologists) has developed a code of ethics for its members. This code sets the standard for ethical behavior in the profession. For example, it requires researchers to provide their subjects with an "informed consent" form that explains subjects' rights, outlines the purpose of the study, describes how the data collected will be used, states whether the subjects' names and other identifying information will be kept confidential, explains what risks participation in the study may entail, and lists some expected outcomes of the research. Based on this information, a potential subject can make an informed decision about whether to participate in a research project.

No code of ethics can cover every conceivable situation a researcher might encounter, but it can provide fairly comprehensive guidelines. That certainly was true for sociologist Ric Scarce. In 1991, intruders took research animals from a laboratory on the campus of Washington State University and damaged about $100,000 worth of property in the laboratory. At the time, Scarce was a doctoral student in sociology at the university. Two years later, he was called before a federal grand jury to answer questions about his research on the animal-rights movement and animal-rights activists. Scarce refused to release the names of those he had interviewed because he had promised his informants confidentiality. He paid dearly for his adherence to the code of ethics, spending over five months in jail for refusing to comply with the grand jury's request. His professional behavior, however, remained above reproach.

The selections in this book may challenge some of your assumptions about how the world works. In fact, what you read within these pages will likely challenge, disturb, amuse, or surprise you. Whatever you find, be prepared for the impact that you may feel when you begin looking at the world you know—or thought you knew—in a new and different way.

References

Berger, P. (1963). Invitation to sociology: A humanistic perspective. New York: Anchor Books.

Chambliss, D. F. (1989). The mundanity of excellence: An ethnographic report on stratification and olympic swimmers. *Sociological Theory, Vol. 7*, 70-86.

Darley, J.M. & Latané, B. (1968). Bystander intervention in emergencies: Diffusion of responsibility. *Journal of Personality and Social Psychology, Vol. 8*, 377-383.

Davis, S. (1990). Men as success objects and women as sex objects: A study of personal advertisements. *Sex Roles: A Journal of Research, Vol. 23*, 43-50.

Fothergill, A. (2003). The stigma of charity: Gender, class, and disaster assistance. *The Sociological Quarterly, Vol. 44*, 659-680.

Mills, C.W. (1959). *The Sociological Imagination*. New York: Oxford University Press.

South, S.J. & Spitze, G. (1994). Housework in marital and nonmarital households. *American Sociological Review, Vol. 59*, 327-347.

The Nature of Symbolic Interactionism

HERBERT BLUMER

Herbert Blumer describes a theoretical perspective called symbolic interactionism and lays out its three premises. As he explains, "The position of symbolic interactionism . . . is that the meaning that things have for human beings are central in their own right." After you read this article, you will not only know what he means by this statement, but you should be able to apply the symbolic interactionist perspective.

The term "symbolic interactionism" [is] a relatively distinctive approach to the study of human group life and human conduct. . . .

Symbolic interactionism rests in the last analysis on three simple premises. The first premise is that human beings act toward things on the basis of the meanings that the things have for them. Such things include everything that the human being may note in his world—physical objects, such as trees or chairs; other human beings, such as a mother or a store clerk; categories of human beings, such as friends or enemies; institutions, as a school or a government; guiding ideals, such as individual independence or honesty; activities of others, such as their commands or requests; and such situations as an individual encounters in his daily life. The second premise is that the meaning of such things is derived from, or arises out of, the social interaction that one has with one's fellows. The third premise is that these meanings are handled in, and modified through, an interpretative process

---

"The Nature of Symbolic Interactionism," by Herbert Blumer, reprinted from *Symbolic Interactionism: Perspective and Method,* 1969. pp. 1-5.

used by the person in dealing with the things he encounters. I wish to discuss briefly each of these three fundamental premises.

It would seem that few scholars would see anything wrong with the first premise—that human beings act toward things on the basis of the meanings which these things have for them. Yet, oddly enough, this simple view is ignored or played down in practically all of the thought and work in contemporary social science and psychological science. Meaning is either taken for granted and thus pushed aside as unimportant or it is regarded as a mere neutral link between the factors responsible for human behavior and this behavior as the product of such factors. We can see this clearly in the posture of psychology and science today. Common to both of these fields is the tendency to treat human behavior as the product of various factors that play upon human beings; concern is with the behavior and with the factors regarded as producing them. Thus, psychologists turn to such factors as stimuli, attitudes, conscious or unconscious motives, various kinds of psychological inputs, perception and cognition, and various features of personal organization to account for given forms or instances of human conduct. In a similar fashion sociologists rely on such factors as social position, status demands, social roles, cultural prescriptions, norms and values, social pressures, and group affiliation to provide such explanations. In both such typical psychological and sociological explanations the meanings of things for the human beings who are acting are either bypassed or swallowed up in the factors used to account for their behavior. If one declares that the given kinds of behavior are the result of the particular factors regarded as producing them, there is no need to concern oneself with the meaning of the things toward which human beings act; one merely identifies the initiating factors and the resulting behavior. Or one may, if pressed, seek to accommodate the element of meaning by lodging it in the initiating factors or by regarding it as a neutral link intervening between the initiating factors and the behavior they are alleged to produce. In the first of these latter cases the meaning disappears by being merged into the initiating or causative factors; in the second case meaning becomes a mere transmission link that can be ignored in favor of the initiating factors.

The position of symbolic interactionism, in contrast, is that the meanings that things have for human beings are central in their own right. To ignore the meaning of the things toward which people act is seen as falsifying the behavior under study. To bypass the meaning in favor of factors alleged to produce the behavior is seen as a grievous neglect of the role of meaning in the formation of behavior.

The simple premise that human beings act toward things on the basis of the meaning of such things is much too simple in itself to differentiate symbolic interactionism—there are several other approaches that share this premise. A major line of difference between them and symbolic interactionism is set by the second premise, which refers to the source of meaning. There are two well-known traditional ways of accounting for the origin of meaning. One of them is to regard meaning as being intrinsic to the thing that has it as being a natural part of the objective makeup of the thing. Thus, a chair is clearly a chair in itself, a cow a cow, a cloud a cloud, a rebellion a rebellion, and so forth. Being inherent in the thing that has it, meaning needs merely to be disengaged by observing the objective thing that has the meaning. The meaning emanates, so to speak, from the thing and as such there is no process involved in its formation; all that is necessary is to recognize the meaning that is there in the thing. It should be immediately apparent that this view reflects the traditional position of "realism" in philosophy—a position that was widely held and deeply entrenched in the social and psychological sciences. The other major traditional view regards "meaning" as a psychical accretion brought to the thing by the person for whom the thing has meaning. This psychical accretion is treated as being an expression of constituent elements of the person's psyche, mind, or psychological organization. The constituent elements are such things as sensations, feelings, ideas, memories, motives, and attitudes. The meaning of a thing is but the expression of the given psychological elements that are brought into play in connection with the perception of the thing; thus one seeks to explain the meaning of a thing by isolating the particular psychological elements that produce the meaning. One sees this in the somewhat ancient and classical psychological practice of analyzing the meaning of an object by identifying the sensations that enter into perception of that object; or in the contemporary practice of tracing the meaning of a thing, such as let us say prostitution, to the attitude of the person who views it. This lodging of the meaning of things in psychological elements limits the processes of the formation of meaning to whatever processes are involved in arousing and bringing together the given psychological elements that produce the meaning. Such processes are psychological in nature, and include perception, cognition, repression, transfer of feelings, and association of ideas.

Symbolic interactionism views meaning as having a different source than those held by the two dominant views just considered. It does not regard meaning as emanating from the intrinsic makeup of the thing that has meaning, nor does it see meaning as arising through a coalescence of psychological elements in the person. Instead, it sees meaning as arising in the process of interaction between people. The meaning of a thing for a person grows out of the ways in which other persons act toward the person with regard to the thing. Their actions operate to define the thing for the person. Thus, symbolic interactionism sees meanings as social products, as creations that are formed in and through the defining activities of people as they interact. This point of view gives symbolic interactionism a very distinctive position, with profound implications that will be discussed later.

The third premise mentioned above further differentiates symbolic interactionism. While the meaning of things is formed in the context of social interaction and is derived by the person from that interaction, it is a mistake to think that the use of meaning by a person is but an application of the meaning so derived. This mistake seriously mars the work of many scholars who otherwise follow the symbolic interactionist approach. They fail to see that the use of meanings by a person in his action involves an interpretative process. In this respect they are similar to the adherents of the two dominant views spoken of above—to those who lodge meaning in the objective makeup of the thing that has it and those who regard it as an expression of psychological elements. All three are alike in viewing the use of meaning by the human being in his action as being no more than an arousing and application of already established meanings. As such, all three fail to see that the use of meanings by the actor occurs through *a process of interpretation.* This process has two distinct steps. First, the actor indicates to himself the things toward which he is acting; he has to point out to himself the things that have meaning. The making of such indications is an internalized social process in that the actor is interacting with himself. This interaction with himself is something other than an interplay of psychological elements; it is an instance of the person engaging in a process of communication with himself. Second, by virtue of this process of communicating with himself, interpretation become a matter of handling meanings. The actor selects, checks, suspends, regroups, and transforms the meanings in the light of the situation in which he is placed and the direction of his action. Accordingly, interpretation should not be regarded as a mere automatic application of established meanings but as a formative process in which meanings are used and revised as instruments for the guidance and formation of action. It is necessary to see that meanings play their part in action through a process of self-interaction.

. . .

Questions

1. What is symbolic interactionism?

2. What are the three premises of symbolic interactionism?

3. Blumer argues that "Symbolic interactionism sees meaning as social products, as creations that are formed in and through the defining activities of people as they interact." What does he mean by this statement?

4. How is a symbolic interactionist approach different from a psychological approach to social phenomenon?

5. Blumer said that "The position of symbolic interactionism...is that the meaning that things have for human beings are central in their own right." Provide an example that illustrates what he means by this statement.

6. What kinds of things would a symbolic interactionist study? Give an example and explain why it is appropriately studied from this perspective.

The Sociologist as Rubbernecker: Photographing the Aftermath of the Red River Valley Flood of 1997

MORTEN G. ENDER, CAROL A. HAGEN, CLIFFORD HAGEN, JR., CORINA A. MORENO-ENDER, AND KATHLEEN A. TIEMANN

Lay-people often wonder how and why sociologists study the things that they do. This article addresses these questions. It also clarifies the difference between journalistic and sociological studies of current events such as floods, wars, or school violence. Finally, the authors show how creative researchers must be in order to study challenging, dangerous, and brief social phenomena.

Curiosity Knocks

For the average American, seeing is believing. We are a visually oriented society, fascinated by spectacle. Extraordinary public events are

---

"The Sociologist as Rubbernecker: Photographing the Aftermath of the Red River Valley Flood of 1997," Morten G. Ender, et al., reprinted from *North Dakota Quarterly*, Vol. 65, No. 4, 1998. pp. 276–285.

routinely captured visually and become emblazoned in our collective memories. These images come to us primarily via mass media—through newspapers, magazines, radio, and television—as people, close enough to bear witness, share their stories and pictures with others. The term *rubberneck* can be used to describe people who bear witness to a spectacle. This term is also applicable to those who walked and drove through the devastated neighborhoods of Grand Forks, North Dakota, and East Grand Forks, Minnesota, after the Red River Valley Flood of 1997. *Webster's New World Dictionary* defines a rubberneck as "a person who stretches his [sic] head to gaze about in curiosity . . ." (Neufeldt, 1988:1172). The key word in this definition is curiosity, especially as it relates to interest about an atypical event.

For those unable to bear witness, the journalist becomes a conduit between the interested public and an event. The journalist finds the story, provides facts about the event, and relates it verbally and visually to us, the public. Indeed, the visual evidence of "being there" is not only saved for posterity through journalistic efforts, but it allows us to participate in the historical event with others. But we are sociologists, not journalists. Therefore, our curiosity motivated us to go beyond bearing witness, to the spectacle of the flood, to analyze it systematically.

Sociological Curiosity

Unlike the layperson or the journalist, a sociologist is a rubbernecker with a plan. Sociologists are concerned with more than witnessing an event of historical or cultural significance and perhaps documenting it via amateur video or in still photographs. We do not simply provide some human-interest feature for others to functionally gauge their own experience on some subjective or objective level. We analyze, interpret, put into perspective, and focus on the interrelationships among the phenomena. For example, Laud Humphreys taught us a great deal about deviance by becoming an observer of the sexual encounters that occurred between men in pubic restrooms during the 1960s (Humphreys 1989). He took voyeurism to a higher level and connected his findings to deviance in general. The result was the eradication of many stereotypes about the kinds of men who engaged in sexual encounters in public restrooms. Some social situations, such as those described by Humphreys, do not allow us to use the traditional "scientific" methods where we test theoretically driven hypotheses in a fairly controlled environment.

Sometimes, sociologists must simply jump into the fray. A classic example serves as illustration. In his award-winning book, *Everything in Its Path: Destruction of Community Following the Buffalo Creek Flood,* uncovering prolonged trauma that followed a flash flood in West Virginia, sociologist Kai Erikson notes that some situations are too pressing to allow for objective social science, at least early on in a project. As he put it, ". . . traditional methods of sociology do not really equip one to study discrete moments in the flow of human experience" (1976:13).

So too is our experience. We sought to put into sociological perspective the events that unfolded after the flood of the Red River Valley during the spring and summer of 1997. The immediacy of the flood, our personal experiences and losses from the flood, our professional training, and our penchant for inquisitiveness brought us together in an attempt to understand how the flood affected residents of Grand Forks and East Grand Forks. The photographs that accompany this article are part of a larger project that focuses on the graffiti that emerged on houses, personal effects, and sign boards after the flood (see Hagen, Ender, Tiemann, & Hagen, 1998). We had to capture this graffiti quickly as we anticipated its removal within a few short weeks from the berms and when the condemned homes on which it appeared would be demolished. Our curiosity got the best of us. We moved beyond the sensation of the river which flowed over our community and pursued our interests and the serendipitous set of patterns that emerged: a flood, rural America, and graffiti formed an unprecedented dalliance.

The Red River and Spray Paint

The residents of the Red River Valley aren't the first to experience people craning their necks for a view of their disaster. Smith and Belgrave (1995), in their study of people's accounts following Hurricane Andrew in Florida, document rubbernecking:

> The enormity and extent of the hurricane damage was an irresistible draw. The appearance in devastated areas of empty-handed voyeurs added indignity to the pain of those living there, creating resentment. As Rachel [an interviewee] observed, "I felt really invaded. I was angry at these assholes out there, knowing that if they are out there looking at us, they didn't lose anything." Individuals and families in their automobiles gawking at the misery of others for their own entertainment and the continual helicopters . . . were also a part of the problem. (255)

HOME
SWEET
HOME

GO HOME

Because we are aware of how people felt about the rubberneckers, this essay is our attempt to let the "Rachels" and other Greater Grand Forks community members know that we were not all empty-handed gawkers. Ours was not idle curiosity about a spectacle; we had a plan. Therefore, we want to return, in a small part, some of the words and sentiments of those who survived the flood. We did not steal away your experience with our cameras, we tried to make some sense of it for others and for ourselves.

The Art and Science of Rubbernecking

We combed the streets of Greater Grand Forks on foot, by bicycle, and by car for a number of months after the flood, and we took photographs of murals, of the debris on berms and houses, and of graffiti. We canvassed neighborhoods at various times of the day and night. At times, we felt obtrusive and tried to document the results of the

4 Sale
(AS IS)
make offer
ThE VELVEETA BOX
NO warranty

flood unobtrusively to avoid causing additional pain to those who had already suffered losses. To diffuse situations and manage impressions, one of the authors and his one-year-old son rode their bicycle into some neighborhoods and took pictures figuring that people would be less likely to get angry at a parent on a bicycle with a child in tow who was taking photographs than at people locked inside their cars who cruised by slowly, snapping pictures. After a short while, we became more comfortable as we took photographs. Sometimes people invited us to photograph their personal tragedy and even posed next to the debris that had previously been part of their lives.

We took over 150 slides and collected 290 instances of graffiti from neighborhoods in Grand Forks and East Grand Forks. We found graffiti on homes, garages, and household items such as washers, dryers, refrigerators, freezers, ranges, couches, chairs, hot water heaters, pieces of insulation, buckets, a stove top, and sign-boards. Graffiti was written mostly with spray paint, but sometimes with mud.

Because we are interested in making sense of the flood and the graffiti that appeared after the flood, we read what other researchers had to say about graffiti. This research helped us develop a procedure to study disaster graffiti as a new and singular form of public graffiti. Because they were most helpful in categorizing what we found, we relied heavily upon previously published studies that examined graffiti in public restrooms. We began with 19 subcategories of graffiti and collapsed them into five categories that better organized the data. The final categories included different types of humor, various forms of social and political commentary, statements of frustration, crude drawings, and other miscellaneous forms of graffiti. We have included some examples on the preceeding pages. We hope that our efforts may help readers understand how sociological rubbernecking can help make sense of the artifacts that remain after a devastating event like a flood. Additionally, we hope our efforts have piqued your curiosity about new ways to look at the world.

References

Erikson, K. T. (1976). *Everything in its path: Destruction of community at buffalo creek.* New York: Simon & Schuster.

Ender, M. G., Hagen, C., Hagen, Jr., C. O., & Tiemann, K. A. (1998). Graffiti on the great plains: A social reaction to the red river valley flood of 1997. Paper presented at the Annual Meetings of the American Sociological Association, San Francisco, CA.

Humphreys, L. (1989). The sociologist as voyeur. *Field: Readings on the Field Research Experience,* (126–33). (Eds). C. D. Smith & W. Kornblum. New York: Praeger.

Neufeldt, V., (Ed.) (1988). *Webster's new world dictionary of English.* New York: Simon & Schuster.

Smith, K. J., & Belgrave, L. L. (1995). The reconstruction of everyday life: Experiencing Hurricane Andrew. *Journal of Contemporary Ethnography*, 24(3), 244–69.

Questions

1. What is a "rubbernecker"? Provide an example of a situation in which you were a rubbernecker.

2. How do journalistic studies differ from sociological studies?

3. Some individuals in Grand Forks and East Grand Forks thought that Ender and his colleagues were rubberneckers. What would you say to these residents to help them understand Enders' and his colleagues' intent?

4. Why did the researchers feel uncomfortable documenting the destruction caused by the flood? How would you have felt if you were in their place? What did the researchers do to overcome this problem? What else might they have tried?

5. What methods did the researchers use to study the aftermath of the flood? In your opinion, were these methods useful? What other approaches could the researchers have taken to learn about people's experiences with the flood?

Sense and Nonsense about Surveys

HOWARD SCHUMAN

While many people have had experiences as research subjects, few have had the necessary training to adequately interpret the results reported by the popular media. How, then, can people tell "good" research from "bad" research? In this selection, Howard Schuman offers basic guidelines for evaluating the strength and interpreting the results of surveys and polls.

Surveys draw on two human propensities that have served us well from ancient times. One is to gather information by asking questions. The first use of language around 100,000 years ago may have been to utter commands such as "Come here!" or "Wait!" Questions must have followed soon after: "Why?" or "What for?" From that point, it would have been only a short step to the use of interrogatives to learn where a fellow hominid had seen potential food, a dangerous animal, or something else of importance. Asking questions continues to be an effective way of acquiring information of all kinds, assuming of course that the person answering is able and willing to respond accurately.

The other inclination, learning about one's environment by examining a small part of it, is the sampling aspect of surveys. A taste of something may or may not point to appetizing food. A first inquiry to a stranger, a first glance around a room, a first date—each is a sample of sorts, often used to decide whether it is wise to proceed further. As with questions, however, one must always be aware of the possibility that the sample may not prove adequate to the task.

Sampling: How Gallup Achieved Fame

Only within the past century—and especially in the 1930s and 1940s—were major improvements made in the sampling process that allowed the modern survey to develop and flourish. A crucial change involved recognition that the value of a sample comes not simply from its size but also from the way it is obtained. Every serious pursuit likes to have a morality tale that supports its basic beliefs: witness Eve and the apple in the Bible or Newton and his apple in legends about scientific discovery. Representative sampling has a marvelous morality tale also, with the additional advantage of its being true.

The story concerns the infamous *Literary Digest* poll prediction—based on 10 million questionnaires sent out and more than two million received back—that Roosevelt would lose decisively in the 1936 presidential election. At the same time, George Gallup, using many fewer cases but a much better method, made the more accurate prediction that FDR would win. Gallup used quotas in choosing respondents in order to represent different economic strata, whereas the *Literary Digest* had worked mainly from telephone and automobile ownership lists, which in 1936 were biased toward wealthy people apt to be opposed to Roosevelt. (There were other sources of bias as well.) As a result, the *Literary Digest* poll disappeared from the scene, and Gallup was on his way to becoming a household name.

Yet despite their intuitive grasp of the importance of representing the electorate accurately, Gallup and other commercial pollsters did not use the probability sampling methods that were being developed in the same decades and that are fundamental to social science surveys today. Probability sampling in its simplest form calls for each person in the population to have an equal chance of being selected. It can also be used in more complex applications where the chances are deliberately made to be unequal, for example, when oversampling a minority group in order to study it more closely; however, the chances of being selected must still be known so that they can later be equalized when considering the entire population.

Intuitions and Counterintuitions about Sample Size

Probability sampling theory reveals a crucial but counterintuitive point about sample size: the size of a sample needed to accurately estimate a value for a population depends very little on the size of the population. For example, almost the same size sample is needed to estimate, with a given degree of precision, the proportion of left-handed people in the United States as is needed to make the same estimate for, say, Peoria, Illinois. In both cases a reasonably accurate estimate can be obtained with a sample size of around 1,000. (More cases are needed when extraordinary precision is called for, for example, in calculating unemployment rates, where even a tenth of a percent change may be regarded as important.)

The link between population size and sample size cuts both ways. Although huge samples are not needed for huge populations like those of the United States or China, a handful of cases is not sufficient simply because one's interest is limited to Peoria. This implication is often missed by those trying to save time and money when sampling a small community.

Moreover, all of these statements depend on restricting your interest to overall population values. If you are concerned about, say, left-handedness among African Americans, then African Americans become your population, and you need much the same sample size as for Peoria or the United States.

Who is Missing?

A good sample depends on more than probability sampling theory. Surveys vary greatly in their quality of implementation, and this variation is not captured by the "margin of error" plus/minus percentage figures that accompany most media reports of polls. Such percentages reflect the size of the final sample, but they do not reveal the sampling method or the extent to which the targeted individuals or households were actually included in the final sample. These details are at least as important as the sample size.

When targeted members of a population are not interviewed or do not respond to particular questions, the omissions are a serious problem if they are numerous and if those missed differ from those who are interviewed on the matters being studied. The latter difference can seldom be known with great confidence, so it is usually desirable to keep omissions to a minimum. For example, sampling from telephone directories is undesirable because it leaves out those with unlisted telephones, as well as those with no telephones at all. Many survey reports are based on such poor sampling procedures that they may not deserve to be taken seriously. This is especially true of reports based on "focus groups," which offer lots of human interest but are subject to vast amounts of error. Internet surveys also cannot represent the general population adequately at present, though this is an area where some serious attempts are being made to compensate for the inherent difficulties.

The percentage of people who refuse to take part in a survey is particularly important. In some federal surveys, the percentage is small, within the range of 5 to 10 percent. For even the best non-government surveys, the refusal rate can reach 25 percent or more, and it can be far larger in the case of poorly executed surveys. Refusals have risen substantially from earlier days, becoming a major cause for concern among serious survey practitioners. Fortunately, in recent years research has shown that moderate amounts of nonresponse in an otherwise careful survey seem in most cases not to have a major effect on results. Indeed, even the *Literary Digest*, with its abysmal sampling and massive nonresponse rate, did well predicting elections before the dramatic realignment of the electorate in 1936. The problem is that one can never be certain as to the effects of refusals and other forms of nonresponse, so obtaining a high response rate remains an important goal.

Calling Spirits from the Vasty Deep

Two characters in Shakespeare's *Henry IV* illustrate a pressing problem facing surveys today:

> Glendower: I can call spirits from the vasty deep.
> Hotspur: Why, so can I, or so can any man; But will they come when you do call for them?

New impediments such as answering machines make contacting people more difficult, and annoyance with telemarketing and other intrusions discourages people from becoming respondents. The major academic survey organizations invest significant resources in repeatedly calling people and also in trying to persuade people to be interviewed. Thus far response rates for leading surveys have suffered only a little, but other organizations more limited by time and costs have seen rates plummet.

Fortunately, research about the effect of nonresponse on findings has increased. Two recent articles in *Public Opinion Quarterly* report surprisingly small differences in results from surveys with substantial differences in response rates. One study focuses on the University of Michigan's Survey of Consumers and finds that the number of calls required to complete a single interview doubled from 1979 to 1996. However, controlling for major social background characteristics, the authors also report that stopping calls earlier and making fewer attempts to convert refusals would have had little effect on a key measure, the Index of Consumer Sentiments. In a second study researchers conducted two basically similar surveys: one accepted a 36 percent response rate to conserve time and money; the other invested additional time and resources to obtain a 61 percent response rate. On a wide range of attitude items, the researchers found few noteworthy differences in outcomes due to the large difference in response rates.

It is important to keep in mind that bias due to nonresponse will occur only if non-respondents differ from respondents on the measures of interest and in ways that cannot be controlled statistically. Thus, while high response rates are always desirable in principle, the actual effects of nonresponse call for careful empirical research, not dogmatic pronouncements.

Questions about Questions

Since survey questions resemble the questions we ask in ordinary social interaction, they may seem less problematic than the counterintuitive and technical aspects of sampling. Yet survey results are every bit as dependent on the form, wording and context of the questions asked as they are on the sample of people who answer them.

No classic morality tale like the *Literary Digest* fiasco highlights the question-answer process, but an example from the early days of surveys illustrates both the potential challenges of question writing and the practical solutions.

In 1940 Donald Rugg asked two slightly different questions to equivalent national samples about the general issue of freedom of speech:

- Do you think the United States should forbid public speeches against democracy?
- Do you think the United States should allow public speeches against democracy?

Taken literally, forbidding something and not allowing something have the same effect, but clearly the public did not view the questions as identical. Whereas 75 percent of the public would not allow such speeches, only 54 percent would forbid them, a difference of 21 percentage points. This finding was replicated several times in later years, not only in the United States but also (with appropriate translations) in Germany and the Netherlands. Such "survey-based experiments" call for administering different versions of a question to random subsamples of a larger sample. If the results between the subsamples differ by more than can be easily explained by chance, we infer that the difference is due to the variation in wording.

In addition, answers to survey questions always depend on the form in which a question is asked. If the interviewer presents a limited set of alternatives, most respondents will choose one, rather than offering a different alternative of their own. In one survey-based experiment, for example, we asked a national sample of Americans to name the most important problem facing the country. Then we asked a comparable sample a parallel question that provided a list of four problems from which to choose the most important; this list included none of the four problems mentioned most often by the first sample but instead provided four problems that had been mentioned by fewer than 3 percent of the earlier respondents. The list question also invited respondents to substitute a different problem if they wished (see Table 1). Despite the invitation, the majority of respondents (60 percent) chose one of the rare problems offered, reflecting their reluctance to go outside the frame of reference provided by the question. The form of a question provides the "rules of the game" for respondents, and this must always be kept in mind when interpreting results.

Other difficulties occur with survey questions when issues are discussed quite generally, as though there is a single way of framing them and just two sides to the debate. For example, what is called "the abortion issue" really consists of different issues: the reasons for an abortion, the trimester involved and so forth. In a recent General Social Survey, nearly 80 percent of the national sample supported legal abortion in the case of "a serious defect in the baby," but only 44 percent supported it "if the family has a low income

TABLE 1 *Experimental Variation Between Open and Closed Questions*

A. Open Question	B. Closed Question
"What do you think is the most important problem facing this country today [1986]?"	"Which of the following do you think is the most important problem facing this country today [1986]—the energy shortage, the quality of public schools, legalized abortion, or pollution—or, if you prefer, you may name a different problem as most important." 1. Energy shortage. 2. Quality of public schools. 3. Legalized abortion. 4. Pollution.

Adapted from: H. Schuman and J. Scott, "Problems in the Use of Survey Questions to Measure Public Opinion," *Science* v. 236, pp. 957-959, May 22, 1987.

In a survey experiment, less than 3% of the 171 respondents asked the question on the left volunteered one of the four problems listed on the right. Yet, 60% of the 178 respondents asked the question on the right picked one of those four answers.

and cannot afford any more children." Often what is thought to be a conflict in findings between two surveys is actually a difference in the aspects of the general issue that they queried. In still other cases an inconsistency reflects a type of illogical wish fulfillment in the public itself, as when majorities favor both a decrease in taxes and an increase in government services if the questions are asked separately.

Solutions to the Question Wording Problem

All these and still other difficulties (including the order in which questions are asked) suggest that responses to single survey questions on complex issues should be viewed with considerable skepticism. What to do then, other than to reject all survey data as unusable for serious purposes? One answer can be found from the replications of the forbid/allow experiment above: Although there was a 21 percentage points difference based on question wording in 1940 and a slightly larger difference (24 percentage points) when they experiment was repeated some 35 years later, both the forbid and the allow wordings registered similar declines in Americans' intolerance of speeches against democracy (see Figure 1). No matter which question was used—as long as it was the same one at both times—the conclusion about the increase in civil libertarian sentiments was the same.

More generally, what has been called the "principle of form-resistant correlations" holds in most cases: if question wording (and meaning) is kept constant, differences over time, differences across educational levels, and most other careful comparisons are not seriously affected by specific question wording. Indeed, the distinction between results for single questions and results based on comparisons or associations holds even for simple factual inquiries. Consider, for example, a study of the number of rooms in American houses. No God-given rule states what to include when counting the rooms in a house (bathrooms? basements? hallways?); hence the average number reported for a particular place and time should not be treated as an absolute truth. What we can do, however, is try to apply the same definitions over time, across social divisions, even across nations. That way, we gain confidence in the comparisons we make—who has more rooms than who, for example.

We still face the task of interpreting the meaning of questions and of associations among questions, but that is true in all types of research. Even

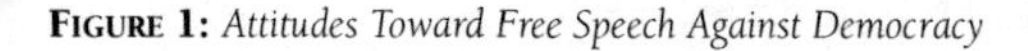

Figure 1: *Attitudes Toward Free Speech Against Democracy*

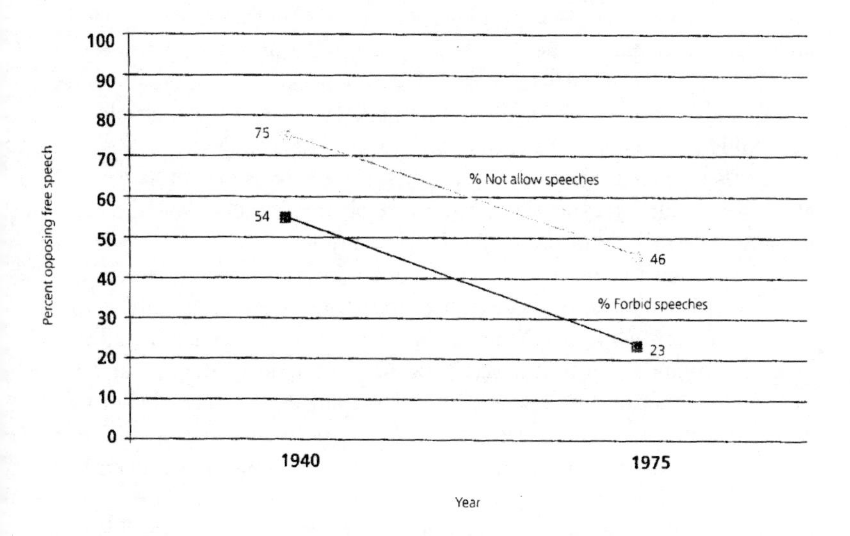

an index constructed from a large number of questions on the basis of a sophisticated statistical calculation called factor analysis inevitably requires the investigator to interpret what it is that he or she has measured. There is no escaping this theoretical challenge, fundamental to all research, whether using surveys or other methods such as field observations.

Survey researchers should also ask several different questions about any important issue. In addition to combining questions to increase reliability, the different answers can be synthesized rather than depending on the angle of vision provided by any single question. A further safeguard is to carry out frequent experiments like that on the forbid/allow wordings. By varying the form, wording, and context of questions, researchers can gain insight into both the questions and the relevant issues. Sometimes variations turn out to make no difference, and that is also useful to learn. For example, I once expected support for legalized abortion to increase when a question substituted *end pregnancy* for the word *abortion* in the phrasing. Yet no difference was found. Today, more and more researchers include survey-based experiments as part of their investigations, and readers should look for these sorts of safeguards when evaluating survey results.

The Need for Comparisons

To interpret surveys accurately, it's important to use a framework of comparative data in evaluating the results. For example, teachers know that course evaluations can be interpreted best against the backdrop of evaluations from other similar courses: a 75 percent rating of lectures as "excellent" takes on a quite different meaning depending on whether the average for other lecture courses is 50 percent or 90 percent. Such comparisons are fundamental for all survey results, yet they are easily overlooked when one feels the urge to speak definitively about public reactions to a unique event.

Comparative analysis over time, along with survey-based experiments, can also help us understand responses to questions about socially sensitive subjects. Experiments have shown that expressions of racial attitudes can change substantially for both black and white Americans depending on the interviewer's race. White respondents, for instance, are more likely to support racial intermarriage when speaking to a black than to a white interviewer. Such self-censoring mirrors variations in cross-race conversations outside of surveys, reflecting not a methodological artifact of surveys but rather a fact of life about race relations in America. Still, if we consider time trends, with the race of interviewer kept constant, we can also see that white responses supporting intermarriage have clearly increased over the past half century (see Table 2), that actual intermarriage rates have also risen (though from a much lower level) over recent years, and that the public visibility of cross-race marriage and dating has also increased. It would be foolish to assume that the survey data on racial attitudes reflect actions in any literal sense, but they do capture important *trends* in both norms and behavior.

Surveys remain our best tool for learning about large populations. One remarkable advantage surveys have over some other methods is the ability to

TABLE 2 *Percent of White Americans Approving or Disapproving of Racial Intermarriage, 1958-1997*

"Do you approve or disapprove of marriage between blacks and whites?"

Year	Approve	Disapprove
1958	4	96
1978	34	66
1997	67	33

Source: Gallup Poll

identify their own limitations, as illustrated by the development of both probability theory in sampling and experiments in questioning. In the end, however, with surveys as with all research methods, there is no substitute for both care and intelligence in the way evidence is gathered and interpreted. What we learn about society is always mediated by the instruments we use, including our own eyes and ears. As Isaac Newton wrote long ago, error is not in the art but in the artificers.

Questions

1. Why did the *Literary Digest* incorrectly predict who would win the 1936 presidential election?
2. What is a probability sample? Why is it used?
3. Explain why it is important to consider "who is missing" when interpreting survey results.
4. According to Schuman, is the way that survey questions are worded important? Why, or why not?
5. Explain why it is important to use comparative data to evaluate the results of a survey. Give an original example to illustrate.

Say What You Mean

G. EVANS WITT

This article reveals that the way researchers phrase a question can make a striking difference in the answers that they receive. Awareness of this fact will make all of us more savvy consumers of the results of polls that we see routinely reported on the nightly news and in the newspaper.

Sometimes, just a word or two makes all the difference. Take "as a person." Add that phrase to a question about Bill Clinton and the President's favorability scores drop 20 points.

Or take the emotion-laden issue of abortion. Do 57 percent of Americans think abortion is wrong? Or do 69 percent think a woman should be able to get an abortion? In fact, both are valid poll results. The difference is all in the way the questions are worded.

Critics often dismiss survey results, saying that people's opinions are being forced into neat little boxes of Yes/No or Favor/Oppose on the questions that overlook the complexity of many issues in these complicated times. What the critics fail to appreciate is how carefully people listen to poll questions when they are asked for their opinion, and how precisely they are trying to respond.

For example, pollsters trying to gauge the public's reaction to various well-known people often use a "favorability" question that is meant to tap into attitudes toward the person overall, not just his or her job performance. The question is usually asked about a list of people, using wording such as "I'd like to get your overall opinion of some people in the news. As I read each name, please say if you have a favorable or unfavorable opinion of this person . . . or if you have never heard of him or her. First. . . ."

"Say What You Mean," by G. Evans Witt, reprinted from *American Demographics*, Vol. 21, No. 2, February 1999. Copyright © by PRIMEDIA/Intertec. p. 23.

But last August, the Gallup Organization conducted a poll for CNN and *USA Today* after President Clinton's grand jury testimony on August 27. With a shorter questionnaire, Gallup simply asked: "Now, thinking about Bill Clinton as a person, do you have a favorable or unfavorable opinion of him?"

That wording—with the magic phrase "as a person"—found a favorability rating for Clinton that was 20 percentage points below that which was found using the longer question the previous week. Gallup did a follow-up survey that showed the change in the wording was responsible for perhaps half of the plunge.

Polls on issues that evoke strong reactions are particularly vulnerable to small changes in wording. At first blush, the poll results regarding gun control and abortion seem to indicate that the American public holds wildly varying views simultaneously.

As part of a regular *Newsweek* poll, Princeton Survey Research Associates asked a series of questions about abortion in late 1998. The response to one question—"Do you personally believe that abortion is wrong?"—seemed to indicate strong support for the pro-life view. A total of 57 percent of the public answered that abortion is wrong. Thirty-six percent said abortion is not wrong. That is solid majority support for the pro-life side. Or so it would appear.

But the very next question found results that the pro-choice side couldn't help but like: "Whatever your own personal view of abortion, do you favor or oppose a woman in this country having the choice to have an abortion with the advice of her doctor?" On this question, 69 percent said they favor a woman having the choice to have an abortion. Only 24 percent said no.

YES, BUT . . .

Do you personally believe that abortion is wrong?

Yes	57 percent
No	36 percent

Whatever your own personal view of abortion, do you favor or oppose a woman in this country having the choice to have an abortion with the advice of her doctor?

Favor	69 percent
Oppose	24 percent

Source: 1998 *Newsweek* poll, by Princeton Survey Research Assoc.

How can these two sets of numbers be reconciled? Isn't the public taking two opposing views on abortion at the same time?

The answer is that the public is listening to the exact questions and giving a nuanced set of answers. It is one thing to be asked if abortion is wrong. But that is not necessarily the same thing as saying a woman should never have the choice to have an abortion under any and all circumstances. For some people, abortion is so wrong that it should never be allowed. For others, their personal opinion on the morality of abortion does not extend to limiting the actions of others.

What's clear is that abortion is a complex and difficult question for many Americans, and they hold complex views on it; no single question can adequately portray those views. The questions that probe into this area must be carefully phrased to pick up these subtleties. Poorly stated or slanted questions simply generate confusing and often meaningless results.

The wording of poll questions is important, whether the issue is abortion, Bill Clinton, what brand of gasoline you buy or what TV show you like. It's impossible to understand a poll's findings without knowing the exact wording of the questions.

The next time someone quotes a poll to you, make sure you ask: "What was the question?"

Questions

1. Why do researchers receive seemingly contradictory responses to their questions about social issues?
2. Why is it so important to know the exact question that was asked when you examine the findings of a poll?
3. Why does Witt argue that critics are wrong to dismiss the results of polls?

4. Find the results of a poll in your local newspaper or a news magazine. What was the question that was asked? Was it biased or slanted in any way? If so, how would you rephrase the question?

5. Write two versions of a question on a subject that might interest students on your campus, or use Witt's questions on abortion. Ask 20 people to respond. Does the wording make a difference in their answers?

Culture

KATHLEEN A. TIEMANN, GENERAL EDITOR

When asked what constitutes culture, many people describe what is more accurately called high culture. They mention opera, painting, ballet, symphonic music—all art forms most often associated with the wealthy. Others, when asked the same question, might describe what is known as popular culture—forms that are created for and enjoyed by a large number of people and often distributed through television and other mass media. These forms might include the latest music video on MTV, the newest clothing fashions, football or basketball games, and so on. Neither of these descriptions, however, fully captures the breadth of how sociologists view culture.

Sociologists define culture as all of the knowledge that we share about how to do things, how to think about the world, and how to navigate our day-to-day existence. Most of this knowledge is unwritten. For instance, consider the knowledge we share about how to "do" Christmas. As Caplow (1984) discovered in his research, there are many unwritten rules about the Christmas season. These rules dictate who should put up a Christmas tree, who should give gifts and to whom, how much you should spend on a gift, and, of course, how to wrap and present gifts. Simply by living and participating in a common culture, we come to learn these kinds of rules. As a result, we also develop a sense that we belong in and are part of a larger group or community.

The average person seldom gives culture much thought, unless something happens that brings him or her face to face with something usually taken for granted. Consider, for example, your reactions to the following situation: You are at a taxi stand, and people behind and around you are shoving their way to the front of the line instead of waiting their turn. Besides getting angry, you would probably also be astounded at this breach of social propriety. Similarly, if you saw your neighbors throw their three-year-old child out of the house, you would likely be horrified, since members of our culture believe that parents should protect and care for their children. The point here is that people who share a culture develop similar expectations, or norms, of what constitutes appropriate behavior.

But notice what would happen if you took the two examples from above and put them in another cultural context. Interestingly, your perceptions of them would change. If you lived in Venice, for instance, fighting your way to the ticket booth to purchase a ticket for the water bus during rush hour would be perfectly normal (especially during tourist season!). If you lived among the Ik tribe of Northern Uganda, believe it or not, you would understand that throwing three-year-old children out of the house goes without comment in that culture. Certainly, we may realize on an intellectual level that people in other parts of the world do things differently than we do. Yet our first reactions to these differences is likely to occur on an emotional level. And it's this very emotion that can cause us to take on an ethnocentric attitude–that is, to judge other cultures on the basis of our own cultural norms.

"Strange Worlds"

To avoid making such judgments, we use something called our sociological imagination to examine norms within their various, unique social contexts. Through this process, we come to understand not only the norms but also the people who live by them. We thus take on a perspective of cultural relativism. To illustrate this point, think about how we view time. Members of Western societies tend to think about time as linear—we can neatly measure it in discrete units like seconds, minutes, hours, days, months, and years. Indeed, we find it difficult to comprehend how anyone could possibly organize his or her day without defining it by the hour and minute hands on a clock or wristwatch. But in Burundi (a country in central Africa), and in many other parts of the world, people do not measure time this way at all. Instead of using "clock time," Burundians live by "event time" (Levine, 1997). Because most residents of Burundi are farmers, they rely on natural cycles to measure and organize their days. Therefore, instead of saying to a friend "Let's meet at ten o'clock," they might say "Let's meet when the cows go out to graze." If they want to meet at midday, they may say that they will meet when "the cows are going to drink in the stream" instead of "at noon" (Levine, 1997, p. 87). In each of these very different cultures, the chosen method of time-keeping makes sense. Because each method is equally useful, each is equally valid.

It can be fascinating to study the "strange worlds" occupied by people dramatically different from us. That's why we are likely to be drawn to stories about people like the Ik, who taunt starving tribe members; the Burundians, who schedule appointments based on the movements of their livestock; or the especially odd Nacirema, those exotic people who bake their heads in ovens and maintain holy shrines in their homes to ward off evil spirits that might make them ill.

As much as we can learn from cultures other than our own, we also have much to gain from studying the "strange worlds" that exist within our own culture. Within any society, there exist many subcultures—groups who have beliefs, values, behaviors, and even a language that set them apart from the dominant or "mainstream" culture. Granted, you might have little interest in studying the subculture of professors (even though, as we all know, professors are fascinating people!). However, you might like to know why college students, lawyers, and other upwardly mobile people get tattoos—which historically have been associated with bikers, prostitutes, prison inmates, and other socially "undesirable" individuals. You might also wonder why some people participate in the "indie" music scene, how gangs can arise within schools or neighborhoods, why women use language differently when they talk to other women than when they communicate with men, or why a growing number of people of all ages participate in the virtual communities that are emerging in cyberspace. All of these are examples of subcultures that exist in our own communities, our own neighborhoods, even our own homes.

Regardless of your specific interests, sociology can deepen your understanding of the importance of culture—your own as well as others'. As you read the articles in this section, try to leave behind your preconceptions about the world. Open yourself to new ways of seeing, living, and thinking. Who knows? You may end up actually appreciating the vast number of ways human societies have chosen to organize themselves based on their shared experiences and expectations.

References

Caplow, T. (1984). Rule enforcement without visible means, Christmas gift giving in Middletown. *American Journal of Sociology 89*, 1310–1317.

Levine, R. (1997). A geography of time. From *A geography of time*. New York: Basic.

Body Ritual Among the Nacirema

HORACE MINER
University of Michigan

As many sociologists will tell you, cross-cultural research is difficult but exciting. Not only might you encounter unusual or disturbing behavior during your research, but you may also find yourself in danger or face-to-face with ethnocentrism—your own, that is. It is easy to judge the rituals, behavior, and general way of life of other peoples as bizarre, strange, or inferior compared to our own. In this reading, Horace Miner lets us confront these issues by allowing us a peek into the lives of the mysterious Nacirema tribe. As you read, note the way the tribe members live, the things that are important to them, and the ways in which they get others to conform to socially approved, but rather odd, behaviors. Would you want to live among the Nacirema?

The anthropologist has become so familiar with the diversity of ways in which different peoples behave in similar situations that he is not apt to be surprised by even the most exotic customs. In fact, if all of the logically possible combinations of behavior have not been found somewhere in the world, he is apt to suspect that they must be present in some yet undescribed tribe. This point has, in fact, been expressed with respect to clan organization by Murdock (1949:71). In this light, the magical beliefs and practices of the Nacirema present such unusual aspects that it seems desirable to

"Body Ritual Among the Nacirema," by Horace Miner, reprinted from *American Anthropologist*, Vol. 58, No. 3, June 1956. pp. 503–507.

describe them as an example of the extremes to which human behavior can go.

Professor Linton first brought the ritual of the Nacirema to the attention of anthropologists twenty years ago (1936:326), but the culture of this people is still very poorly understood. They are a North American group living in the territory between the Canadian Cree, the Yaqui and Tarahumare of Mexico, and the Carib and Arawak of the Antilles. Little is known of their origin, although tradition states that they came from the east. According to Nacirema mythology, their nation was originated by a culture hero, Notgnihsaw, who is otherwise known for two great feats of strength—the throwing of a piece of wampum across the river Po-To-Mac and the chopping down of a cherry tree in which the Spirit of Truth resided.

Nacirema culture is characterized by a highly developed market economy which has evolved in a rich natural habitat. While much of the people's time is devoted to economic pursuits, a large part of the fruits of these labors and a considerable portion of the day are spent in ritual activity. The focus of this activity is the human body, the appearance and health of which loom as a dominant concern in the ethos of the people. While such a concern is certainly not unusual, its ceremonial aspects and associated philosophy are unique.

The fundamental belief underlying the whole system appears to be that the human body is ugly and that its natural tendency is to debility and disease. Incarcerated in such a body, man's only hope is to avert these characteristics through the use of the powerful influences of ritual and ceremony. Every household has one or more shrines devoted to this purpose. The more powerful individuals in the society have several shrines in their houses and, in fact, the opulence of a house is often referred to in terms of the number of such ritual centers it possesses. Most houses are of wattle and daub construction, but the shrine rooms of the more wealthy are walled with stone. Poorer families imitate the rich by applying pottery plaques to their shrine walls.

While each family has at least one such shrine, the rituals associated with it are not family ceremonies but are private and secret. The rites are normally only discussed with children, and then only during the period when they are being initiated into these mysteries. I was able, however, to establish sufficient rapport with the natives to examine these shrines and to have the rituals described to me.

The focal point of the shrine is a box or chest which is built into the wall. In this chest are kept the many charms and magical potions without which no native believes he could live. These preparations are secured from a variety of specialized practitioners. The most powerful of these are the medicine men, whose assistance must be rewarded with substantial gifts. However, the medicine men do not provide the curative potions for their clients, but decide what the ingredients should be and then write them down in an ancient and secret language. This writing is understood only by the medicine men and by the herbalists who, for another gift, provide the required charm.

The charm is not disposed of after it has served its purpose, but is placed in the charm-box of the household shrine. As these magical materials are specific for certain ills, and the real or imagined maladies of the people are many, the charm-box is usually full to overflowing. The magical packets are so numerous that people forget what their purposes were and fear to use them again. While the natives are very vague on this point, we can only assume that the idea in retaining all the old magical materials is that their presence in the charm-box, before which the body rituals are conducted, will in some way protect the worshipper.

Beneath the charm-box is a small font. Each day every member of the family, in succession, enters the shrine room, bows his head before the charm–box, mingles different sorts of holy water in the font, and proceeds with a brief rite of ablution. The holy waters are secured from the Water Temple of the community, where the priests conduct elaborate ceremonies to make the liquid ritually pure.

In the hierarchy of magical practitioners, and below the medicine men in prestige, are specialists whose designation is best translated "holy-mouth-men." The Nacirema have an almost pathological horror of and fascination with the mouth, the condition of which is believed to have a supernatural influence on all social relationships. Were it not for the rituals of the mouth, they believe that their teeth would fall out, their gums bleed, their jaws shrink, their friends desert them, and their lovers reject them. They also believe that a strong relationship exists between oral and moral characteristics. For example, there is a ritual ablution of the mouth for children which is supposed to improve their moral fiber.

The daily body ritual performed by everyone includes a mouth-rite. Despite the fact that these people are so punctilious about care of the mouth, this rite involves a practice which strikes the uninitiated stranger as revolting. It was reported to me that the ritual consists of inserting a small bundle of hog hairs into the mouth, along with certain magical powders and then moving the bundle in a highly formalized series of gestures.

In addition to the private mouth-rite, the people seek out a holy-mouth-man once or twice a year. These practitioners have an impressive set of paraphernalia, consisting of a variety of augers, awls, probes, and prods. The use of these objects in the exorcism of the evils of the mouth involves almost unbelievable ritual torture of the client. The holy-mouth-man opens the client's mouth and, using the above-mentioned tools, enlarges any holes which decay may have created in the teeth. Magical materials are put into these holes. If there are no naturally occurring holes in the teeth, large sections of one or more teeth are gouged out so that the supernatural substance can be applied. In the client's view, the purpose of these ministrations is to arrest decay and to draw friends. The extremely sacred and traditional character of the rite is evident in the fact that the natives return to the holy-mouth-men year after year, despite the fact that their teeth continue to decay.

It is to be hoped that, when a thorough study of the Nacirema is made, there will be careful inquiry into the personality structure of these people. One has but to watch the gleam in the eye of a holy-mouth-man, as he jabs an awl into an exposed nerve, to suspect that a certain amount of sadism is involved. If this can be established, a very interesting pattern emerges, for most of the population shows definite masochistic tendencies. It was to these that Professor Linton referred in discussing a distinctive part of the daily body ritual which is performed only by men. This part of the rite involves scraping and lacerating the surface of the face with a sharp instrument. Special women's rites are performed only four times during each lunar month, but what they lack in frequency is made up in barbarity. As part of this ceremony, women bake their heads in small ovens for about an hour. The theoretically interesting point is that what seems to be a preponderantly masochistic people have developed sadistic specialists.

The medicine men have an imposing temple, or *latipso,* in every community of any size. The more elaborate ceremonies required to treat very sick patients can only be performed at this temple. These ceremonies involve not only the thaumaturge but a permanent group of vestal maidens who move sedately about the temple chambers in distinctive costume and headdress.

The *latipso* ceremonies are so harsh that it is phenomenal that a fair proportion of the really sick natives who enter the temple ever recover. Small children whose indoctrination is still incomplete have been known to resist attempts to take them to the temple because "that is where you go to die." Despite this fact, sick adults are not only willing but eager to undergo the protracted ritual purification, if they can afford to do so. No matter how ill the supplicant or how grave the emergency, the guardians of many temples will not admit a client if he cannot give a rich gift to the custodian. Even after one has gained admission and survived the ceremonies, the guardians will not permit the neophyte to leave until he makes still another gift.

The supplicant entering the temple is first stripped of all his or her clothes. In everyday life the Nacirema avoids exposure of his body and its natural functions. Bathing and excretory acts are performed only in the secrecy of the household shrine, where they are ritualized as part of the body-rites. Psychological shock results from the fact that body secrecy is suddenly lost upon entry into the *latipso.* A man, whose own wife has never seen him in an excretory act, suddenly finds himself naked and assisted by a vestal maiden while he performs his natural functions into a sacred vessel. This sort of ceremonial treatment is necessitated by the fact that the excreta are used by a diviner to ascertain the course and nature of the client's sickness. Female clients, on the other hand, find their naked bodies are subjected to the scrutiny, manipulation and prodding of the medicine men.

Few supplicants in the temple are well enough to do anything but lie on their hard beds. The daily ceremonies, like the rites of the holy-mouth-men, involve discomfort and torture. With ritual precision, the vestals awaken their miserable charges each dawn and roll them about on their beds of pain while performing ablutions, in the formal movements of which the maidens are highly trained. At other times they insert magic wands in the supplicant's mouth or force him to eat substances which are supposed to be healing. From time to time the medicine men come to their clients and jab magically treated needles into their flesh. The fact that these temple ceremonies may not cure, and may even kill the neophyte, in no way decreases the people's faith in the medicine men.

There remains one other kind of practitioner, known as a "listener." This witch-doctor has the power to exorcise the devils that lodge in the heads of people who have been bewitched. The Nacirema believe that parents bewitch their own children. Mothers are particularly suspected of putting a curse on children while teaching them the secret body rituals. The counter-magic of the witch-doctor is unusual in its lack of ritual. The patient simply tells the "listener" all his troubles and fears, beginning with the earliest difficulties he can remember. The memory displayed by the Nacirema in these exorcism sessions is truly remarkable. It is not uncommon for the patient to bemoan the rejection he felt upon being weaned as a babe, and a few individuals even see their troubles going back to the traumatic effects of their own birth.

In conclusion, mention must be made of certain practices which have their base in native esthetics but which depend upon the pervasive aversion to the natural body and its functions. There are ritual fasts to make fat people thin and ceremonial feasts to make thin people fat. Still other rites are used to make women's breasts larger if they are small, and smaller if they are large. General dissatisfaction with breast shape is symbolized in the fact that the ideal form is virtually outside the range of human variation. A few women afflicted with almost inhuman hypermammary development are so idolized that they make a handsome living by simply going from village to village and permitting the natives to stare at them for a fee.

Reference has already been made to the fact that excretory functions are ritualized, routinized, and relegated to secrecy. Natural reproductive functions are similarly distorted. Intercourse is taboo as a topic and scheduled as an act. Efforts are made to avoid pregnancy by the use of magical materials or by limiting intercourse to certain phases of the moon. Conception is actually very infrequent. When pregnant, women dress so as to hide their condition. Parturition takes place in secret, without friends or relatives to assist, and the majority of women do not nurse their infants.

Our review of the ritual life of the Nacirema has certainly shown them to be a magic-ridden people. It is hard to understand how they have managed to exist so long under the burdens which they have imposed upon themselves. But even such exotic customs as these take on real meaning when they are viewed with the insight provided by Malinowski when he wrote (1948:70):

> Looking from far and above, from our high places of safety in the developed civilization, it is easy to see all the crudity and irrelevance of magic. But without its power and guidance early man could not have mastered his practical difficulties as he has done, nor could man have advanced to the higher stages of civilization.

References

Linton, R. (1936). *The study of man*. New York: D. Appleton-Century Co.

Malinowski, B. (1948). *Magic, science, and religion*. Glencoe, IL: The Free Press.

Murdock, G. P. (1949). *Social structure*. New York: The Macmillan Co.

Questions

1. We might find many things strange about the Nacirema. What might the Nacirema find strange about us? List three possibilities and explain your choices.
2. Use the reading to explain and cite examples of the following concepts: value, norm, and sanction.
3. What benefit might we derive from studying the Nacirema way of life?
4. Miner studied the Nacirema from an anthropological perspective; as a sociologist who wants to understand the Nacirema, what would you do differently in studying them?
5. What role does the listener play in Nacirema culture?
6. Explain the role of magic in the daily lives of the Nacirema.
7. Many readers finish this article without realizing that "Nacirema" is "American" spelled backwards. Why did Miner write about Americans as if we were a strange tribe? What insights do we gain about ourselves by taking this perspective?

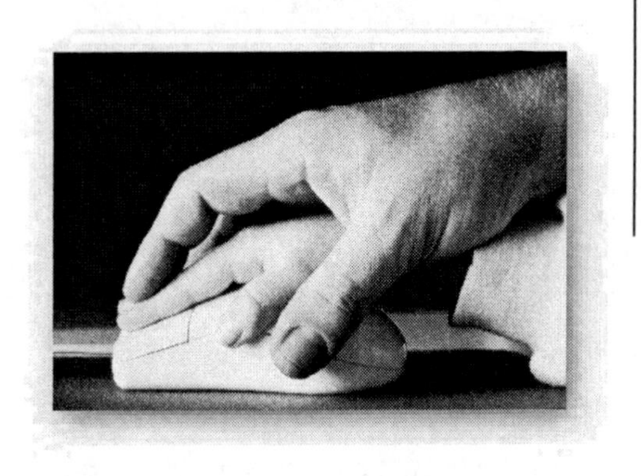

Socialization

Ralph B. McNeal, Jr., General Editor

Everybody has a particular image of "who" they are. For some of us, the adjectives that we use to describe ourselves—such as intelligent, athletic, pretty, musical, funny, and witty—are quite positive. For others, the adjectives are primarily negative, such as slow, clumsy, ugly, and mean. However, most people describe themselves with a mix of positive and negative adjectives. The socialization process is an important area of study for sociologists because it helps explain *how* we come to perceive ourselves as we do. More technically, socialization is the process "through which individuals acquire a self-identity and the physical, mental, and social skills needed for survival in society" (Kendall, 1999, p. 72). Socialization is complicated, takes place in numerous arenas of our lives, and continues throughout our lifespan.

According to some researchers, socialization is the internalization of reality (Berger & Luckman, 1966). This means that individuals are born as "blank slates," in a sense, and learn the necessities of life through myriad encounters and interactions with others. For example, people are not born valuing democracy, honesty, athleticism, or intellect. They are taught by the society they live in to value specific attributes. This is the basis of socialization. The socialization process thus begins the day a child is born and continues throughout the entire lifecourse.

To better understand why socialization is so fundamental, we only have to look at how pervasive it is in our lives. For most of us, the process is indeed a lifelong one. To be sure, there have been rare cases in which individuals have been raised in near total isolation. The most infamous example, at least as far as the field of sociology is concerned, is that of "Anna" (Davis, 1947). Anna lived the first six years of her life having almost no contact with other human beings. When she was found, she demonstrated few of the mental and social skills that we think of as characterizing human beings. Her situation, though tragic, provided one of the earliest sociological case studies on the negative effects of isolation on human development and on the stages of socialization throughout the lifecourse. While Anna never developed enough socially to match her biological age, she did eventually learn some language and other key elements of human behavior.

A Complex Process

This study revealed the importance of initial human interaction on social development. For many individuals, this early experience takes place in the family (often considered the primary source of socialization). As we begin to grow and develop, other institutions—such as school and media—come to the fore and contribute more to the socialization process. These other institutions have less emotional influence on us and thus are often considered secondary sources of socialization.

The fact that socialization occurs throughout the lifecourse is especially relevant, because it means that individual's perceptions and identities are continually shaped. As an example of this continuity, you need only to consider your own sense of self or identity. While you were in high school, how did you think of yourself? Were you athletic? Were you intelligent? Through what processes did you come to think of yourself in these terms? Now that you are in college, how has your identity changed? Much of your sense of identity during high school initially stemmed from family influences. Later in your life, your self-image derives more from peer group influences.

Understanding socialization can be particularly difficult. This is because the role of each of these "socializing" institutions is not always uniform or clear. To illustrate, what exactly does your peer group contribute to your self-image? What do the schools you have attended contribute? The complexity and lack of clarity regarding the content that these institutions transmit can make the socialization process seem haphazard and confusing at times. In studying this phenomenon, sociologists seem most fascinated by instances in which the socialization process has broken down. But how should we interpret these situations? For example, deviant behavior can be thought of as either the failure to be properly socialized *or* the successful socialization of a person into a deviant peer group.

The Power of Peer Groups

As an example of how peer groups and school affect our sense of self, consider the socialization of young people into gender roles. As many researchers have found, schools often play a central part in this process. Specifically, American society teaches girls to value their appearance and boys to value their physical strength or their intellect; girls also learn to be obedient, while boys learn to be inquisitive; girls are taught to value interdependence, while boys are taught to value autonomy. Indeed, in many middle and high schools, the most popular girls are pretty and well behaved, while the popular boys are captains of sports teams.

However, not every school exhibits this pattern of socialization, nor does each student within a given school fit the template. Because socialization is a fluid and ever changing process, it is subject to variation, which manifests itself in gender, race, social class, or cultural differences. But despite such differences, the *process* of socialization is remarkably similar to for each individual.

As we've seen, peer groups exert more influence on the socialization process as we go through our lives. Even later in adulthood, our self-image can be highly influenced—even transformed—by those around us. One study (Schmid & Jones, 1991) provided an excellent example of how resocialization can take place in a total institution (that is, an institution that governs all aspects of a person's daily life such as prison). As this study revealed, most prisoners emerge from incarceration with identities that are distinctive, permanent blends of their preprison identities and their prison experiences. This kind of drastic resocialization occurs in other total institutions as well, such as mental hospitals and the military.

When Socialization Fails: A Challenge for Researchers

Given the lifelong course of the socialization process, the complexity of what we learn as we mature, and the shifting impact of various institutions on our self-image during our lives, it is not surprising that socialization often fails. Why do some small children intentionally inflict harm on animals, for example? Why do some adults deliberately hurt children? Why is violence on the rise in American society? On a more subtle level, why are people increasingly concerned about the seeming lack of values in America's young people? Why do we often find ourselves asking what went wrong?

Sociologists who recognize the complexities inherent in the socialization process try to design studies that take these complexities into account. In their research, they tend to focus on the dynamics of the socialization process, instances in which the process goes awry, the impact of various social institutions on the process, and ways in which self-identity changes during the lifecourse. In lay terms, sociologists thus explore "who we are" (i.e., our self-identity), "how we have come to be that way" (i.e., the socialization process), and "who we might yet become" (i.e., the resocialization process).

References

Berger, P., & Luckman, T. (1966). Socialization: The internalization of reality. In P. Berger & T. Luckman (Eds), *The social construction of reality: A treatise in the sociology of knowledge*. Garden City, New York: Doubleday.

Davis, K. (1947). Final note on a case of extreme isolation. *American Journal of Sociology, 52*, 432-437.

Kendall, D. (1999). *Sociology in our times*. New York: Wadsworth.

Schmid, T., & Jones, R. (1991). Suspended identity: Identity transformation in a maximum security prison. *Symbolic Interaction, Vol. 14*, No. 4, pp. 415-432.

Final Note on a Case of Extreme Isolation

Kingsley Davis
Princeton University

Kingsley Davis's work is a classic examination of early socialization and the effect of delayed human contact. In this piece, he briefly reviews the story of a girl named Anna, who was virtually isolated from all human contact and affection until she was six years old. Davis then compares Anna's life history and subsequent development to that of another young girl who experienced similar circumstances. Davis concludes that socialization can occur at various stages of the lifecourse, a finding that stands in stark contrast to a more traditional psychological explanation.

. . .

Early in 1940 there appeared in this *Journal* an account of a girl called Anna.[1] She had been deprived of normal contact and had received a minimum of human care for almost the whole of her first six years of life. At that time observations were not complete and the report had a tentative character. Now, however, the girl is dead, and, with more information available,[2] it is possible to give a fuller and more definitive description of the case from a sociological point of view.

Anna's death, caused by hemorrhagic jaundice, occurred on August 6, 1942. Having been born on March 1 or 6,[3] 1932, she was approximately ten and a half years of age when she died. The previ-

---

"Final Note on a Case of Extreme Isolation," by Kingsley Davis, reprinted from *American Journal of Sociology*, vol. 52, 1947. pp. 432–447.

ous report covered her development up to the age of almost eight years; the present one recapitulates the earlier period on the basis of new evidence and then covers the last two and a half years of life.

Early History

The first few days and weeks of Anna's life were complicated by frequent changes of domicile. It will be recalled that she was an illegitimate child, the second such child born to her mother, and that her grandfather, a widowed farmer in whose house her mother lived, strongly disapproved of this new evidence of the mother's indiscretion. This fact led to the baby's being shifted about.

Two weeks after being born in a nurse's private home, Anna was brought to the family farm, but the grandfather's antagonism was so great that she was shortly taken to the house of one of her mother's friends. At this time a local minister became interested in her and took her to his house with an idea of possible adoption. He decided against adoption, however, when he discovered that she had vaginitis. The infant was then taken to a children's home in the nearest large city. This agency found that at the age of only three weeks she was already in a miserable condition, being "terribly galled and otherwise in very bad shape." It did not regard her as a likely subject for adoption but took her in for a while anyway, hoping to benefit her. After Anna had spent nearly eight weeks in this place, the agency notified her mother to come to get her. The mother responded by sending a man and his wife to the children's home with a view to their adopting Anna, but they made such a poor impression on the agency that permission was refused. Later the mother came herself and took the child out of the home and then gave her to this couple. It was in the home of this pair that a social worker found the girl a short time thereafter. The social worker went to the mother's home and pleaded with Anna's grandfather to allow the mother to bring the child home. In spite of threats, he refused. The child, by then more than four months old, was taken to another children's home in a nearby town.

A medical examination at this time revealed that she had impetigo, vaginitis, umbilical hernia, and a skin rash.

Anna remained in this second children's home for nearly three weeks, at the end of which time she was transferred to a private foster home. Since, however, the grandfather would not, and the mother could not, pay for the child's care, she was finally taken back as a last resort to the grandfather's house (at the age of five and a half months). There she remained, kept on the second floor in an attic-like room because her mother hesitated to incur the grandfather's wrath by bringing her downstairs.

The mother, a sturdy woman weighing about 180 pounds, did a man's work on the farm. She engaged in heavy work such as milking cows and tending hogs and had little time for her children. Sometimes she went out at night, in which case Anna was left entirely without attention. Ordinarily, it seems, Anna received only enough care to keep her barely alive. She appears to have been seldom moved from one position to another. Her clothing and bedding were filthy. She apparently had no instruction, no friendly attention.

It is little wonder that, when finally found and removed from the room in the grandfather's house at the age of nearly six years, the child could not talk, walk, or do anything that showed intelligence. . . .

Anna's condition when found, and her subsequent improvement, have been described in the previous report. It now remains to say what happened to her after that.

Later History

In 1939, nearly two years after being discovered, Anna had progressed, as previously reported, to the point where she could walk, understand simple commands, feed herself, achieve some neatness, remember people, etc. But she still did not speak, and though she was much more like a normal infant of something over one year of age in mentality, she was far from normal for her age.

On August 30, 1939, she was taken to a private home for retarded children, leaving the country home where she had been for more than a year and a half. In her new setting she made some further progress, but not a great deal. In a report of an examination made November 6 of the same year, the head of the institution pictured the child as follows:

> Anna walks about aimlessly, makes periodic rhythmic motions of her hands, and, at intervals, makes guttural and sucking noises. She regards her hands as if she had seen them for the first time. It was impossible to hold her attention for more than a few seconds at a time—not because of distraction due to external stimuli but because of her inability to concentrate. She ignored the task in hand to gaze vacantly about the room. Speech is entirely lacking. Numerous unsuccessful attempts have been made with her in the hope of developing initial sounds. I do not believe that this failure is due to negativism or deafness but that she is not sufficiently developed to accept speech at this time. . . . The prognosis is not favorable. . . .

More than five months later, on April 25, 1940, a clinical psychologist, the late Professor Francis N. Maxfield, examined Anna and reported the following: large for her age; hearing "entirely normal," vision apparently normal; able to climb stairs; speech in the "babbling stage" and "promise for developing intelligible speech later seems to be good." He said further that "on the Merrill-Palmer scale she made a mental score of 19 months. On the Vineland social maturity scale she made a score of 23 months."[4]

. . . Professor Maxwell gave it as his opinion at that time that Anna would eventually "attain an adult mental level of six or seven years."[5]

The school for retarded children, on July 1, 1941, reported that Anna had reached 46 inches in height and weighed 60 pounds. She could bounce and catch a ball and was said to conform to group socialization, though as a follower rather than a leader. Toilet habits were firmly established. Food habits were normal, except that she still used a spoon as her sole implement. She could dress herself except for fastening her clothes. Most remarkable of all, she had finally begun to develop speech. She was characterized as being at about the two-year level in this regard. She could call attendants by name and bring in one when she was asked to. She had few complete sentences to express her wants. The report concluded that there was nothing peculiar about her, except that she was feeble-minded—"probably congenital in type."[6]

A final report from the school, made on June 22, 1942, and evidently the last report before the girl's death, pictured only a slight advance over that given above. It said that Anna could follow directions, string beads, identify a few colors, build with blocks, and differentiate between attractive and unattractive pictures. She had a good sense of rhythm and loved a doll. She talked mainly in phrases but would repeat words and try to carry on a conversation. She was clean about clothing. She habitually washed her hands and brushed her teeth. She would try to help other children. She walked well and could run fairly well, though clumsily. Although easily excited, she had a pleasant disposition.

Interpretation

Such was Anna's condition just before her death. It may seem as if she had not made much progress, but one must remember the condition in which she had been found. One must recall that she had no glimmering of speech, absolutely no ability to walk, no sense of gesture, not the least capacity to feed herself even when the food was put in front of her, and no comprehension of cleanliness. She was so apathetic that it was hard to tell whether or not she could hear. And all this at the age of nearly six years. Compared with this condition, her capacities at the time of her death seem striking indeed, though they do not amount to much more than a two-and-a-half-year mental level. One conclusion therefore seems safe, namely, that her isolation prevented a considerable amount of mental development that was undoubtedly part of her capacity. Just what her original capacity was, of course, is hard to say; but her development after her period of confinement (including the ability to walk and run, to play, dress, fit into a social situation, and, above all, to speak) shows that she had at least this much capacity—capacity that never could have been realized in her original condition of isolation.

A further question is this: What would she have been like if she had received a normal upbringing from the moment of birth? A definitive answer would have been impossible in any case, but even an approximate answer is made difficult by her early death. If one assumes, as was tentatively surmised in the previous report, that it is "almost impossible for any child to learn to speak, think, and act like a normal person after a long period of early isolation," it seems likely that Anna might have had a normal or near-normal capacity, genetically speaking. On the other hand, it was pointed out that Anna represented "a marginal case, [because] she was discovered before she had reached six years of age," an age "young enough to allow for some plasticity."[7] While admitting, then, that Anna's isolation *may* have been the major cause (and was certainly a minor cause) of her lack of rapid mental progress during the four and a half years following her rescue from neglect, it is necessary to entertain the hypothesis that she was congenitally deficient.

In connection with this hypothesis, one suggestive though by no means conclusive circumstance needs consideration, namely, the mentality of Anna's forebears. Information on this subject is easier to obtain, as one might guess, on the mother's than on the father's side. Anna's maternal grandmother, for example, is said to have been college educated and wished to have her children receive a good education, but her husband, Anna's stern grandfather, apparently a shrewd, hard-driving, calculating farmowner, was so penurious that her ambitions in this direction were thwarted. Under the circumstances her daughter (Anna's mother) managed, despite having to do hard work on the farm, to complete the eighth grade in a country school. Even so, however, the daughter was evidently not very smart. "A schoolmate of [Anna's mother] stated that she was retarded in school work;

was very gullible at this age; and that her morals even at this time were discussed by other students." Two tests administered to her on March 4, 1938, when she was thirty-two years of age, showed that she was mentally deficient. On the Stanford Revision of the Binet-Simon Scale her performance was equivalent to that of a child of eight years, giving her an I.Q. of 50 and indicating mental deficiency of "middle-grade moron type."[8]

As to the identity of Anna's father, the most persistent theory holds that he was an old man about seventy-four years of age at the time of the girl's birth. If he was the one, there is no indication of mental or other biological deficiency, whatever one may think of his morals. However, someone else may actually have been the father.

To sum up: Anna's heredity is the kind that *might* have given rise to innate mental deficiency, though not necessarily.

Comparison with Another Case

Perhaps more to the point than speculations about Anna's ancestry would be a case for comparison. If a child could be discovered who had been isolated about the same length of time as Anna but had achieved a much quicker recovery and a greater mental development, it would be a stronger indication that Anna was deficient to start with.

Such a case does exist. It is the case of a girl found at about the same time as Anna and under strikingly similar circumstances. . . .

Born apparently one month later than Anna, the girl in question, who has been given the pseudonym Isabelle, was discovered in November, 1938, nine months after the discovery of Anna. At the time she was found she was approximately six and a half years of age. Like Anna, she was an illegitimate child and had been kept in seclusion for that reason. Her mother was a deaf-mute, having become so at the age of two, and it appears that she and Isabelle had spent most of their time together in a dark room shut off from the rest of the mother's family. As a result Isabelle had no chance to develop speech; when she communicated with her mother, it was by means of gestures. . . . Her behavior toward strangers, especially men, was almost that of a wild animal, manifesting much fear and hostility. In lieu of speech she made only a strange croaking sound. In many ways she acted like an infant. . . . At first it was even hard to tell whether or not she could hear, so unused were her senses. Many of her actions resembled those of deaf children.

It is small wonder that, once it was established that she could hear, specialists working with her believed her to be feeble-minded. . . .

In spite of this interpretation, the individuals in charge of Isabelle launched a systematic and skillful program of training. It seemed hopeless at first. The approach had to be through pantomime and dramatization, suitable to an infant. It required one week of intensive effort before she even made her first attempt to vocalization. Gradually she began to respond, however, and, after the first hurdles had at last been overcome, a curious thing happened. She went through the usual stages of learning characteristic of the years from one to six not only in proper succession but far more rapidly than normal. In a little over two months after her first vocalization she was putting sentences together. Nine months after that she could identify words and sentences on the printed page, could write well, could add to ten, and could retell a story after hearing it. Seven months beyond this point she had a vocabulary of 1,500–2,000 words and was asking complicated questions. Starting from an educational level of between one and three years (depending on what aspect one considers), she had reached a normal level by the time she was eight and a half years old. In short, she covered in two years the stages of learning that ordinarily require six. . . . [9]

When the writer saw Isabelle a year and a half after her discovery, she gave him the impression of being a very bright, cheerful, energetic little girl. She spoke well, walked and ran without trouble, and sang with gusto and accuracy. Today she is over fourteen years old and has passed the sixth grade in a public school. Her teachers say she participates in all school activities as normally as other children. . . .

Clearly the history of Isabelle's development is different from that of Anna's. In both cases there was an exceedingly low, or rather blank, intellectual level to begin with. In both cases it seemed that the girl might be congenitally feeble minded. In both a considerably higher level was reached later on. But the Ohio girl achieved a normal mentality within two years, whereas Anna was still marked inadequate at the end of four and a half years. This difference in achievement may suggest that Anna had less initial capacity. But an alternative hypothesis is possible.

One should remember that Anna never received the prolonged and expert attention that Isabelle received. The result of such attention, in the case of the Ohio girl, was to give her speech at an early stage, and her subsequent rapid development seems to have been a consequence of that. "Until Isabelle's speech and language development, she had all the characteristics of a feeble-minded child." Had Anna, who, from the standpoint of psychometric tests and early history, closely resembled this girl at the start, been given a mastery of speech at an earlier point by intensive training, her subsequent development might have been much more rapid. . . .

Consideration of Isabelle's case serves to show, as Anna's case does not clearly show, that isolation up to the age of six, with failure to acquire any form of speech and hence failure to grasp nearly the whole world of cultural meaning, does not preclude the subsequent acquisition of these. Indeed, there seems to be a process of accelerated recovery in which the child goes through the mental stages at a more rapid rate than would be the case in normal development. Just what would be the maximum age at which a person could remain isolated and still retain the capacity for full cultural acquisition is hard to say. Almost certainly it would not be as high as age fifteen; it might possibly be as low as age ten. Undoubtedly various individuals would differ considerably as to the exact age.

Anna's not an ideal case for showing the effects of extreme isolation, partly because she was possible deficient to begin with, partly because she did not receive the best training available, and partly because she did not live long enough. Nevertheless, her case is instructive when placed in the record with numerous cases of extreme isolation. This and the previous article about her are meant to place her in the record. It is to be hoped that other cases will be described in the scientific literature as they are discovered (as unfortunately they will be), for only in these rare cases of extreme isolation is it possible "to observe *concretely separated* two factors in the development of human personality which are always otherwise only analytically separated, the biogenic and the sociogenic factors."[10]

Endnotes

[1]Davis, K. (1940, January). Extreme social isolation of a child, *American Journal of Sociology*, 45, 554–565.

[2]Sincere appreciation is due to the officials in the Department of Welfare, Commonwealth of Pennsylvania, for their kind co-operation in making available the records concerning Anna and discussing the case frankly with the writer. . . .

[3]The records are not clear as to which day.

[4]Letter to one of the state officials in charge of the case.

[5]*Ibid.*

[6]Progress report of the school.

[7]Davis, *op. cit.*, p. 564.

[8]The facts set forth here as to Anna's ancestry are taken chiefly from a report of mental tests administered to Anna's mother by psychologists at a state hospital where she was taken for this purpose after the discovery of Anna's seclusion. This excellent report was not available to the writer when the previous paper on Anna was published.

[9]Mason, M. K. (1942). Learning to speak after six and one-half years of silence, *Journal of Speech Disorders*, 7, 295–304.

[10]Singh & Zingg, *op cit.*, pp. xxi–xxii, in a foreword by the writer.

Questions

1. How did the early experiences of the two young girls in the article differ prior to their discovery? How were they alike?

2. How did the two girls' experiences differ after their discovery? In other words, were there systematic differences in their training and education? If so, what were they, and how could these differences have affected the girls?

3. Anna had very little exposure to any human contact, while Isabelle likely had some contact with her mother, who was a deaf mute. To what degree could the developmental differences between Anna and Isabelle have stemmed from differences in mental ability? To what degree could these differences be explained by the varied contact that the girls had with other human beings?

Social Networks: The Value of Variety

BONNIE ERICKSON

Bonnie Erickson observes that people are happier and healthier when they have close family, friends, and confidants who know and care about them; but she also notes that people do better when they know many people casually. The value of diversity in people's social networks not only contributes to good health, but it also spills over into other parts of life. After reading this article, you'll interpret the old saying "It's not what you know, but who you know" a little differently.

Having close kin and intimate friends helps with many things, from coping with everyday problems to living longer. But what about the hundreds of more casual connections individuals have? What of acquaintances, workmates and neighbors? We tend to make such fast friends easily and lose them without noticing. Nonetheless, these seemingly thin social bonds are quite valuable when they are diverse.

Variety is the key. Knowing many kinds of people in many social contexts improves one's chances of getting a good job, developing a range of cultural interests, feeling in control of one's life and being healthy. Sometimes knowing many kinds of people is helpful because it improves the chances of having the right contact for some purpose: hearing of an attractive job opening, borrowing a lawnmower, getting the home cleaned.

Network variety can also be useful in itself, for example in jobs that call for diverse contacts. Either way, the critical matter is the variety of acquaintances and not the mere number.

Understanding Acquaintanceship

Sociologists have measured acquaintance networks by focusing on occupations. People in different occupations differ from each other in many important ways. The work we do reflects much of our pasts, such as schooling and

Reprinted from *Contexts* (2003), by permission of the University of California Press.

family background, and shapes the ways we live, such as tastes and lifestyles. Generally, someone who knows people in diverse kinds of jobs will thereby know people who are diverse in many respects. The standard strategy is to present a respondent with a list of occupations that range from very high to very low in prestige, and ask whether the respondent knows anyone in each. The greater number of occupations within which a respondent has a contact, the more the variety in the respondent's social network.

Researchers using this measure have found interesting differences between respondents in different nations. For example, a study in Albany, New York and a study in East Germany before the fall of the Communist regime each asked respondents about the same 10 occupations: Did they know anyone who was a lawyer, small business owner, teacher, engineer, motor mechanic, secretary, bookkeeper/office clerk, salesperson, porter/janitor or waiter?

The average respondent in Albany knew someone in 4.5 of these occupations, compared to an average of 3.8 for East Germans, so the American networks were about 20 percent more diverse. This is not surprising given that East Germans were wary of strangers in a totalitarian society in which about one in ten people in every work group was an informant for the secret police.

Such acquaintances are a more diverse set than are the few people to whom we feel really close—both because weak ties greatly outnumber strong ones, and because our close ties are usually limited to people very much like ourselves. For example, when I studied the private security industry in Toronto I asked whether people knew close friends, relatives, or anyone at all in each of 19 occupations. My respondents knew relatives, on average, in about two of these occupations, close friends in about half a dozen and anyone at all in about a dozen.

In every country that has been studied in this way, being of higher status goes with having a wider variety of acquaintances. In the Toronto security industry, business owners had contacts in 15 occupations, managers in 13, supervisors 10, and mere employees 9. In Hungary, before and even more so after the end of Communism, wealthier people had more diverse networks than the less wealthy. In Taiwan, more highly educated people have more diverse acquaintances than the less educated, and men have more diverse acquaintances than women do. In general, every kind of social advantage tends to generate a network advantage, which in turn helps the socially advantaged to stay ahead.

Networks and Jobs

Diverse networks can help people to get good jobs. Having a variety of acquaintances improves a jobseeker's chances of having one really useful contact, and variety itself is a qualification for some upper-end jobs.

People in North America find their jobs with the help of a contact roughly half the time. We might assume that such helpers must be close friends and relatives willing to work hard for the jobhunter. But this is not the usual story in Western nations. Close friends and kin want to help, but often cannot do very much because they are too much alike: they move in the same social circles and share information and influence, so they can do little for the candidate beyond what he or she can do alone. But acquaintances are more varied, less like each other, more likely to have new information and more likely to include people highly-placed enough to influence hiring. Thus family and close friends provide fewer jobs (and often worse jobs) than do people outside the intimate circle. This is the surprising finding that Mark Granovetter called "the strength of weak ties" (the title of one of the most frequently cited articles in social science).

The strength of strong ties applies best to the few people at the top, because they have highly-placed kin and friends who collect a lot of information and can exert a lot of influence. In general, more highly-placed people can connect a jobseeker to more highly-placed jobs, and one big advantage of having a diverse network is the improved chance of knowing such a useful contact. The Albany study found that people with more diversified acquaintances were more likely to get help from contacts holding more prestigious jobs, which led in turn to getting a job with higher prestige. On the other hand, for most people, using a friend or relative as a contact meant using someone with a lower-ranking job, and hence getting a worse job. For the few who came from privileged backgrounds, all kinds of helpers—friends, relatives or acquaintances—were in high-status positions on average, and all those kinds of contacts helped them get good jobs.

Having a diverse set of acquaintances matters where there is a fairly free market in jobs and a fairly rich supply of jobs. If jobs are scarce, those in the know will hoard access to good ones for people they care about the most, so strong ties are more valuable in these circumstances. In non-market systems run by the state, the private use of personal contacts to get jobs may be risky: networking subverts state power and policy, and influential people may not want to be responsible for the occupational or political errors of acquaintances whom they help. Well-placed people still provide personal help, but mainly to jobseekers or intermediaries whom they know well and can trust. Thus studies show that both the Chinese and the East Germans (before the change of regime) used strong ties the most, far more often than in the West.

Diversified acquaintances are valuable as an ensemble when employers want to recruit both a person and the person's contacts, to make his or her network work for the organization. This is especially true for higher-level jobs because it is only higher-level jobs that include consequential responsibility for the "foreign affairs" of the organization. For example, in my study of the private security industry in Toronto, I asked employers how they hired for jobs from security guard up to manager and asked whether the employer required "good contacts" for these positions. For lower-level jobs, they did not. But for upper-level jobs, employers often did want people with contacts they could use to monitor the industry and its environment, to get information, to recruit new customers and to maintain good relationships with powerful outsiders such as the police.

When employers think of good contacts, what do they mean? In a word, variety. Employers named desirable contacts of many kinds (in their own industry, government, the police, senior management, etc.) and sometimes explicitly wanted variety as such ("all available"). The more varied a person's network, the more that network can do for the organization.

Employees with more network variety got jobs with higher rank and higher income. This was true whether or not people got those jobs through someone they knew. Again, a network of acquaintances is more useful than one of intimates, because acquaintances have the diversity employers seek.

Does all this add up to "it's not what you know, but who you know?" Not really. Sometimes what you know is critical. Even in the security industry, which has no formal certifications, employers often want to hire people with contacts and skills, not contacts instead of skills. Because employers look for both, using personal connections helps most to get a job at the top or bottom of the ladder, not in the middle. At the bottom, skill requirements are modest. Employers just want a reliable employee and jobseekers just want an adequate job. Using contacts is one cheap way to make this match.

At the top, skill requirements are important but also hard to measure (how do you know whether someone will be a dynamic manager with current knowledge of the market, for example?) so employers look for prospects they know or candidates recommended by people they trust. In the middle, skill requirements are serious and fairly easy to measure through credentials (like a recent computer programming degree from a good school) or experience (like a strong track record in sales), so who the candidate knows matters less.

Networks and Health

Knowing people is important in getting a job, but it also matters for other areas of our lives that are less obvious, such as good health. Research has long shown that having close friends and family is good for a person's health. People who say they have someone they can count on feel less depressed, get less physically ill and live longer than those who do not. The newer news is that having a variety of acquaintances also improves health. In a study of a Toronto social movement, I asked people about both the diversity of their contacts outside the group and the diversity of their contacts within the group. I found that people with more diversified general networks were less depressed, and people with more diverse contacts in the group more often felt that participation had improved their health. Such findings may seem odd, because our intimates play a more obvious role in our health. We discuss our health concerns with those we trust and get care from those who care about us.

Acquaintances make more subtle contributions in small, invisible increments over the long run. One such contribution is a sense of control over one's life, a well-documented source of good health. People who feel more in control are less depressed just because of that, since feeling pushed around is a miserable and unwelcome experience. Moreover, having a sense of control encourages people to tackle problems they encounter, so they cope better with stress. This valuable sense of control grows with the diversity of acquaintances.

People with diverse contacts consciously adapt to different situations and manage conflicting obligations. They have to decide whom to see, how to act appropriately with others differing in their expectations, how to balance sometimes conflicting demands. As they navigate their intricate options, they develop a well-grounded sense of control over the lives. Thus I found that members with more diversified acquaintances outside the Toronto movement felt more in control of their lives overall, and members with more diversified acquaintances within the group more often felt that participation had empowered them.

Acquaintance diversity also contributes to being better informed about health. People with wider networks are better informed about most things, but they may not realize how many of their good health practices go back to a thousand tiny nudges from casual conversations. They may know that they are committed to pushing down the broccoli and getting some exercise, while forgetting how many acquaintances mentioned the importance of such healthy habits. My study of the security industry shows a clear link between diversity and information flow, not only about health, but on a variety of topics. People with more varied connections knew more about each of several different kinds of things: the arts (books and artists), popular culture (sports stars), and business culture (business magazines and restaurants suited to power dining).

Feeling in control and being well-informed both flow from the diversity of the whole ensemble of acquaintances. But health, like work, sometimes benefits from a varied network because varied connections are more likely to include particular useful ones. For example, people who knew many kinds of people in the social movement group were much more likely to get some help with health (from organic vegetables to massage) from associates in the group. They knew what to look for and whom to trust to provide it.

Diverse networks also improve people's health indirectly, by helping them get ahead economically, and wealthier people tend to be healthier people. But the connection between wealth and health might suggest that all these benefits of having a variety of acquaintances might really just reflect the advantages of high social position. People with more network variety, better jobs, more feelings of control and better health may be that way because they come from more privileged circumstances. It is important to note, therefore, that all the studies that I have described have taken into account other characteristics of individuals, such as educational attainment and gender. Nonetheless, the diversity of acquaintanceship itself improves health and happiness.

What Next?

Other possible benefits of network variety are yet to be studied. Students of politics have speculated that interacting with a range of people expands one's sources of political information and activity, and increases tolerance for others different from oneself—but this is only speculation at present because political research has focused exclusively on close relationships such as the handful of people with whom a person discusses important matters.

Another critical avenue for future work is the way in which we think about and measure network diversity. At present, almost all studies focus on the variety of occupations within which a respondent knows someone. This works very well, because occupation goes with so many important differences of resources, views, lifestyles and so on. But occupation is not the only way in which the social world is carved up into different kinds of people—gender and ethnicity also shape networks.

For instance, men occupy more powerful positions in organizations, so knowing a variety of men may help one's job search more than knowing a wide variety of women. But women take more responsibility for health, including the health of others, so knowing a good range of women may be better for one's health than knowing many kinds of men. In countries like the United States or Canada, ethnic groups have distinctive cultures and, sometimes, even labor markets. Knowing a variety of people in an ethnic group may lead to better jobs within the ethnic economy, to richer knowledge of the ethnic culture, to better access to alternative medicines and to feeling better about the group. At the same time, having acquaintances exclusively in an ethnic group may cut one off from broader social benefits.

Indeed, there are many kinds of network variety: variety of occupation, gender, ethnicity and much more. Each probably goes with a somewhat different menu of benefits. Future research should elaborate on the finding that, not only is knowing people good for you, but knowing many different kinds of people is especially good for you.

Questions

1. What is the value of variety in our social networks?
2. Define the "strength of weak ties" and the "strength of strong ties." Clarify how each is useful in your life.
3. Describe how social networks promote good health. What is more important in promoting good health—acquaintances or intimates? Explain your answer.
4. Evaluate the statement "It's not what you know, but who you know," and give an example from your own life to illustrate.

Gemeinschaft and Gesellschaft

FERDINAND TÖNNIES

In this excerpt from his book Community and Society, *German sociologist Ferdinand Tönnies presents two models of Tönnies societal organization that he calls* Gemeinschaft *and* Gesellschaft. *He uses these concepts to describe types of human grouping and stages of societal growth. As you read this selection, consider the advantages and disadvantages of each model of societal organization.*

Human wills stand in manifold relations to one another. Every such relationship is a mutual action, inasmuch as one party is active, or gives, while the other party is passive, or receives. These actions are of such a nature that they tend either toward preservation or destruction of the other will or life; that is, they are either positive or negative. This study will consider as its subject of investigation only the relationships of mutual affirmation. Every such relationship represents unity in plurality or plurality in unity. It consists of assistance, relief, services, which are transmitted back and forth from one party to another and are to be considered as expressions of wills and their forces. The group which is formed through this positive type of relationship is called an association *(Verbindung)* when conceived of as a thing or being which acts as a unit inwardly and outwardly. The relationship itself, and also the resulting association, is conceived of either as real and organic life—this is the essential characteristic of

---

the Gemeinschaft (community); or as imaginary and mechanical structure—this is the concept of Gesellschaft (society). . . .

All intimate, private, and exclusive living together, so we discover, is understood as life in Gemeinschaft (community). Gesellschaft (society) is public life—it is the world itself. In Gemeinschaft with one's family, one lives from birth on, bound to it in weal and woe. One goes into Gesellschaft as one goes into a strange country. A young man is warned against bad Gesellschaft, but the expression bad Gemeinschaft violates the meaning of the word. Lawyers may speak of domestic (*häusliche*) Gesellschaft, thinking only of the legalistic concept of social association; but the domestic Gemeinschaft, or home life with its immeasurable influence upon the human soul, has been felt by everyone who ever shared it. Likewise, a bride or groom knows that he or she goes into marriage as a complete Gemeinschaft of life. A Gesellschaft of life would be a contradiction in and of itself. One keeps or enjoys another's Gesellschaft, but not his Gemeinschaft in this sense. One becomes a part of a religious Gemeinschaft; religious Gesellschaften (associations or societies), like any other groups formed for given purposes, exist only in so far as they, viewed from without, take their places among the institutions of a political body or as they represent conceptual elements of a theory; they do not touch upon the religious Gemeinschaft as such. There exists a Gemeinschaft of language, of folkways or mores, or of beliefs; but, by way of contrast, Gesellschaft exists in the realm of business, travel, or sciences. So of special importance are the commercial Gesellschaften; whereas, even though a certain familiarity and Gemeinschaft may exist among business partners, one could indeed hardly speak of commercial Gemeinschaft. To make the word combination "joint-stock Gemeinschaft" would be abominable. On the other hand, there exists a Gemeinschaft of ownership in fields, forest, and pasture. The Gemeinschaft of property between man and wife cannot be called Gesellschaft of property. Thus many differences become apparent.

In the most general way, one could speak of a Gemeinschaft comprising the whole of mankind, such as the Church wishes to be regarded. But human Gesellschaft is conceived as mere coexistence of people independent of each other. . . .

Gemeinschaft is old; Gesellschaft is new as a name as well as a phenomenon. . . . [Says] Bluntschli *(Slaalswörterbuch IV)*, "finds its natural foundation in the folkways, mores, and ideas of the third estate. It is not really the concept of a people *(Volks-Begriff)* but the concept of the third estate . . . Its Gesellschaft has become the origin and expression of common opinion and tendencies . . . Wherever urban culture blossoms and bears fruits, Gesellschaft appears as its indispensable organ. The rural people know little of it." On the other hand, all praise of rural life has pointed out that the Gemeinschaft among people is stronger there and more alive; it is the lasting and genuine form of living together. In contrast to Gemeinschaft, Gesellschaft is transitory and superficial. Accordingly, Gemeinschaft should be understood as a living organism, Gesellschaft as a mechanical aggregate and artifact.

. . .

The Gemeinschaft by blood, denoting unity of being, is developed and differentiated into Gemeinschaft of locality, which is based on a common habitat. A further differentiation leads to the Gemeinschaft of mind, which implies only co-operation and co-ordinated action for a common goal. Gemeinschaft of locality may be conceived as a community of physical life, just as Gemeinschaft of mind expresses the community of mental life. In conjunction with the others, this last type of Gemeinshaft represents the truly human and supreme form of community. Kinship Gemeinschaft signifies a common relation to, and share in, human beings themselves, while in Gemeinschaft of locality such a common relation is established through collective ownership of land; and, in Gemeinschaft of mind, the common bond is represented by sacred places and worshiped deities. All three types of Gemeinschaft are closely interrelated in space as well as in time. They are, therefore, also related in all such single phenomena and in their development, as well as in general human culture and its history. Wherever human beings are related through their wills in an organic manner and affirm each other, we find one or another of the three types of Gemeinschaft. Either the earlier type involves the later one, or the later type has developed to relative independence from some earlier one. It is, therefore, possible to deal with (1) kinship, (2) neighborhood, and (3) friendship as definite and meaningful derivations of these original categories.

. . .

The theory of the Gesellschaft deals with the artificial construction of an aggregate of human beings which superficially resembles the Gemeinschaft in so far as the individuals live and dwell together peacefully. However, in the Gemeinschaft they remain essentially united in spite of all separating factors, whereas in the Gesellschaft they are essentially separated in spite of all uniting factors. In the Gesellschaft, as contrasted with the Gemeinschaft, we find no actions that can be derived from an a priori and necessarily existing unity; no actions, therefore, which manifest the will and the spirit of the unity even if performed by the individual; no actions which, in so far as they are performed by the individual, take place on behalf of those united with him. In the Gesellschaft such actions do not exist. On the contrary, here everybody is by himself and isolated, and there exists a condition of tension against all others. Their spheres of activity and power are sharply separated, so that everybody refuses to everyone else contact with and admittance to his sphere; i. e., intrusions are regarded as hostile acts. Such a negative attitude toward one another becomes the normal and always underlying relation of these power-endowed individuals, and it characterizes the Gesellschaft in the condition of rest; nobody wants to grant and produce anything for another individual, nor will he be inclined to give ungrudgingly to another individual, if it be not in exchange for a gift or labor equivalent that he considers at least equal to what he has given. It is even necessary that it be more desirable to him than what he could have kept himself; because he will be moved to give away a good only for the sake of receiving something that seems better to him.

. . .

In the conception of Gesellschaft, the original or natural relations of human beings to each other must be excluded. The possibility of a relation in the Gesellschaft assumes no more than a multitude of mere persons who are capable of delivering something, and consequently of promising something. Gesellschaft as a totality to which a system of conventional rules applies is limitless; it constantly breaks through its chance and real boundaries. In Gesellschaft every person strives for that which is to his own advantage and he affirms the actions of others only in so far as and as long as they can further his interest. Before and outside of convention and also before and outside of each special contract, the relation of all to all may therefore be conceived as potential hostility or latent war. Against this condition, all agreements of the will stand out as so many treaties and peace pacts. This conception is the only one which does justice to all facts of business and trade where all rights and duties can be reduced to mere value and definitions of ability to deliver. Every theory of pure private law or law of nature understood as pertaining to the Gesellschaft has to be considered as being based upon this conception.

. . .

Since all relations in the Gesellschaft are based upon comparison of possible and offered services, it is evident that the relations with visible, material matters have preference, and that mere activities and words form the foundation for such relationships only in an unreal way. In contrast to this, Gemeinschaft as a bond of "blood" is in the first place a physical relation, therefore expressing itself in deeds and words. Here, the common relation to the material objects is of a secondary nature, and such objects are not exchanged as often as they are used and possessed in common. . . .

Questions

1. What is Gemeinschaft?

2. What is Gesellschaft? How does it differ from Gemeinschaft?

3. Tönnies links Gemeinschaft to friendship and family and Gesellschaft to business and commerce. Could the opposite argument be made? Explain why or why not.
4. Which form of societal organization does Tönnies seem to prefer? Which form do you prefer? Explain why.

Characteristics of Bureaucracy

MAX WEBER

One of Max Weber's better known contributions to sociology is his work on formal organizations, particularly bureaucracy. In this selection, he describes the essential elements of bureaucracy as well as the functions of these elements. While reading this selection, ask yourself how accurately Weber's portrayal of bureaucracy reflects understandings of bureaucracy today.

Modern officialdom functions in the following specific manner:

I. There is the principle of fixed and official jurisdictional areas, which are generally ordered by rules, that is, by laws or administrative regulations.

1. The regular activities required for the purposes of the bureaucratically governed structure are distributed in a fixed way as official duties.

2. The authority to give the commands required for the discharge of these duties is distributed in a stable way and is strictly delimited by rules concerning the coercive means, physical, sacerdotal, or otherwise, which may be placed at the disposal of officials.

3. Methodical provision is made for the regular and continuous fulfillment of these duties and for the execution of the correspon-

---

"Characteristics of Bureaucracy," by Max Weber, reprinted from *Max Weber: Essays in Sociology*, translated and edited by H.H. Gerth and C. Wright Mills, 1946.
 pp. 196–198.

ding rights; only persons who have the generally regulated qualifications to serve are employed.

In public and lawful government these three elements constitute "bureaucratic authority." In private economic domination, they constitute bureaucratic "management." Bureaucracy, thus understood, is fully developed in political and ecclesiastical communities only in the modern state, and, in the private economy, only in the most advanced institutions of capitalism. Permanent and public office authority, with fixed jurisdiction, is not the historical rule but rather the exception. This is so even in large political structures such as those of the ancient Orient, the Germanic and Mongolian empires of conquest, or of many feudal structures of state. In all these cases, the ruler executes the most important measures through personal trustees, table-companions, or court-servants. Their commissions and authority are not precisely delimited and are temporarily called into being for each case.

II. The principles of office hierarchy and of levels of graded authority mean a firmly ordered system of super- and subordination in which there is a supervision of the lower offices by the higher ones. Such a system offers the governed the possibility of appealing the decision of a lower office to its higher authority, in a definitely regulated manner. With the full development of the bureaucratic type, the office hierarchy is monocratically organized. The principle of hierarchical office authority is found in all bureaucratic structures: in state and ecclesiastical structures as well as in large party organizations and private enterprises. It does not matter for the character of bureaucracy whether its authority is called "private" or "public."

When the principle of jurisdictional "competency" is fully carried through, hierarchical subordination—at least in public office—does not mean that the "higher" authority is simply authorized to take over the business of the "lower." Indeed, the opposite is the rule. Once established and having fulfilled its task, an office tends to continue in existence and be held by another incumbent.

III. The management of the modern office is based upon written documents ("the files"), which are preserved in their original or draught form. There is, therefore, a staff of subaltern officials and scribes of all sorts. The body of officials actively engaged in a "public" office, along with the respective apparatus of material implements and files, make up a "bureau." In private enterprise, "the bureau" is often called "the office."

In principle, the modern organization of the civil service separates the bureau from the private domicile of the official, and, in general, bureaucracy segregates official activity as something distinct from the sphere of private life. Public monies and equipment are divorced from the private property of the official. This condition is everywhere the product of a long development. Nowadays, it is found in public as well as in private enterprises; in the latter, the principle extends even to the leading entrepreneur. In principle, the executive office is separated from the household, business from private correspondence, and business assets from private fortunes. The more consistently the modern type of business management has been carried through the more are these separations the case. The beginnings of this process are to be found as early as the Middle Ages.

It is the peculiarity of the modern entrepreneur that he conducts himself as the "first official" of his enterprise, in the very same way in which the ruler of a specifically modern bureaucratic state spoke of himself as "the first servant" of the state.[1] The idea that the bureau activities of the state are intrinsically different in character from the management of private economic offices is a continental European notion and, by way of contrast is totally foreign to the American way.

IV. Office management, at least all specialized office management—and such management is distinctly modern—usually presupposes thorough and expert training. This increasingly holds for the modern executive and employee of private enterprises, in the same manner as it holds for the state official.

V. When the office is fully developed, official activity demands the full working capacity of the official, irrespective of the fact that his obligatory time in the bureau may be firmly delimited. In the normal case, this is only the product of a long development, in the public as well as in the private office. Formerly, in all cases, the normal state of affairs was reversed: official business was discharged as a secondary activity.

VI. The management of the office follows general rules, which are more or less stable, more or less exhaustive, and which can be learned. Knowledge of these rules represents a special technical learning which the officials possess. It involves jurisprudence, or administrative or business management.

The reduction of modern office management to rules is deeply embedded in its very nature. The theory of modern public administration, for instance, assumes that the authority to order certain matters by decree—which has been legally granted to public authorities—does not entitle the bureau to regulate the matter by commands given for each case, but only to regulate the matter abstractly. This stands in extreme contrast to the regulation of all relationships through individual privileges and bestowals of favor, which is absolutely dominant in patrimonialism, at least in so far as such relationships are not fixed by sacred tradition.

. . .

Endnote

[1]Frederick II of Prussia.

Questions

1. According to Weber, what are the three main elements of a bureaucracy?
2. To what degree do these elements apply to public enterprises? What about private enterprises?
3. What are the benefits and costs of hierarchical authority structures in a bureaucratic organization?
4. To what degree does Weber's conceptualization of bureaucracy apply to contemporary organizations?

Bureaucracy in Process

PETER M. BLAU, Columbia University

MARSHALL W. MEYER, Cornell University

Bureaucracy characterizes most contemporary organizations. In our everyday interactions, we benefit from the efficiency that bureaucracy affords. Unfortunately, we also experience the rigidity of its rules and regulations. However, most of us pay little attention to the more informal processes that unfold within a bureaucracy. In this selection, Peter Blau and Marshall Meyer discuss the relationship between the formal bureaucratic structure and these informal processes. Despite the latter, most of us still think of bureaucracies as cumbersome, rigid, and inefficient.

A bureaucracy in operation appears quite different from the abstract portrayal of its formal structure. Many official rules are honored in the breach; the members of the organization act as human beings—often friendly and sometimes disgruntled—rather than like dehumanized impersonal machines.

But this contradiction between official requirements and actual conduct in bureaucracies may be more apparent than real. Perhaps the violation of some rules is inconsequential for the organization, and the essential regulations are regularly obeyed.

. . .

"Bureaucracy in Process," by Peter M. Blau and Marshall W. Meyer, reprinted from *Bureaucracy in Modern Society*, Second Edition, 1971.

In a Police Department

The police in a small town may believe that they are treating equals equally even when they do not treat everybody the same (by, for example, an arrest). With their more intimate knowledge of the community, they can make more discriminating judgments about who is equal to whom.

In Brighton, for example, there was a series of incidents involving a Peeping Tom. The police knew the culprit, a minor executive of an important local firm. When such an incident was reported the police would call the man's wife and tell her, "Your husband's at it again." An arrest, they told the interviewer, would be difficult to make because the victim would often be reluctant to sign a complaint, but a serious effort to secure an arrest, to say nothing of the arrest itself, would make public the behavior of the culprit and no doubt cost him his job. The embarrassment of being reported to his wife was punishment enough. On another occasion the police found the daughter of a prominent local citizen staggering drunk down the street at night with practically no clothes on. They brought her to the station and, although she was very abusive, made no arrest. Instead, the police photographed her in her disorderly condition and showed the picture to her parents to convince them of the seriousness of the problem and to induce them to "do something." The incident was kept out of the town newspaper, which ordinarily prints almost all local police news. At the same time, the officers involved were disgusted to encounter a family that "had everything" but could not handle its own children. "Most of these kids could be straightened out at home if the parent only took the time to give them a little disciplining," said one office, "but you don't find that much anymore." Nonetheless, they were sure they had done the right thing, because they had no further trouble with the young lady.

Officers who stop motorists for traffic violations will take into account who is involved, and his attitude, in determining whether a ticket should be issued. One patrolman told an interviewer that if the driver is a doctor or a clergyman, "We just like to warn (them) to slow down for their own good; they may be tired and in a hurry to get home from the hospital."

A traffic ticket once issued in Brighton cannot be fixed—it is a numbered form, all of which must be accounted for to the state. But the police are aware that people who feel unjustly ticketed will try to intervene with the judge or with other town leaders. A senior police officer explained what usually happens: "I can't do anything about a traffic ticket. The judge, he can . . . do anything he wants with it . . . I'm glad. I'd just as soon not get involved in that. I will write a note to the judge asking for leniency in certain cases. I had one involving . . . a big political figure. . . . When it came in I got a phone call saying that, 'Do you know that one of your men just ticketed X's car?' I told him I couldn't do anything about it, but that I would write a letter to the judge explaining what had happened and ask him to go easy. I'm not sure what happened, but I imagine the judge probably dismissed or suspended (the sentence)."

A small department may be more sensitive to circumstances of personality and politics, but by the same token this sensitivity need have nothing to do—indeed, it would create problems if it *did* have something to do—with vulgar bribery. A bribe induces an officer to act other than as his duty requires. Its value requires that an officer have something to sell—freedom from an arrest he is otherwise empowered to make—and that a citizen be willing to buy. Ideally, the transaction should be secret; even if higher police officials were willing to tolerate it, they could rarely do so publicly, and few important citizens concerned about their reputation want to be known in a small town as persons who buy special privileges. But keeping secrets in a small town is not easy. More important, it is not necessary—the officer rarely has anything to sell because his superiors expect him to treat "somebodies" different from "nobodies." A prominent man who is drunk in a public place will, unless he behaves in an extraordinary manner, be taken home or turned over to friends. A shabbily dressed itinerant with no family or friends who commits the same offense will be arrested—there is no place to take him, it is unlikely that embarrassment or a hangover will prove an effective punishment, and he may, lacking a place to stay, hurt himself or endanger others.[1]

Organization of Work Groups

When we examine sufficiently small segments of bureaucracies to observe their operations in detail, we discover patterns of activities and interactions that cannot be accounted for by the official structure. Whether the work group is part of the armed forces, a factory, civil service, or the police, it is characterized by a network of informal relations and a set of unofficial practices which have been called its "informal organization." This concept calls attention to the fact that deviations from the formal blueprint are socially organized patterns and not merely the consequence of fortuitous personality differences. . . .

Regularities do not occur accidentally. That official rules bring them about is expected, but what is the source of those regularities in social conduct that do not reflect official standards? They are also the result of normative standards, but standards that have emerged in the work group itself rather than having been officially instituted by superiors or formal blueprints. In the course of social interaction to work, there arise patterned expectations and norms, which find expression in a network of social relationships and in prevailing practices. . . .

To be effective, social norms must be enforceable. Unless a member of a formal organization conforms with its official regulations to a certain minimum degree, he will be expelled. The reverse of this statement is also true: unless expulsion is a serious threat, the prevalence of conformity cannot be assured. The individual's motivation to remain part of the organization makes him subject to its control. Salaried employees are more dependable than unpaid volunteers in large part because economic dependence is a reliable mechanism for interesting the members of the organization in keeping their positions. The same principle holds for the enforcement of unofficial norms. Whereas the work group does not have the power to remove one of its members from his job and deprive him of his income, it can ostracize him and thereby exclude him from genuine group membership. But for such exclusion to be a threat that discourages deviant tendencies, the individual must first wish to be included in the group. If a person did not care about maintaining congenial relations with his co-workers, being cold-shouldered by them would neither disconcert him nor deter him from disregarding their social norms; and for him it would be "their" norms rather than "ours."

This is the reason why the existence of social cohesion is so significant for work groups. Strong mutual ties between the members of a group make each interested in maintaining his position in the group. In this situation, unofficial norms can readily be enforced, and it is rarely necessary to resort to the extreme penalty of ostracism, since lesser sanctions suffice to sustain conformity. If an individual violates a norm highly valued by the other members of the group, they will become less friendly towards him; this is virtually an automatic reaction when somebody's behavior displeases us. Such a change in interpersonal relationships endangers the individual's standing in the group and induces him, if he is identified with the group, to refrain from similar violations in the future in order to regain the favor of his colleagues or, at least, to prevent his relations with them from deteriorating further.

. . .

Social scientists often set up a dichotomy between the informal and the formal organization and attempt to place every observation into one of these pigeonholes. This procedure can only be misleading, since the distinction is an analytical one: there is only one actual organization. When government agents make official decisions in the course of informal discussions, their conduct cannot meaningfully be classified as belonging to either the formal or the informal organization. . . . Official as well as unofficial standards, formal as well as informal social relations, affect the ways in which the daily operations in work groups become organized, but the result is *one* social organization in each work group, not two.

Bureaucratic Ideologies

Social processes in bureaucracies modify their structures and operations. Some of these processes make the organization more flexible and responsive to changing conditions, such as the informal modifications of formal procedures that emerge, but other bureaucratic processes engender rigidities and resistance to change. The popular stereotype of bureaucracy exaggerates the rigidity. . . of formal organizations, but it is not without considerable basis in fact. One important organizational process that engenders rigidity is the tendency, in large bureaucracies, for organizational ideologies to develop that take precedence over original goals, distort perceptions, and typically create resistance to change by sanctifying the existing state of affairs. It should be emphasized that concern here is not with the pathologies of individual bureaucrats but rather with organizational processes that lead to the shaping of conduct by ideologies or myths instead of by initial objectives and external realities. An ideology may be confined to a particular organization and glorify its traditions; or it may pertain to administrative practice in general and be widely accepted in many organizations.

. . .

The Myth of "Scientific Management"

In the early part of this century, an ideology concerning administrative practices developed which went under the label of "scientific management," and which influenced management in many industrial organizations. Scientific management has attempted to rationalize industrial production and administration by discovering and applying the most efficient methods of operations.[2] Time-and-motion studies are a well-known illustration of this approach: the motions required by the most skilled workers for performing a given task in the shortest possible time are determined, and these exact motions are taught to other workers. But, as a well-known industrial sociologist points out, "managerial technologists have been far more successful in demonstrating the efficient procedures for maximum productivity than they have been in getting such procedures accepted by workers."[3] This failure of scientific management was the inevitable result of its assumption, most evident in "scientific" wage incentive systems, that rational economic interests alone govern the conduct of employees and of its neglect of social factors. To administer a social organization according to purely technical criteria of rationality is irrational because the nonrational aspects of social conduct are ignored.

From an abstract standpoint, the most traditional method of effecting uniformity and coordination in a large organization would appear to be to devise efficient procedures for every task and to insist that they be strictly followed. In practice, however, such a system would not function effectively for several reasons. One is that it implicitly assumes that management is omniscient. No system of rules and supervision can be so finely spun that it anticipates all exigencies that may arise. Changes in external conditions create new administrative problems, and the very innovations introduced to solve them often have unanticipated consequences that produce further problems. For example, the interviewers in a public employment agency were evaluated on the basis of the number of applicants for jobs they interviewed per month. As jobs became scarce after World War II, interviewers, induced by this method of evaluation to work fast, tended to dismiss clients for whom jobs could not be located quickly. In the interest of effective employment services, it was necessary to discourage such tendencies. For this purpose, a new method of evaluation, based primarily on the number of applicants placed in jobs, was instituted. This innovation did motivate interviewers to exert greater efforts to find jobs for clients, but it also gave rise to competition for the slips of paper on which job openings were recorded, which interviewers sometimes even hid from one another. These competitive practices were naturally a new obstacle to efficient operations. In response to the emergent problem, the most cohesive group of interviewers developed cooperative norms and successfully suppressed competitive tendencies, with the result that productive efficiency increased.[4] Unless the members of the organization have the freedom and initiative to deal with operating problems as they come up, efficiency will suffer.

Moreover, some impediments to operating efficiency cannot be eradicated by official decree. This is the case with respect to the anxieties and feelings of *anomie* (a state of feeling isolated and disoriented) that often arise among the lower echelons of bureaucratic hierarchies. Informal relations in cohesive work groups reduce such disruptive tensions. But once cohesive groups exist in the bureaucracy, as we have seen, they will develop their own standards of conduct and enforce them among their members. Administrative efficiency cannot be served by ignoring the fact that the performance of individuals is affected by their relations with colleagues, but only by taking cognizance of the fact and attempting to create those conditions in the organization that lead to unofficial practices which further rather than hinder the achievement of its objectives.

Finally, in a democratic culture, where independence of action and equality of status are highly valued, detailed rules and close supervision are resented, and resentful employees are poorly motivated to perform their duties faithfully and energetically. A striking contrast exists between the rigorous discipline employees willingly impose upon themselves because they realize that their work requires strict operating standards, and their constant annoyance at being hamstrung by picayune rules that they experience as arbitrarily imposed upon them. . . .

Let us conclude this discussion with a reexamination of the concept of bureaucracy. Bureaucracies can be defined as formally established organizations designed to maximize administrative efficiency. In other words, they are characterized by formalized procedures for mobilizing and coordinating the collective efforts of many, usually specialized, individuals and subgroups in the pursuit of organizational objectives. However, social processes arise within the formal structure that modify it. Although the formally established structure and procedures are designed to further efficiency, some of these emergent processes defeat the formal design and create bureaucratic rigidity which interferes with adaptation to changing conditions and impedes efficiency. Other internal processes have the opposite effect and create informal adjustments to new situations and problems that arise, thus furthering effective operations. A fundamental dilemma of bureaucratic administration is that the very arrangements officially instituted to improve efficiency often have by-products that impede it. Centralized authority, even if it results in superior decisions, undermines the ability of middle managers to assume responsibilities. Detailed rules, even if they improve performance, prevent adaptation to changing situations. Strict discipline, even if it facilitates managerial direction, creates resentments that reduce effort. Generally, there are no formal arrangements that can assure efficiency because it depends on flexible adjustments to varying and changing conditions in the organization. What formal arrangements can and should do, however, is create conditions in the organization that foster processes of adjustment. The main task of management is not to lay down rules on how to do the work but to maintain conditions in which adjustments spontaneously occur when new problems arise and to protect these conditions from bureaucratic processes of ossification.

Endnotes

[1]Wilson, J. Q. (1968). *Varieties of police behavior.* Cambridge, MA: Harvard University Press, 220–222. Copyright, 1968, by the President and Fellows of Harvard College. By permission.

[2]See Taylor, F. W. (1911). *The principles of scientific management.* New York: Harper & Brothers.

[3]Moore, W. E. (1947). *Industrial relations and the social order.* New York: Macmillan, 190.

[4]See Blau, *op. cit.*, 57–81.

Questions

1. Define bureaucracy. Provide examples of each element of bureaucracy from either your college/university setting or your place of employment.
2. How do the formal and informal organizational structures in a bureaucracy differ? How are they alike?
3. How do Blau and Meyer explain deviations in behavior away from the formal organizational structure?
4. What role does ideology play in a bureaucracy? How does ideology affect the formal and informal operations of a bureaucracy?
5. Define "scientific management." How is scientific management related to bureaucratic structure? How do formal and informal operations affect the efficiency of "scientific management"?
6. Explain how the formal and informal processes associated with bureaucracy pertain to an experience you have had while in college. Examples might involve financial aid or registration, among other aspects of college life.

The Meaning of Social Control

PETER BERGER

In this selection, Peter Berger introduces the concept of social control. He is primarily interested in explaining how informal social control mechanisms, such as jobs and families, constrain human behavior in everyday interactions. While he covers some important domains, he is not writing for college students and thus ignores the role of student in his treatment. As you read the piece, ask yourself how the student role may also qualify as a form of social control. Specifically, how does it shape your own behavior?

. . .

Social control is one of the most generally used concepts in sociology. It refers to the various means used by a society to bring its recalcitrant members back into line. No society can exist without social control. Even a small group of people meeting occasionally will have to develop their mechanisms of control if the group is not to dissolve in a very short time. It goes without saying that the instrumentalities of social control vary greatly from one social situation to another. Opposition to the line in a business organization may mean what personnel directors call a terminal interview, and in a criminal syndicate a terminal automobile ride. Methods of control vary with the purpose and character of the group in question. In either case, control mechanisms function to eliminate undesirable personnel and

---

"The Meaning of Social Control," by Peter Berger, reprinted from *Invitation to Sociology: A Humanistic Perspective*, 1963, Anchor Books/Doubleday. pp. 66-92. www.randomhouse.com

(as it was put classically by King Christophe of Haiti when he had every tenth man in his forced-labor battalion executed) "to encourage the others."

The ultimate and, no doubt, the oldest means of social control is physical violence. In the savage society of children it is still the major one. But even in the politely operated societies of modern democracies the ultimate argument is violence. No state can exist without a police force or its equivalent in armed might. This ultimate violence may not be used frequently. There may be innumerable steps before its application, in the way of warnings and reprimands. But if all the warnings are disregarded, even in so slight a matter as paying a traffic ticket, the last thing that will happen is that a couple of cops show up at the door with handcuffs and a Black Maria. Even the moderately courteous cop who hands out the initial traffic ticket is likely to wear a gun—just in case. And even in England, where he does not in the normal course of events, he will be issued one if the need arises. . . .

. . . In any functioning society violence is used economically and as a last resort, with the mere threat of this ultimate violence sufficing for the day-to-day exercise of social control. For our purposes in this argument, the most important matter to underline is that nearly all men live in social situations in which, if all other means of coercion fail, violence may be officially and legally used against them.

If the role of violence in social control is thus understood, it becomes clear that the, so to speak, penultimate means of coercion are more important for more people most of the time. While there is a certain uninspired sameness about the methods of intimidation thought up by jurists and policemen, the less-than-violent instrumentalities of social control show great variety and sometimes imagination. Next in line after the political and legal controls one should probably place economic pressure. Few means of coercion are as effective as those that threaten one's livelihood or profit. Both management and labor effectively use this threat as an instrumentality of control in our society. But economic means of control are just as effective outside the institutions properly called the economy. Universities or churches use economic sanctions just as effectively in restraining their personnel from engaging in deviant behavior deemed by the respective authorities to go beyond the limits of the acceptable. It may not be actually illegal for a minister to seduce his organist, but the threat of being barred forever from the exercise of his profession will be a much more effective control over this temptation than the possible threat of going to jail. It is undoubtedly not illegal for a minister to speak his mind on issues that the ecclesiastical bureaucracy would rather have buried in silence, but the chance of spending the rest of his life in minimally paid rural parishes is a very powerful argument indeed. Naturally such arguments are employed more openly with economic institutions proper, but the administration of economic sanctions in churches or universities is not very different in its end results from that used in the business world.

Where human beings live or work in compact groups, in which they are personally known and to which they are tied by feelings of personal loyalty (the kind that sociologists call primary groups), very potent and simultaneously very subtle mechanisms of control are constantly brought to bear upon the actual or potential deviant. These are the mechanisms of persuasion, ridicule, gossip and opprobrium. It has been discovered that in group discussions going on over a period of time individuals modify their originally held opinions to conform to the group norm, which corresponds to a kind of arithmetic mean of all the opinions represented in the group. Where this norm lies obviously depends on the constituency of the group. For example, if you have a group of twenty cannibals arguing over cannibalism with one noncannibal, the chances are that in the end he will come to see their point and, with just a few face-saving reservations (concerning, say, the consumption of close relatives), will go over completely to the majority's point of view. But if you have a group discussion between ten cannibals who regard human flesh aged over sixty years as too tough for a cultivated palate and ten other cannibals who fastidiously draw the line at fifty, the chances are that the group will eventually agree on fifty-five as the age that divides the *déjeuner* from the *débris* when it comes to sorting out prisoners. Such are the wonders of group dynamics. What lies at the bottom of this apparently inevitable pressure towards consensus is probably a profound human desire to be accepted, presumably by whatever group is around to do the accepting. This desire can be manipulated most effectively, as is well known by group therapists, demagogues and other specialists in the field of consensus engineering.

Ridicule and gossip are potent instruments of social control in primary groups of all sorts. Many societies use ridicule as one of the main controls over children—the child conforms not for fear of punishment but in order not to be laughed at. Within our own larger culture, "kidding" in this way has been an important disciplinary measure among Southern Negroes. But most men have experienced the freezing fear of making oneself ridiculous in some social situation. Gossip, as hardly needs elaboration, is especially effective in small communities, where most people live their lives in a high degree of social visibility and inspectability by their neighbors. In such communities gossip is one of the principal channels of communication, essential for the maintenance of the social fabric. Both ridicule and gossip can be manipulated deliberately by any intelligent person with access to their lines of transgression.

Finally, one of the most devastating means of punishment at the disposal of a human community is to subject one of its members to systematic opprobrium and ostracism. It is somewhat ironic to reflect that this is a favorite control mechanism with groups opposed on principle to the use of violence. An example of this would be "shunning" among the Amish Mennonites. An individual who breaks one of the principal tabus of the group (for example, by getting sexually involved with an outsider) is "shunned." This means that, while permitted to continue to work and live in the community, not a single person will speak to him ever. It is hard to imagine a more cruel punishment. But such are the wonders of pacifism. . . .

It is possible, then, to perceive oneself as standing at the center (that is, at the point of maximum pressure) of a set of concentric circles, each representing a system of social control. The other ring might well represent the legal and political system under which one is obligated to live. This is the system that, quite against one's will,

will tax one, draft one into the military, make one obey its innumerable rules and regulations, if need be put one in prison, and in the last resort will kill one. One does not have to be a right-wing Republican to be perturbed by the ever-increasing expansion of this system's power into every conceivable aspect of one's life. A salutary exercise would be to note down for the span of a single week all the occasions, including fiscal ones, in which one came up against the demands of the politico-legal system. The exercise can be concluded by adding up the sum total of fines and/or terms of imprisonment with disobedience to the system might lead to. The consolidation, incidentally, with which one might recover from this exercise would consist of the recollection of law-enforcement agencies are normally corrupt and of only limited efficiency.

Another system of social control that exerts its pressures towards the solitary figure in the center that is of morality, custom and manners. Only the most urgent-seeming (to the authorities, that is) aspects of this system are endowed with legal sanctions. This does not mean, however, that one can safely be immoral, eccentric or unmannered. At this point all the other instrumentalities of social control go into action. Immorality is punished by loss of one's job, eccentricity by the loss of one's chances of finding a new one, bad manners by remaining uninvited and uninvitable in the groups that respect what they consider good manners. Unemployment and loneliness may be minor penalties compared to being dragged away by the cops, but they may not actually appear so to the individuals thus punished. Extreme defiance against the *mores* of our particular society, which is quite sophisticated in its control apparatus, may lead to yet another consequence—that of being defined, by common consent, as "sick.". . .

But in addition to these broad coercive systems that every individual shares with vast numbers of fellow controlees, there are other and less extensive circles of control to which he is subjected. His choice of an occupation (or, often more accurately, the occupation in which he happens to end up) inevitably subordinates the individual to a variety of controls, often stringent ones. There are the formal controls of licensing boards, professional organizations and trade unions—in addition, of course, to the formal requirements set by his particular employers. Equally important are the informal controls imposed by colleagues and co-workers. Again, it is hardly necessary to elaborate overly on this point. The reader can construct his own examples—the physician who participates in a prepaid comprehensive health insurance program, the undertaker who advertises inexpensive funerals, the engineer in industry who does not allow for planned obsolescence in his calculations, the minister who says that he is not interested in the size of the membership of his church (or rather, the one who acts accordingly—they nearly all say so), the government bureaucrat who consistently spends less than his allotted budget, the assembly-line worker who exceeds the norms regarded as acceptable by his colleagues, and so on. Economic sanctions are, of course, the most frequent and effective ones in these instances—the physician finds himself barred from all available hospitals, the undertaker may be expelled from his professional organization for "unethical conduct," the engineer may have to volunteer for the Peace Corps, as may the minister and the bureaucrat (in, say, New Guinea, where there is as yet no planned obsolescence, where Christians are few and far between, and where the governmental machinery is small enough to be relatively rational), and the assembly-line worker may find that all the defective parts of machinery in the entire plant have a way of congregating on his workbench. But the sanctions of social exclusion, contempt and ridicule may be almost as hard to bear. Each occupational role in society, even in very humble jobs, carries with it a code of conduct that is very hard indeed to defy. Adherence to this code is normally just as essential for one's career in the occupation as technical competence or training. . . .

Finally, the human group in which one's so-called private life occurs, that is the circle of one's family and personal friends, also constitutes a control system. It would be a grave error to assume that this is necessarily the weakest of them all just because it does not possess the formal means of coercion of some of the other control systems. It is in this circle that an individual normally has his most important social ties. Disapproval, loss of prestige, ridicule or contempt in this intimate group has far more serious psychological weight than the same reactions encountered elsewhere. It may be economically disastrous if one's boss finally concludes that one is a worthless nobody, but the psychological effect of such a judgment is incomparably more devastating if one discovers that one's wife has arrived at the same conclusion. What is more, the pressures of this most intimate control system can be applied at those times when one is least prepared for them. At one's job one is usually in a better position to embrace oneself, to be on one's guard and to pretend than one is at home. Contemporary American "familism," a set of values that strongly emphasizes the home as a part of refuge from the tensions of the world and of personal fulfillment, contributes effectively to this control system. The man who is at least relatively prepared psychologically to give battle in his office is willing to do almost anything to preserve the precarious harmony of his family life. Last but not least, the social control of what German sociologists have called the "sphere of the intimate" is particularly powerful because of the very factors that have gone into its construction in the individual's biography. A man chooses a wife and a good friend in acts of essential self-definition. His most intimate relationships are those that he must count upon to sustain the most important elements of his self-image. To risk, therefore, the disintegration of these relationships means to risk losing himself in total way. It is no wonder then that many an office despot promptly obeys his wife and cringes before the raised eyebrows of his friends.

If we return once more to the picture of an individual located at the center of a set of concentric circles, each one representing a system of social control, we can understand a little better that location in society means to locate oneself with regard to many forces that constrain and coerce one. The individual who, thinking consecutively of all the people he is in a position to have to please, from the Collector of Internal Revenue to his mother-in-law, gets the idea that all of society sits right on top of him had better not dismiss that idea as a momentary neurotic derangement. The sociologist, at any rate, is likely to strengthen him in this conception, no matter what other counselors may tell him to snap out of it.

. . .

The sanctions of society are able at each moment of existence to isolate us among our fellow men, to subject us to ridicule, to deprive us of our sustenance and our liberty, and in the last resort to deprive us of life itself. The law and the morality of society can produce elaborate justifications for each one of these sanctions, and most of our fellow men will approve if they are used against us in punishment for our deviance. Finally, we are located in society not only in space but in time. Our society is a historical entity that extends temporally beyond any individual biography. Society antedates us and it will survive us. It was there before we were born and it will be there after we are dead. Our lives are but episodes in its majestic march through time. In sum, society is the walls of our imprisonment in history.

Questions

1. Define social control.
2. Explain how economic mechanisms or constraints can be effective forms of social control. Under what circumstances might economic constraints be more or less effective?
3. There are various forms of social control including violence, politics, economic structures, social ostracism or isolation, and moral constraints. If you had to rank these from most to least effective, how would you do it? Why?
4. In our everyday interactions, we face numerous constraints on our behavior. Berger mentions occupation as one of these. If you assume that your occupation is that of "student," explain how this role may serve as a mechanism of social control.

5. Peer groups also constrain our behavior. Explain how this happens. How does peer group compare with family unit as a source of social control?

Race and Class in the American Criminal Justice System

DAVID COLE

In his book No Equal Justice, *David Cole examines inequality in the criminal justice system, paying particular attention to inequities toward race and class. In this selection, he carefully summarizes his major themes and findings. He contends that inequities exist because "our criminal justice system affirmatively depends on inequality." He further argues that inequality in the judicial arena widens the already growing gap between whites and blacks, and between rich and poor, in other areas of society.*

The most telling image from the most widely and closely watched criminal trial of our lifetime is itself an image of people watching television. On one half of the screen black law students at Howard Law School cheer as they watch the live coverage of a Los Angeles jury acquitting O. J. Simpson of the double murder of his ex-wife and her friend. On the other half of the screen, white students at George Washington University Law school sit shocked in silence as they watch the same scene. The split-screen image captures in a moment the division between white and black Americans on the question of O. J. Simpson's guilt. And that division in turn reflects an even deeper divide on the issue of the fairness and legitimacy of American criminal justice.

Before, during, and after the trial, about three quarters of black citizens maintained that Simpson was not guilty, while an equal fraction of white citizens deemed him guilty. More people paid attention to this trial than any other in world history, but neither the DNA evidence nor the dubious reliability of Los Angeles detective Mark Fuhrman altered either group's views on guilt or innocence.

In some respects, the racially divided response to the verdict was understandable. For many black citizens, the acquittal was a sign of hope, or at least payback. For much of our history, the mere allegation that a black man had murdered two white people would have been sufficient grounds for his lynching. Until very recently, the jury rendering judgment on O. J. Simpson would likely have been all white; Simpson's jury, by contrast, consisted of nine blacks, two whites, and an Hispanic. And the prosecution was poisoned by the racism of the central witness, Detective Mark Fuhrman, who had, among other things, called blacks "niggers" on tape and then lied about it on the stand. To many blacks, the jury's "not guilty" verdict demonstrated that the system is not *always* rigged against the black defendant, and that was worth cheering.

The white law students' shock was also understandable. The evidence against Simpson was overwhelming. Simpson's blood had been found at the scene of the murders. The victims' blood had been found in Simpson's white Bronco and on a sock in Simpson's bedroom. And a glove found at Simpson's home had, as prosecutor Marcia Clark put it in her closing argument to the jury, "all of the evidence on it: Ron Goldman, fibers from his shirt; Ron Goldman's hair; Nicole's hair; the defendant's blood; Ron Goldman's blood; Nicole's blood; and the Bronco fiber."[1] The defense's suggestion that the Los Angeles Police Department somehow planted all of this evidence ran directly contrary to their simultaneous (and quite effective) demonstration of the LAPD's "keystone cops" incompetence. To many whites, it appeared that a predominantly black jury had voted for one of their own, and had simply ignored the overwhelming evidence that Simpson was a brutal double murderer.

But there is a deep irony in these reactions. Simpson, of course, was atypical in every way. The very factors that played to his advantage at trial generally work to the disadvantage of the vast majority of black defendants. Simpson had virtually unlimited resources, a jury that identified with him along racial grounds, and celebrity status. Most black defendants, by contrast, cannot afford any attorney, much less a "dream team." Their fate is usually decided by predominantly or exclusively white juries. And most black defendants find that their image is linked in America's mind not with celebrity, but with criminality.

At the same time, the features that worked to Simpson's advantage, and that occasioned such outrage among whites, generally benefit whites. Whites have a disproportionate share of the wealth in our society, and are more likely to be able to buy a good defense; white defendants generally face juries composed of members of their own race; and a white person's face is not stereotypically associated with crime. Thus, what dismayed whites in Simpson's case is precisely what generally works to their advantage, while what blacks cheered is what most often works to their disadvantage.

Had Simpson been poor and unknown, as most black (and white) criminal defendants are, everything would have been different. The case would have garnered no national attention. Simpson would have been represented by an overworked and underpaid public defender who would not have been able to afford experts to examine and challenge the government's evidence. No one would have conducted polls on the case, and the trial would not have been televised. In all likelihood, Simpson would have been convicted in short order, without serious testing of the evidence against him or the methods by which it was obtained. Whites would have expressed no outrage that a poor black defendant had been convicted, and blacks would have had nothing to cheer about. That, not *California v. O. J. Simpson,* is the reality in American courtrooms across the country today.

In other words, it took an atypical case, one in which minority race and lower socioeconomic class did *not* coincide, in which the defense outperformed the prosecution, and in which the jury was predominantly black, for white people to pay attention to the role that race and class play in criminal justice. Yet the issues of race and class are present in every criminal case, and in the vast majority of cases they play out no more fairly. Of course, they generally work in the opposite direction: the prosecution outspends and outperforms the defense, the jury is predominantly white, and the defendant is poor and a member of a racial minority. In an odd way, then, the Simpson case brought to the foreground issues that lurk beneath the entire system of criminal justice. The system's legitimacy turns on equality before the law, but the system's reality could not be further from that ideal. As Justice Hugo Black wrote over 40 years ago: "There can be no equal justice where the kind of trial a man gets depends on the amount of money he has." He might well have added, "or the color of his skin." Where race and class affect outcomes, we cannot maintain that the criminal law is just.

Equality, however, is a difficult and elusive goal. In our nation, it has been the cause of a civil war, powerful political movements, and countless violent uprisings. Yet the gap between the rich and the poor is larger in the United States today than in any other Western industrialized nation,[2] and has been steadily widening since 1968.[3] In 1989, the wealthiest 1% of U.S. households owned nearly 40% of the nation's wealth. The wealthiest 20% owned more than 80% of the nation's wealth. That leaves precious little for the rest.[4] The income and wealth gap correlates closely with race. Minorities' median net worth is less than 7% that of whites.[5] Nine percent of white families had incomes below the poverty level in 1992, while more than 30% of black families and 26.5% of Hispanic families fell below that level.[6] The consequences of the country's race and class divisions are felt in every aspect of American life, from infant mortality and unemployment, where black rates are double white rates;[7] to public education, where the proportion of black children educated in segregated schools is increasing;[8] to housing, where racial segregation is the norm, integration the rare exception.[9] Racial inequality . . . remains to this day the most formidable of our social problems.

This inequality is in turn reflected in statistics on crime and the criminal justice system. The vast majority of those behind bars are poor; 40% of state prisoners can't even read; and 67% of prison inmates did not have full-time employment when they were arrested. The per capita incarceration rate among blacks is seven times that among whites. African Americans make up about 12% of the general population, but more than half of the prison population. They serve longer sentences, have higher arrest and conviction rates, face higher bail amounts, and are more often the victims of police use of deadly force than white citizens. In 1995, one in three young black men between the ages of 20 and 29 was imprisoned or on parole or probation. If incarceration rates continue their current trends, one in four young black males born today will serve time in prison during his lifetime (meaning that he will be convicted and sentenced to more than one year of incarceration). Nationally, for every one black man who graduates from college, 100 are arrested.[10]

In addition, poor and minority citizens are disproportionately victimized by crime. Poorer and less educated persons are the victims of violent crime at significantly higher rates than wealthy and more educated persons.[11] African Americans are victimized by robbery at a rate 150% higher than whites; they are the victims of rape, aggravated assault, an armed robbery 25% more often than whites.[12] Homicide is the leading cause of death among young black men.[13] Because we live in segregated communities, most crime is intraracial; the more black crime there is, the more black victims there are. But at the same time, the more law enforcement resources we direct toward protecting the black community from crime, the more often black citizens, especially those living in the inner city, will find their friends, relatives, and neighbors behind bars.

. . . While our criminal justice system is explicitly based on the premise and promise of equality before the law, the administration of criminal law—whether by the officer on the beat, the legislature, or the Supreme Court—is in fact predicated on the exploitation of inequality. My claim is not simply that we have ignored inequality's effects within the criminal justice system, nor that we have tried but failed to achieve equality there. Rather, I contend that *our criminal justice system affirmatively depends on inequality.* Absent race and class disparities, the privileged among us could not enjoy as much constitutional protection of our liberties as we do; and without those disparities, we could not afford the policy of mass incarceration that we have pursued over the past two decades.

White Americans are not likely to want to believe this claim. The principle that all are equal before the law is perhaps the most basic American law; it is that maxim, after all, that stands etched atop the Supreme Court's magnificent edifice. The two most well-known Supreme Court decisions on criminal justice stand for equality before the law, and that is why they are so well known. In *Gideon v. Wainwright,* the Court in 1963 held that states must provide a lawyer at state expense to all defendants charged with a serious crime who cannot afford to hire their own lawyer. . . . Three years later, in *Miranda v. Arizona,* the Court required the police to provide poor suspects with an attorney at state expense and to inform all suspects of their rights before questioning them in custody. In these landmark decisions, the Court sought to ameliorate societal inequalities—both among suspects and between suspects and the state—that undermined the criminal justice system's promise of equality. As the Court stated in *Miranda,* "[w]hile authorities are not required to relieve the accused of his poverty, they have the obligation not to take advantage of indigence in the administration of justice."

The prominence of these decisions, however, is misleading. They were both decided by the Supreme Court under Chief Justice Earl Warren, at a time when the Court was solidly liberal and strongly committed to racial and economic equality. At virtually every juncture since *Gideon* and *Miranda,* the Supreme Court has undercut the principle of equality reflected in those decisions, and has itself "take[n] advantage of indigence in the administration of justice." Today, those decisions stand out as anomalies. *Gideon* is a symbol of equality unrealized in practice; poor defendants are nominally entitled to the assistance of counsel at trial, but the Supreme Court has failed to demand that the assistance be meaningful. Lawyers who have slept through testimony or appeared in court drunk have nonetheless been deemed to have provided their indigent clients "effective assistance of counsel." And today's Court has so diluted *Miranda* that the decision has had little effect on actual police integration practices.

The exploitation of inequality in criminal justice is driven by the need to balance two fundamental and competing interests: the protection of constitutional rights, and the protection of law-abiding citizens from crime. Virtually all constitutional protections in criminal justice have a cost: they make the identification and prosecution of suspected criminals more difficult. Without a constitutional requirement that police have probable cause and a warrant before they conduct searches, for example, police officers would be far more effective in rooting out and stopping crime. Without jury trials, criminal justice administration would be much more efficient. But if police could enter our homes whenever they pleased, we would live in a police state, with no meaningful privacy protection. And absent jury trials, the community would have little check on overzealous prosecutors. Much of the public and academic debate about criminal justice focuses on where we should draw the line between law enforcement interests and constitutional protections. Liberals tend to argue for more rights-protective rules, while conservatives tend to advocate rules that give law enforcement more leeway. But both sides agree, at least in principle, that the line should be drawn in the same place for everyone.

In fact, however, we have repeatedly mediated the tension not by picking one point on the continuum, but in effect by picking two points—one for the more privileged and educated, the other for the poor and less educated. For example, the Supreme Court has ruled that the Fourth Amendment bars police from searching luggage, purses, or wallets without a warrant that is based on probable cause to believe evidence of a crime will be found. But at the same time, the Court permits police officers to approach any citizen—without any basis for suspicion—and request "consent" to search. The officer need not inform the suspect that he has a right to say no. This tactic, not surprisingly, is popular among the police, and is disproportionately targeted at young black men, who are less likely to assert their right to say no. In this way, the privacy of the privileged is guaranteed, but the police still get their evidence, and society does not have to pay the cost in increased crime of extending to everyone the right to privacy that the privileged enjoy. This pattern is repeated throughout the criminal justice system: the Court affirms a constitutional right, but in a manner that effectively protects the right only for the privileged few, while as a practical matter denying the right to those who are less privileged. By exploiting society's "background" inequality, the Court sidesteps the difficult question of how much constitutional protection we could afford if we were willing to ensure that it was enjoyed equally by all people.

Nor is the Supreme Court alone in exploiting inequality in this way. If there is a common theme in criminal justice policy in America, it is that we consistently seek to avoid difficult trade-offs by exploiting inequality. Politicians impose the most serious criminal sanctions on conduct in which they and their constituents are least likely to engage. Thus, a predominantly white Congress has mandated prison sentences for the possession and distribution of crack cocaine one hundred times more severe than the penalties for powder cocaine. African Americans comprise more than 90% of those found guilty of crack cocaine crimes, but only 20% of those found guilty of powder cocaine crimes. By contrast, when white youth began smoking marijuana in large numbers in the 1960s and 1970s, state legislatures responded by reducing penalties and in some states effectively decriminalizing marijuana possession. More broadly, it is unimaginable that our country's heavy reliance on incarceration would be tolerated if the black/white incarceration rates were reversed, and whites were incarcerated at seven times the rate that blacks are. The white majority can "afford" the costs associated with mass incarceration because the incarcerated mass is disproportionately nonwhite.

Similarly, police officers routinely use methods of investigation and interrogation against members of racial minorities and the poor that would be deemed unacceptable if applied to more privileged members of the community. "Consent" searches, pretextual traffic stops, and "quality of life" policing are all disproportionately used against black citizens. Courts assign attorneys to defend the poor in serious criminal trials whom the wealthy would not hire to represent them in traffic court. And jury commissioners and lawyers have long engaged in discriminatory practices that result in disproportionately white juries.

These double standards are not, of course, explicit; on the face of it, the criminal law is color-blind and class blind. But in a sense, this only makes the problem worse. The rhetoric of the criminal justice system sends the message that our society carefully protects everyone's constitutional rights, but in practice the rules assure that law enforcement prerogatives will generally prevail over the rights of minorities and the poor. By affording criminal suspects substantial constitutional protections in theory, the Supreme Court validates the results of the criminal justice system as fair. That formal fairness obscures the systemic concerns that ought to be raised by the fact that the prison population is overwhelmingly poor and disproportionately black.

I am not suggesting that the disproportionate results of the criminal justice system are wholly attributable to racism, nor that the double standards are intentionally designed to harm members of minority groups and the poor. Intent and motive are notoriously difficult to fathom, particularly where there are multiple actors and decisionmakers. . . . In fact, I think it more likely that the double standards have developed because they are convenient mechanisms for avoiding hard questions about competing interests, and it is human nature to avoid hard questions. But whatever the reasons, we have established two systems of criminal justice: one of the privileged, and another for the less privileged. Some of the distinctions are based on race, others on class, but in no true sense can it be said that all are equal before the criminal law. Thus, I take issue with those, like Professor Randall Kennedy, who argue that as long as we can rid the criminal justice system of *explicit* and *intentional* considerations of race, we will have solved the problem of inequality in criminal justice.[14] . . . To suggest that a "color-blind" set of rules is sufficient is to ignore the lion's share of inequality that pervades the criminal justice system today. The disparities I discuss are built into the very structure and doctrine of our criminal justice system, and unless and until we acknowledge and remedy them, we will have "no equal justice."

Equality in criminal justice does not necessarily mean more rights for the criminally accused. Indeed, I think it likely that were we to commit ourselves to equality, the substantive scope of constitutional protections accorded to the accused would be reduced, not expanded. If we had to pay full cost, in law enforcement terms, for the constitutional rights we now claim to protect, the scope of those constitutional rights would probably be cut back for all. But at least we would then strike the balance between law enforcement and constitutional rights honestly. . . .

No one disputes that the criminal justice system's legitimacy depends on equality before the law. . . . There are . . . strong pragmatic reasons for responding to inequality in criminal justice, because a criminal justice system based on double standards both fuels racial enmity and encourages crime.

The racially polarized reactions to the Simpson case illustrate a deep and longstanding racial divide on issues of criminal justice: blacks are consistently more skeptical of the criminal justice system than whites. A long history of racially discriminatory practices in criminal law enforcement has much to do with this skepticism, but it is not just a matter of history: the double standards we rely on today in drawing the lines between rights and law enforcement reinforce black alienation and distrust. Because criminal law governs the most serious sanctions that a society can impose on its members, inequity in its administration has especially corrosive consequences. Perceptions of race and class disparities in the criminal justice system are at the core of the race and class divisions in our society.

The perception and reality of double standards also contribute to the crime problem by eroding the legitimacy of the criminal law and undermining a cohesive sense of community. As any wise ruler knows (and many ineffective despots learn), the most effective way to govern is not through brute force or terror, but by fostering broad social acceptance for one's policies. Where a community accepts the social rules as legitimate, the rule will be largely self-enforcing. Studies have found that most people obey the law not because they fear formal punishment—the risk of actually being apprehended and punished is infinitesimal for all crimes other than murder—but because they and their peers have accepted and internalized the rules, and because they do not want to let their community down. The rules will be accepted, and community pressure to conform will be effective, only to the extent that "the community" believes that the rules are just and that the authority behind them is legitimate. Thus, although the double standards . . . were adopted for the purpose of *reducing* the costs of crime associated with protecting constitutional rights, . . . in the end they undermine the criminal justice system's legitimacy, and thereby *increase* crime and its attendant costs.

When significant sectors of a community view the system as unjust, law enforcement is compromised in at least two ways. First, people feel less willing to cooperate with the system, whether by offering leads to police officers, testifying as witnesses for the prosecution, or entering guilty verdicts as jurors. Second, and more importantly, people are more likely to commit crimes, precisely because the laws forbidding such behavior have lost much of their moral force. When the law loses its moral force, the only deterrents that remain are the strong-arm methods of conviction and imprisonment. We should not be surprised, then, that the United States has the second highest incarceration rate of all developed nations. And it should be no wonder that black America, which has been most victimized by the inequalities built into the criminal justice system, is simultaneously most plagued by crime and most distrustful of criminal law enforcement.

What is to be done? . . . The first step, of course, is to recognize the scope of the problem. Although African-Americans are generally skeptical of the criminal justice system's fairness, their skepticism is not shared by the white majority, nor apparently by the courts. Until now, the courts and legislatures have been extremely reluctant even to allow the issue of inequality in criminal justice to be aired, and have instead impermissibly exploited inequality to make the hard choices of criminal justice seem easier. . . . A realistic response to crime, and in the end our society's survival as a cohesive community, depend on a candid assessment of the uses of inequality in criminal justice.

The second step is to eliminate the double standards. This turns out to be rather straightforward in some instances, but difficult if not impossible in others. We could certainly require, for example, that police officers seeking consent to search informed citizens that they have the right to say no. But wealthy defendants will always be able to outspend poor defendants; not everyone can afford Johnny Cochran. Even an *attempt* to limit such disparities would be a reversal of the current approach, however, which affirmatively exploits them. Such reforms are necessary if the criminal justice system is to regain the legitimacy so critical to effective law enforcement.

But restoring legitimacy through adjusting the rules that govern criminal law enforcement will not be nearly enough. The double standards have also had a devastating impact on black communities, particularly in poor, inner-city enclaves. The racial divide fostered and furthered by inequality in criminal justice has contributed to a spiral of crime and decay in the inner city, corroding the sense of belonging that encourages compliance with the criminal law. Therefore, we cannot limit ourselves to restoring the criminal law's legitimacy, but must also seek to restore the communities that have been doubly ravaged by crime and the criminal justice system. To accomplish this, we must both reinforce and support community-building organizations in the inner cities, and change the way we respond to crime itself.

These remedies go hand in hand. In order to adopt a more effective approach to criminal punishment, we must rebuild communities. In order to rebuilt communities, we must forego our reliance on mass incarceration—a policy that has robbed inner-city neighborhoods of whole generations of young men. We respond to crime today in a self-defeating way, by stigmatizing criminals, cutting them off from their communities, and fostering criminal subcultures that encourage further criminal behavior. In doing so, we undermine one of the most important deterrents to crime: a sense of belonging to a law-abiding community. By the same token, to the extent that we reinforce and reify divisions between individuals and communities, and between the law-enforcing and law-breaking communities, we encourage continuing criminal behavior. If we are to reduce criminal recidivism, we must adopt measures that seek to reintegrate offenders into the community, and that reinforce social ties within and across communities.

This is an ambitious agenda. But unless all Americans begin to see the problem of inequality in criminal justice as their own, and unless we take responsible measures to respond to it, America's crime problem and racial divide will only get worse.

Endnotes

[1]Toobin, J. (1995, October 23). A horrible human event. *The New Yorker,* 40.

[2]Bradsher, K. (1995, April 17). Gap in wealth in U.S. called widest in West. *N.Y. Times,* p. A1; Bradsher, K. (1995, August 14). Low ranking for poor American children. *N.Y. Times,* p. A9.

[3]Holmes, S. A. (1996, June 20). Income disparity between poorest and richest rises. *N.Y. Times,* p. A1.

[4]Johnson, E. W. (1997, October 4). Corporate soulcraft in the age of brutal markets. *Business Ethics Quarterly,* 7(4).

[5]Bureau of the Census, U.S. Dept of Commerce. *Statistical Abstract of the United States—1993,* 477 (Table 753).

[6]Id. at 47 (Table 50), 471 (Table 741), 473 (Table 743).

[7]In 1993, the infant mortality rate among whites was 6.8 deaths per 1,000 live births, while the rate among blacks was 16.5 deaths per 1,000 births. U.S. Dept. of Commerce, *Statistical Abstract of the United States—1996,* 93 (Table 127) (Infant Morality Rates, by Race). From 1980 to 1995, the unemployment rate among blacks has always been at least twice that among whites. In 1995, unemployment among blacks was 10.4%, and among whites was 4.9%. Id. at 413 (Table 64) (Unemployed Workers—Summary: 1980 to 1995).

[8]Orfield, G., Bachmeier, M. D., James, D. R., & Eitle, T. (1997, April 5). Deepening segregation in American public schools (Harvard Project on School Desegregation.)

[9]Massey, D. and Denton, N. (1993). *American apartheid: Segregation and the making of the underclass.* Cambridge, MA: Harvard University Press.

[10]Lewen, D. C. (1993). Curing America's addiction to prisons. 20 Fordham Urb. L.J. 641, 646; Tonry, M. (1995). *Malign neglect—Race, crime and punishment in America.* New York: Oxford University Press; Butterfield, F. (1998, August 9). Prison population growing although crime rate drops, 19; Bureau of Justice Statistics. (1996). *Sourcebook of criminal justice statistics—1995,* 474; See also Ayres, I., & Waldfogel, J. (1994). A market test for race discrimination in bail setting. *Stan. L. Rev.*, 46; Maurer, M., & Huling, T. (1995, October 1).*Young black Americans and the criminal justice system: Five years later* (The Sentencing Project); Gates Jr., H. L. (1996, April 29/May 6). The charmer. *The New Yorker*; Mustard, D. B. (1997). Racial, ethnic and gender disparities in sentencing: Evidence from the U.S. federal courts. University of Georgia Economics Working Paper, 97–458.

[11]Bachman, R. (1992, June). U.S. Department of Justice, Bureau of Justice Statistics. *Crime victimization in city, suburban, and rural areas: National crime victimization survey report.*

[12]Hagan, J. and Peterson, R. (1995). Criminal inequality in America. In J. Hagan & R. Peterson, (Eds.), *Crime and Inequality* (25). Stanford: Stanford University Press.

[13]Id. at 16.

[14]Kennedy, R. (1997). *Race, crime and the law.* New York: Pantheon.

Questions

1. Summarize the major differences in how blacks and whites perceive the criminal justice system. Are there any similarities? If so, what are they?

2. To what degree do the inequalities in the criminal justice system reflect inequality in other areas of American society (e.g., housing, education, etc.)? Can Cole's belief that inequality is structurally inherent in the criminal justice system be extended to other areas?

3. According to Cole, how do double standards serve to worsen crime? What other effects do double standards have on minorities' communities?

4. Why does Cole claim that key legislative or legal precedents, such as *Gideon vs. Wainwright* (court-provided attorney for the indigent) and *Miranda vs. Arizona* (rights before questioning), are misleading and only give the impression of equity?

5. According to Cole, why is the court's decision to allow certain types of investigations inherently discriminatory? Why are there drastic differences in sentencing for specific types of crime (e.g., crack-cocaine possession versus powder-cocaine possession)? Are there any reasons, other than those provided by Cole, that might explain these apparent inequities?

Stratification

Ralph B. McNeal, Jr., General Editor

What do you think of when you see the word "stratification"? What about if you see the phrase "class inequality"? Perhaps these terms make you think of homeless people living under bridges, poor people sitting on front porches in the Deep South during the heat of summer, or the proverbial "bag-lady" often depicted on television. Most likely, these terms do *not* bring to mind the exorbitantly rich who vacation in Vail in the winter and Barbados in the summer, and who live at "home" during the rest of the year. For some reason, we tend to think of stratification as being nearly synonymous with poverty, without recognizing the opposite end of the spectrum.

To understand stratification from a sociological perspective, you need only think about the maxim "He who has the gold, makes the rules." In other words, people who have money also wield power. Indeed, we can trace some of the earliest sociological work on stratification to Karl Marx's writings on systems of inequality (Marx, 1867). This nineteenth-century German theorist believed that the economic system of capitalism separates the populace into two distinct groups, the bourgeoisie or "true capitalists" (those who own the means of production) and the proletariat (the workers who labor for the owners). He also later defined a third group, the "lumpen proletariat" (the unemployed or unemployable). Marx's terms broadly fit our common conceptualization of "class"; that is, the upper class (the "haves") and the lower classes (the "have-nots"). This conceptualization of society inherently emphasizes conflict between the groups and, in fact, is commonly referred to as the "conflict perspective" among sociologists.

The famed sociologist Max Weber (1968) offered a different conceptualization of social class. Weber contended that social class should not be defined based on one's relationship to the means of production. Instead, he argued, class consists of three interrelated components: wealth, power, and prestige. Wealth can be thought of as the total resources a person has at his or her disposal (not just income). Power is a person's ability to get his or her way despite resistance—an ability that often accompanies positions of leadership in government, business, or the military. Prestige is the social status (or the respect, admiration, and envy of others) that derives from one's occupation (e.g., doctor, lawyer, congressman) or some other source (such as family surname). Weber's framework aligns closely with the conceptualization of class used by sociologists today, though Marx's model has by no means disappeared.

Sociologist C. Wright Mills (1959) contributed yet another noteworthy framework to the study of stratification. For Mills, in order to understand stratification, we must first examine the interrelationships among corporate, political, and military leaders. This triumvirate, which Mills labeled the "power elite," holds most of the power in any given society, but especially in industrialized and post-industrialized ones.

Who Has the Power?

Whatever particular approaches theorists might take on the concept of social stratification, there are at least two central questions facing anyone studying inequality and stratification. These are: "Who holds the power?" and "Who makes the rules?" And these questions apply both within *and* between societies. As "globalization," or the increasing connectedness of economies and societies worldwide, continues into the 21st century, studying stratification within just one society seems less and less relevant and appropriate. Understanding the relationships *between* societies has led to the emergence of a framework that categorizes various societies into underdeveloped, developing, and developed nations. From this perspective, those who have the "gold" are the developed nations, which often systematically control and exploit underdeveloped nations.

If we focus on the micro level (i.e., within one society), we again tend to emphasize economic inequality. For example, anyone who grows up in the United States is told that America is "the land of opportunity"—an almost magical realm where people can make a name and place for themselves by dint of skill, hard work, and tenacity. We can think of this as "contest mobility"; that is, you get ahead by working harder or being smarter than the next guy. However, hard facts reveal that hurdles in the form of birthright, gender, and race (to name just a few) can actually exclude even the most talented individuals from the "American Dream."

For example, consider your birthright, or the circumstances into which you were born. Is your family of origin wealthy or poor? Studies suggest that, no matter which socioeconomic class you are born into, you will likely stay within that class throughout your life. Think about how often you hear stories about children following in the family "business," whether that business is assembly-line work, mining, teaching, banking, doctoring, or politics. Not surprisingly, our occupational choices, as well as our overall life expectations, largely reflect the influence of our parents. If parents *expect* their children to pursue a certain path, oftentimes the children *will* pursue that path.

If this is true, then by definition there is little social mobility. By and large, the rich continue to be rich, and the poor continue to be poor. Research not only confirms this, but it also reveals that the gap between the rich and the poor in the United States is actually growing (Reich, 1990). Many studies have focused on the dynamics that widen the gap between the upper and lower tiers in American society. For example, in 1970, those making the most money (the top 5 percent of the U.S. population) brought home 6.3 times more income than the poorest in society. By 1998, this ratio had increased from 6.3 to 8.2. This means that the upper fifth of all households in 1998 earned 49.2 percent of all income, while the lower fifth of all households earned just 3.6 percent of the economic "pie" (U.S. Census Bureau, 1999). Despite numerous reforms and initiatives intended to equalize things, the rich are getting richer faster than the poor are breaking out of poverty.

Gender, Race, and Ethnicity

In addition to economic power, gender, race, and ethnicity play a central role in social stratification. To see how demographic attributes such as gender and race are interrelated with social class, we have only to consider the following numbers. In 1998, females earned 73 cents on the dollar compared to men (Weinberg, 1999). That same year, the average household income for blacks was $25,400, for Hispanics $28,300, and for whites $42,400 (Weinberg, 1999). Clearly, prejudice and discrimination are closely intertwined with social class in American society: To put it in harsh but realistic terms, to be white and/or male is good, but to be a minority and/or female is not.

Sociologists who study stratification try to understand it cross-sectionally (i.e., at one point in time) as well as longitudinally (i.e., over a specific time span). Some sociologists seek simply to understand the processes by which societies become stratified. For others, understanding these processes is a means to a more important end: bringing about much-needed social change. Social stratification is a complex phenomenon, often encompassing many facets of life. By reading the articles in this section, you will be taking the first step toward understanding this fascinating yet troublesome aspect of human life.

References

Marx, K. (1967). *Capital: A critique of political economy.* (F. Engels, ed.). New York: International Publishers (orig. pub. 1867).

Mills, C. W. (1959). *The power elite.* Fair Lawn, NJ: Oxford University Press.

Reich, R. (1990). Why the rich are getting richer and the poor poorer. *Utne Reader, 37*, 42-49.

U.S. Census Bureau. (1999). *Selected measures of household income dispersion: 1967-1998.* Published September 1999; <http://www.census.gov/hhes-/income/income98/in98dis.html>

Weber, M. (1968). *Economy and society.* (G. Roth & G. Wittich, trans.). New York: Bedminster Press (orig. pub. 1922).

Weinberg, D. (1999, September 30). *Income and poverty 1998 - Press briefing.* U.S. Census Bureau.

Making Ends Meet on a Welfare Check

KATHRYN EDIN AND LAURA LEIN

This selection is a compelling look at how welfare mothers sustain their families on various cash and non-cash assistance. Kathryn Edin and Laura Lein portray what living on welfare is like. Having conducted research through in-depth interviews, they detail how much money "welfare mothers" spend each month on basic necessities. They then contrast the families' expenses with the amount of support they receive through various funding mechanisms including welfare, food stamps, Section 8 housing assistance, and Aid to Families with Dependent Children (AFDC). Edin and Lein observe the discrepancy between the families' necessary expenses and their income and ask the logical question, How do welfare mothers "make the ends meet?"

Along Minnesota's Highway 72—which runs between the Canadian border town of Rainy River and Bemidji, Minnesota—a large, crudely lettered billboard greets the southbound traveler:

WELCOME TO MINNESOTA

LAND OF 10,000 TAXES

BUT WELFARE PAYS GOOD

Antiwelfare sentiment is common among Minnesotans, who live in a state with high personal income taxes and cash welfare benefits substantially above the national median. But even in southern states, where cash welfare benefits are very low and taxes modest, citizens are likely to denigrate welfare. In 1990, about 40 percent of respondents in each region told interviewers from the National Opinion Research Center that the United States spends too much on welfare.[1] In 1994, another nationally representative survey found that 65 percent of Americans believed welfare spending was too high (Blendon et al. 1995).

Legislators recognize welfare's unpopularity. In the first half of the

1990s, several states cut benefits, and all let their value lag behind inflation. In addition, most states applied for federal waivers to experiment with benefit limitations or sanctions not allowed by the old federal rules. Some states established a "family cap," which, denied additional cash to mothers who had another child while receiving welfare. In other states, mothers whose children were truant from school lost a portion of their cash grant. Furthermore, under the new federal rules, all states must limit the amount of time a mother spends on welfare to five years.

Public dissatisfaction with welfare persists despite the fact that cash benefits to welfare recipients have declined by more than 40 percent in real terms since the mid-1970s (Blank 1994, 179). The reasons for the continuing public discontent throughout this period are complex, but probably rest on the widespread belief that the federal welfare entitlement perpetuated laziness and promiscuity (Bobo and Smith 1994; Page and Shapiro 1992).[2] Lazy women had babies to get money from the welfare system, the story went, and then let lazy boyfriends share their beds and live off their benefits. These lazy and immoral adults then raised lazy and immoral children, creating a vicious cycle of dependency.

Those who have promoted this view include the news media and talk show hosts, but social scientists also have contributed. The most widely known "scientific" argument was developed by Charles Murray, who in 1984 claimed that welfare actually makes the poor worse off. Federal welfare became too generous during the 1960s and 1970s, Murray argued, and began to reward unwed motherhood and indolence over marriage and jobs (Murray 1984). Social scientists spent much of the late 1980s attempting to discover whether Murray was right. Typically, economists judged the merits of the claim by estimating the disincentive effects of more or less generous state welfare benefits on work (for a review of this literature, see Moffitt 1992). Other researchers attempted to measure the effect of varying state benefits on marriage, divorce, and remarriage (Bane and Ellwood 1994).

The task we set for ourselves in this chapter is a more fundamental one. In order to assess whether any welfare program is too generous, one must compare its benefits to the cost of living faced by that program's recipients. An obvious starting point is to ask how much families headed by single mothers spend each month to make ends meet, and how that income compares with what they receive from welfare.

How Much do Welfare-Reliant Mothers Spend?

In 1992, Donna Carson, a forty-year-old African American mother of two living in San Antonio, characterized herself as "ambitious and determined." She had spent most of her adult life playing by the rules. After high school graduation, she got a job and got married. She conceived her first child at age twenty-five, but her husband left before the child was born. Soon after her son's birth, she arranged for her mother to take care of him and went back to work. Because she did not have to pay for child care, her wages from her nurse's aide job combined with the child support she received from her ex-husband were enough to pay the bills. Ten years later, when she turned thirty-six, she had a second child. This time she was not married to the father. Carson's mother was willing to watch this child as well, so again she returned to work. Shortly thereafter, Carson's father's diabetes worsened and both of his legs were amputated. Her mother was overwhelmed by the tragedy and checked herself into a psychiatric hospital, leaving Carson to care for her two children and her disabled father alone. Seeing no other way out, she quit her job and turned to welfare. That was 1989.

Three years later, when we were talking with her, Carson was still on welfare, and her budget was tight. Her typical monthly expenditures were about $920 a month. One-third of that amount went to rent and utilities, another third went to food, and the rest went to cover her children's clothing, their school supplies, her transportation, and all the other things the family needed. Her combined monthly benefits from AFDC and food stamps, however, came to only $477.

Some months, she received a "pass through" child support payment of $50 from the father of her first child, who was legally obligated to pay. Although this payment did not reduce her AFDC benefits, her food stamps did go down by about $15 every time she received it. The father of her second child bypassed the formal child support system and paid her $60 directly each month. To get the rest of the money she needed, Carson took care of a working neighbor's child during the day. This neighbor could pay only $100 a month, but gave her the money in cash so that Carson's welfare caseworker could not detect the earnings and reduce her check. She got the rest of the money she needed from her father, who paid her $250 in cash each month to care for him.

TABLE 1 *Monthly Expenses of 214 AFDC Recipients: Means and Standard Deviations*

	Mean	SID
Housing costs	$213	$187
Food costs	262	112
Other necessities	336	176
Medical	18	43
Clothing	69	62
Transportation	62	83
Child care	7	32
Phone	31	35
Laundry/toiletries/cleaning supplies	52	31
Baby care	18	32
School supplies and fees	14	48
Appliance and furniture	17	39
Miscellaneous	47	59
Nonessentials	64	63
Entertainment	20	31
Cable TV	6	14
Cigarettes and alcohol	22	30
Eat out	13	27
Lottery costs	3	16
TOTAL EXPENSES	876	283

Source: Authors' calculations using Edin and Lein survival strategies data.
Note: The mean family size is 3.17 people. Numbers do not total due to rounding.

Though Carson had more personal tragedy than most, her budget was similar to that of most other welfare recipients we talked with. Table 1 gives the monthly expenses of the 214 welfare-reliant mothers we interviewed (and their 464 children). It shows that our respondents averaged $213 a month on housing, $262 on food, $336 on other necessary expenses, and $64 on items that were arguably not essential—a total of $876 for an average family of 3.17 people.[3]

Housing Expenses

The housing expenses of welfare-reliant families varied substantially. This variation depended on whether recipients paid market rent, had a housing subsidy in a public housing project or a private building (Section 8), or shared housing with a relative or friend. Donna Carson paid market rent, which in San Antonio was quite low but still higher than what most mothers pay in subsidized units. However, apartments that meet the physical criteria required for Section 8 tended to be in neighborhoods with less access to public transportation than the neighborhoods where housing projects were generally located, so these families usually had to maintain an automobile. Consequently, while public housing and Section 8 residents paid roughly the same amount for housing, Section 8 families spent far more for transportation.

In most cases, the welfare-reliant families who shared housing with a friend or relative were able to split the rent, utilities, telephone bill, and other household expenses. Thus, their expenses for rent and these other items were relatively low. About half of those who shared housing lived with one or both parents. The other half lived with siblings or friends. Mothers who lived with a parent usually made only token contributions toward the rent and took some portion of the responsibility for utilities and household maintenance. Most lived with their parents precisely because they could not afford to maintain their own households. Those who lived with a sibling or friend usually paid half of the household expenses. Sometimes, however, mothers "rented" only a portion of the living space (a single room, for example) and paid only a quarter or a third of the household costs.[4]

Food Expenses

Food expenditures averaged $262 a month for the welfare-reliant families we interviewed. This means that these mothers spent $19 per person on food in a typical week. This amount is nearly identical to the federal government's cheap food plan (the "thrifty food budget"), which uses as its base what poor mothers bought for their families in the 1950s and adjusts the prices in that "basket" for inflation each year (Ruggles 1990; Schwarz and Volgy 1992). The average weekly food stamp allotment for the families we interviewed, however, was slightly lower than this amount—$16 per person. This is because we oversampled mothers with housing subsidies to try to find mothers who could live on their benefits alone, and they do not qualify for the maximum amount of food stamps (food stamps are adjusted for living costs). This meant that the average mother had to cover $40 of food expenses each month with income from some source other than food stamps.[5]

Food stamp benefits also varied with family income, including cash welfare. In the lowest AFDC benefit states, therefore, families could receive up to $292 a month in food stamps for a family of three, or $21 per person per week in 1991, and families in these sites who reported no outside income received this maximum. Most found it sufficient to cover the bulk of their food expenditures. Families in states that paid more generous welfare benefits received roughly 30 cents less in food stamps for each additional dollar in cash welfare benefits. Because of this, hardly anyone who lived outside the South could pay their food bills with food stamps alone.[6] In San Antonio, food stamps covered 99 percent of respondents' average food expenditures; in Charleston, 88 percent; in Chicago, 80 percent; and in high-benefit Boston, only 65 percent.

Other Expenses

Besides housing and food, clothing took the next biggest bite out of the average family's monthly budget, followed by transportation, laundry and toiletries, telephone charges, medical expenses, baby care, and appliance and furniture costs. On average, welfare reliant mothers spent $69 a month on clothing. This means that the mothers with whom we spoke typically purchased $261 worth of shoes, coats, and other apparel for each family member in a year.[7] Most of this was for their children, since children continually grow out of their clothing.

Welfare-reliant mothers employed a number of strategies to contain their clothing expenditures. Virtually all purchased some of their clothing at thrift or second-hand stores, and most scoured neighborhood yard sales. During our interviews, many mothers proudly showed us their second-hand buys: a barely worn pair of name-brand jeans or a winter coat that was practically new and only a bit too small. A mother's largest expense in the clothing category was for children's shoes. Children not only went through two or more pairs of shoes a year, but shoes in children's sizes and in good condition were seldom available at neighborhood thrift stores. Winter coats, hats, mittens, and boots were also expensive, and most children grew out of them every other winter. Thus in the winter months, clothing needs could become an added hardship. One mother told us,

> In the winter months, I have had to keep my children at home on the really cold days because I didn't have warm enough clothes to dress them. I have learned to swallow my pride, though, and go to the second-hand shops and try to get the right kind of winter clothes for the boys.

The welfare-reliant mothers we interviewed felt that second-hand clothing was acceptable for younger children, whose peers were still largely unconcerned with appearance. One mother told us,

> For shopping I go to yard sales and the Salvation Army for Jay's clothes. Fortunately, he isn't the type of kid who always has to have Nike sneakers or he won't go to school. I get him K-Mart ones, or I go to the used clothes store [on] Belmont [Avenue]. I probably spend $200 a season on new clothes for him, but some of those he can wear from season to season.

Other mothers reported that their older children—especially high school boys—felt they could not maintain their self-respect or the respect of their peers while wearing K-Mart shoes to school. Some mothers felt that if they did not purchase name-brand sneakers, an athletic jacket, or other popular items for their teenagers, their children might be lured into criminal activity so they could buy these items themselves:

> My boy, he sees these kids that sell drugs. They can afford to buy these [tennis shoes] and he can't. So I have my little side-job and [I buy them for him]. You got to do it to keep them away from drugs, from the streets.

One mother told us that in order to buy her child a $50 pair of tennis shoes, she ate only one meal a day for a month. The savings in her food bill were enough to cover the purchase of the shoes. Most mothers in her neighborhood did not feel it was necessary to go hungry to meet their children's clothing needs, because they could generate the extra cash in other ways, which we discuss later.

Mothers who bought new clothing generally had to put the clothing on layaway. They paid a small portion of the purchase price each month. Some others found professional shoplifters who would note the children's sizes, shoplift the clothing, and sell it for a fraction of the ticket price to the mother.

Transportation cost the average welfare-reliant family $62 a month. Families living in Charleston (where there was little access to public transportation) and families living outside central cities spent more because they had to maintain automobiles or pay for taxis. At the time of our interviews, welfare rules limited the value of a family's automobile to $2,500. This meant that mothers had older cars, which generally required more frequent repair and got poorer gas mileage. All of the states we studied had mandatory insurance laws, and respondents told us that minimum insurance coverage cost at least $40 a month. In addition, Chicago and metropolitan Boston required that families purchase city stickers to park on the street, and South Carolina taxed the value of a family's car each year.

Although mothers who had access to public transportation spent less than those mothers who maintained cars, bus and subway transportation cost the average mother who used it more than $60 a month. Few mothers lived in areas where they could walk to the laundromat or the grocery store. In neighborhoods that provided these amenities, rents were higher. Since few mothers could afford child care, a shopping trip required that mothers bring their children with them and pay the bus or subway fares for the older children as well (younger children often ride free).

Laundry, toiletries, and cleaning supplies also constituted a significant proportion of monthly expenses. Some mothers washed their clothing in the bathtub and let it air-dry in their apartment or outside. This was a time-consuming task, however, and mothers complained that their clothes did not get as clean as machine-washed clothing. A few mothers owned or rented their own washers and dryers, but most used local laundromats. Because most families' clothing stock was slim (for example, two or three pairs of pants for each person was typical), mothers usually washed their clothing once each week or more. Laundromat prices varied, but mothers seldom spent less than $6 for coin machines each time they visited the laundromat, for roughly three loads.

All told, the welfare-reliant mothers had to spend $23 in a typical month to wash and dry their clothing and an additional $29 on toiletries and cleaning supplies. Food stamps could not be used to purchase toiletries or cleaning supplies, so mothers had to pay for sponges, cleaning fluids, dishwashing liquid, hand and laundry soap, bleach, toilet paper, hair care products, deodorant, disposable razors, and feminine products with cash.

Ninety-two percent of our sample had telephone service for at least part of the year. On average, families spent $31 monthly on telephone charges. Twenty-six percent of the welfare recipients had their phone disconnected at least once during the past year because of nonpayment. When mothers ran short of money, they were usually more willing to do without a phone than to neglect rent, utilities, food, clothing, transportation, or other essentials. Basic service charges also varied widely by site. in San Antonio, where basic local service cost about $12 a month, families spent only $18 a month for phone-related costs. In all other sites, comparable service ranged from $20 to $25 a month, and families spent much more. These costs included not only charges for local and long-distance calls but connection and reconnection charges as well. Although not strictly necessary for a family's material well-being, mothers without telephones had a difficult time maintaining contact with welfare caseworkers and their children's schools. It was also more difficult to apply for jobs because prospective employers could not reach them to set up an interview. Some solved this dilemma by sharing a phone with a neighbor; messages left with neighbors, however, were not always promptly forwarded.

Medicaid, the government's health insurance program for low-income families, offered free emergency care and routine physician care. All the households in our welfare-reliant sample were covered by Medicaid. Over-the-counter medicines and other medical services, however, were not covered and constituted another $18 of the average welfare-reliant mother's monthly budget. These expenses included routine drugstore costs, such as those for pain relievers, cough syrup, adhesive bandages, vitamin tablets, or other medicines families frequently used. In addition, few state Medicaid programs pay for prescription birth control pills, abortions, antidepressants, or other mental health drugs. Nor do most Medicaid plans pay for dental care, except for emergency oral surgery.

Diapers and other baby care products cost an average welfare-reliant family $18 a month (37 percent of the welfare recipients in our sample had babies in diapers). Welfare-reliant mothers with infants and young toddlers typically received formula, milk, eggs, and cheese from WIC (Women's, Infants', and Children's nutritional program). Most mothers told us, however, that they were usually one or two cans short of formula each month and had to purchase them at the grocery store. In addition, WIC does not provide disposable diapers, which constituted roughly 80 percent of the cash welfare-reliant mothers had to spend on baby care. Only a tiny minority of the mothers we interviewed used cloth diapers; although cheaper than disposables, cloth diapering was not practicable for mothers who relied on laundromats. In addition, mothers who used cloth diapers reported substantial upfront costs (they had to buy the diapers), and these mothers spent substantially more for laundry supplies than other mothers. Mothers also averaged $14 a month on school-related expenses and $7 a month on child care.

Appliances and furniture cost the typical family another $17 a month. Generally mothers purchased both new and used furniture and appliances with installment payments. Because they could not get bank credit, these mothers would often arrange credit at local thrift shops and "rent-to-own" furniture stores. Although local thrift stores did not generally apply finance charges to mothers' purchases (they usually held the item until it was fully paid for), rent-to-own furniture stores did. Because the latter stores charged very high interest rates and allowed long repayment periods, mothers sometimes ended up paying two to three times the actual value of the item. Meanwhile, mothers who missed a payment could have the furniture repossessed, losing whatever equity they had built up.

Miscellaneous items in the families' budgets included check-cashing fees and fees for money orders, debt service, burial insurance (discussed later in this chapter), and haircuts. These items totaled $47 in the average month.

Nonessentials

Entertainment cost the typical family $20 each month and was usually limited to video rentals; occasionally it included movies, trips to amusement parks, and travel (mothers sometimes sent their children to relatives during the summer). Mothers spent an average of $22 for cigarettes and alcohol each month, mostly on cigarettes. Mothers seldom bought their own alcohol, and those who drank depended on boyfriends, friends, and family members to pay for their drinks. This was also true for most mothers who used marijuana or other drugs. In addition, mothers spent an average of $3 a month for the lottery, $6 a month for cable television, and $13 a month to eat out. All told, the typical welfare-reliant family spent $64 a month on these nonnecessary items, or about 7 percent of their total budget.[8] Although not physical necessities, the items met crucial psychological needs.

Although the mothers in our sample worried about day-to-day material survival, most saw survival as having broader "psychological" and "social" dimensions. One mother commented:

> You know, we live in such a materialistic world. Our welfare babies have needs and wants too. They see other kids going to the circus, having toys and stuff like that. You gotta do what you gotta do to make your kid feel normal. There is no way you can deprive your child.

This woman's statement captures a common sentiment among the welfare recipients we interviewed: children need to have an occasional treat, and mothers who refuse them may deprive their offspring of normalcy. Even among Mexican American mothers in San Antonio, who spent less than any of the other welfare-reliant mothers, one family in six paid a small monthly fee for a basic cable subscription. These mothers told us they saw the cable subscription as a cheap way of keeping their kids off the streets and out of trouble.

The mothers themselves needed an occasional boost too. Many reported that by spending small amounts on soda pop, cosmetics, cigarettes, alcohol, or the lottery, they avoided feeling like they were "completely on the bottom," or that their lives were "completely hopeless." When we asked respondents if they could do without them, they replied that these items gave them some measure of self-respect, and without them they would lose hope of bettering their situations:

> I never buy for myself, only for my son. Well, I take that back. I allow myself two of what I guess you would call luxuries. Well, I guess three. First, I buy soda pop. I do not eat meals hardly ever, but I always have to have a can of Pepsi in my hand. I drink Pepsi nonstop. My boyfriend, he buys it for me by the case 'cause he knows how much I like it, and I guess it's the pop that gives me my energy for dealing with my son—you know, the sugar and caffeine and stuff.
>
> And then I treat myself to the cigarettes. Without the smoking, I would just worry all the time about how we was going to eat and would never relax. I feel like I deserve some little pleasure, you know, and so those cigarettes keep me up, keep me feeling that things aren't so bad.
>
> And the other thing is, I buy my cosmetics. I mean, I go around feeling so low all the time, and the makeup makes me feel, you know, better about myself. I feel like I'm not so poor when I can buy myself some cosmetics at the discount house.

The few respondents who spent money on alcohol reported similar sentiments:

> Oh, sometimes, you know, just to relax or somethin', I just go out and have a few. And when I'm really low, I sometimes go out and tie one on, if you know what I mean. Sometimes I think I'll go crazy all day in the house if I can't get out once in a while. I just couldn't take it.

Although few mothers played the lottery with any regularity, those who did also viewed it as a sort of escape:

> I just can't afford not to buy some tickets when the pot gets real big. I sometimes buy five tickets if I can afford it. I like to plan what I'm going to do with it, you know, fantasize and stuff—dream of what it would be like to own nice things and such.

. . .

How do Welfare-Reliant Mothers Make Ends Meet?

No one without substantial assets can spend more than they take in for long. The welfare-reliant women we interviewed had few savings, no IRA accounts, no stocks or bonds, and no valuable assets. If they had and if their caseworkers had known, they would have been ineligible for welfare. When they ran out of cash and food stamps, those who did not have a generous parent or boyfriend worked at regular or informal jobs. They also had to "work" the system, making sure that neither their earnings nor the contributions they received came to the attention of the welfare department. If they reported such income, their welfare checks would soon be reduced by almost the full amount of this income, leaving them as poor as before.

Table 2 shows that, on average, cash welfare, food stamps, and SSI covered only about three-fifths of welfare-reliant mothers' expenses.[9] A small amount also came from the earned income tax credit (EITC) for wages earned in the prior year. From our conversations with mothers, we learned that they made up the remaining gap by generating extra cash, garnering in-kind contributions, and purchasing stolen goods at below market value. We found it difficult to estimate, however, how much each mother saved by using the latter two techniques. Therefore, we only present figures for those strategies that generated extra cash.

Earnings from reported work, unreported work (off the books or under a false identity), or work in the underground economy (selling sex, drugs, or stolen goods) made up 15 percent of welfare-reliant mothers' total income.[10] Another chunk (17 percent) came from members of their personal networks and went unreported. Agency-based contributions—usually cash contributions, direct payment of mothers' bills, or the portion of student grants and loans that could be squeezed for extra household cash after paying for tuition and books—covered the last 4 percent of the average welfare-reliant mother's budget.

To get a clearer sense how welfare-reliant mothers generated extra income, Table 2 also shows the degree to which mothers relied on various sources of income each month. By definition, all the mothers we coded as welfare-reliant received something from the AFDC program. Table 2 shows that almost all of them also received food stamps (95 percent), compared with 87 percent of welfare recipients nationwide (U.S. House of Representatives 1993, 711).[11] Nine percent of the sample received SSI or payments for the care of foster children. Seven percent received money from the EITC because they reported income from work during the previous calendar year.

Table 2 gives further detail on how mothers' earnings from work contributed to their family budgets. Five percent worked in the formal economy at reported jobs, compared with 6 percent nationally (U.S. House of

TABLE 2 *Survival Strategies of 214 Welfare-Reliant Mothers*

Variable	Amount of Income Generated Through Each Survival Strategy	Percentage of Total Budget	Percent of Mothers Engaging in Each Survival Strategy[a]
TOTAL EXPENSES	$876	100%	N/A
Housing costs	213	24	N/A
Food costs	262	30	N/A
Other necessities	336	39	N/A
Nonessentials	64	7	N/A
Welfare benefits	565	64	N/A
AFDC	307	35	100%
Food stamps	222	25	95
SSI	36	4	9
EITC	3	2	7
Work-based strategies	128	15	46
Reported work	19	2	5
Unreported work	90	10	39
Underground work	19	2	8
Network-based strategies	151	17	77
Family and friends	62	7	46
Men	95	11	52
Boyfriends	56	6	29
Absent fathers	39	4	33
Covert system	33	4	23
Formal system	7	1	14
Agency-based strategies	37	4	31
TOTAL INCOME	883	100%	N/A

Source: Authors' calculations using Edin and Lein survival strategies data.
Note: These income-generating strategies do not include in-kind contributions or purchasing goods illegally because these figures were difficult to estimate. Columns do not total due to rounding.
[a]The sum of the percentages exceeds the total because some mothers engaged in more than one strategy.

Representatives 1993, 696). Others were also working and not reporting it. Approximately two-fifths (39 percent) worked off the books or under a false identity to generate additional income, and 8 percent worked in the underground economy selling sex, drugs, or stolen goods. (The percentages do not sum to 46 percent because some mothers engaged in more than one strategy.) Table 2 also shows that 77 percent of mothers were currently receiving covert contributions from family, boyfriends, or absent fathers in order to make ends meet.[12] Nearly half (46 percent) of welfare-reliant mothers relied on family and friends for financial help each month. Even more, 52 percent, received help from a man: 29 percent from boyfriends on a regular basis, 14 percent through the formal child support collection system, and 23 percent from the fathers of their children on a covert basis. In addition, 31 percent received cash, voucher, or direct assistance in paying a bill from a community group, charity, or student aid program.

. . .

Surviving on Welfare

Americans have long worried that welfare benefits are too generous. Many hear about high rates of out-of-wedlock births among the poor and conclude that welfare contributes to the problem. A more fundamental question is how individual welfare recipients actually use the government support they receive? What standard of living do welfare benefits afford single mothers?

We have attempted to answer this question by interviewing 214 welfare-reliant mothers about what they spent to keep their families together. We also examined the level of welfare benefits available to the mothers. We found that for most welfare-reliant mothers food and shelter alone cost almost as much as these mothers received from the government. For more than one-third, food and housing costs exceeded their cash benefits, leaving no extra money for uncovered medical care, clothing, and other household expenses. When we added the costs of other necessities to the mothers' budgets, it was evident that virtually all welfare-reliant mothers experienced a wide gap between what they could get from welfare and what they needed to support their families. In fact, with only one exception, we met no welfare mother who was making ends meet on her government check alone. Mothers filled the gap through reported and unreported work and through handouts from family, friends, and agencies. Finally, we asked the difficult question of whether welfare-reliant mothers' expenditures were truly necessary. We found that our mothers' budgets were far below the household budgets collected by the Consumer Expenditure Survey in 1991 for single-parent families. Our welfare-reliant mothers also spent less than the lowest income group the CES interviewed. Our conclusion is that the vast majority of our welfare-reliant mothers' expenses were at the very low end of widely shared national consumption norms.

Despite spending far more than their welfare benefits, many of the families we interviewed experienced serious material hardship. Variations in benefit levels had real consequences for welfare-reliant single mothers and their children. Lower benefits substantially increased material hardship as did having larger families. Life on welfare, it seems, was an exceedingly tenuous affair.[13] An articulate Chicago respondent put it this way:

> I don't understand why [Public Aid is] punishing people who are poor if you want to mainstream them. If indeed, the idea is to segregate, to be biased, to create a widening gap between the haves and the have-nots, then the welfare system is working. If it is to provide basic needs, not just the financial but psychological and social needs of every human being, then the system fails miserably.

Endnotes

[1]In 1994, 49 percent of Americans thought that welfare programs discouraged people from working, and two-thirds believed that welfare encouraged women to have more children than they would have had if welfare were not available (Blendon and others 1995).

[2]These responses were gathered during the center's General Social Survey.

[3]Due to rounding, these estimates do not total $876.

[4]We did not include any teenage mothers living at home. Mothers under age eighteen constitute only a tiny portion of all mothers on the welfare rolls (U.S. House of Representatives 1995, table 10-27). We did interview seventeen teenage mothers and found that they paid almost none of their own bills because most of them lived rent-free with their mothers while they tried to finish school. Therefore, these teenage mothers could not construct a household budget.

[5]Nor could families with housing subsidies, disability income, or reported outside income buy all of their food with food stamps.

[6]There is a reduction in food stamp benefits as cash benefits rise.

[7](69/3.17)*12

[8]In terms of nonnecessary spending, more than a third of families spent nothing whatsoever on entertainment during the previous year, two-thirds never ate out;

nearly half had spent nothing on cigarettes or alcohol during the year; and four-fifths had gone without cable television.

[9]Four percent of all welfare-reliant families received either SSI or survivor's benefits (U.S. House of Representatives 1993, 719).

[10]For those mothers who sold illegal drugs, a small personal supply was sometimes an in-kind benefit of the job.

[11]These small differences are due to the fact that we did not interview any teenage recipients, who often lived with better-off family members and were thus not eligible for food stamps.

[12]Fourteen percent had received payments through the Child Support Enforcement system in the last year, which was slightly above the national average of 12 percent for welfare recipients (U.S. Department of Health and Human Services 1990, 43).

[13]Whereas Charles Murray portrayed an overly generous welfare system that kept the poor in poverty because it rewarded their indolence, mothers saw welfare as a stingy and punishing system that placed them and their children in a desperate economic predicament.

Questions

1. Why do Americans generally resent welfare assistance programs and welfare recipients?

2. How large is the discrepancy between the funds needed for self-sufficiency and the level of assistance welfare families receive?

3. Do you see any places where welfare mothers could cut their monthly budgets to survive on welfare assistance? Would eliminating certain items be sufficient to get their expenses under budget?

4. Most college students live on what they perceive to be a "bare bones" budget. Find out how much welfare assistance you would qualify for in your residential state. How far above or below this threshold are your current expenses? What in your own monthly budget would you need to eliminate to survive on welfare assistance?

5. What do you speculate are the causes for people living on welfare assistance? Think of causes that include cultural, structural, and normative factors.

Did Welfare Reform Work? Implications for 2002 and Beyond

SANDRA HOFFERTH

In 1996, President Clinton signed a welfare reform bill with the intention of ending welfare "as we know it." Since then, the media often features stories about ex-welfare recipients who are now employed, calling welfare reform a success. The reality for people who have left welfare, however, is more complex. Many, working at very low wages, still do not earn enough to escape poverty, and many others have lost the jobs that liberated them from governmental assistance. In this article, Sandra Hofferth refers to an established survey, the Panel Study of Income Dynamics, to address whether welfare reform really worked.

Former president Bill Clinton entered office vowing to "end welfare as we know it." Yet in 1996, the Clinton administration was deeply divided into liberal and conservative camps over the welfare reform bill Congress had passed. Would the law's stringent limits encourage welfare recipients to be more self-sufficient, as conservative proponents of welfare reform argued, or would it simply punish them and harm their children, as liberal opponents protested? Clinton bet on the first outcome and signed the act. Several architects of the liberal alternative plan resigned in protest. The jury is still out on the great federal welfare reform experiment of 1996, even as a decision to extend it looms in 2002. But states' experiments with welfare policies during the 1990s can tell us much about what works and what does not.

At first glance, the conservative approach seems to have been vindicated; welfare rolls dropped sharply by the end of Clinton's term—49 percent between 1994 and 1999. But skeptics reply that this felicitous turn of events would not have happened without economic prosperity. The policy may have given people a push, but the economy pulled them into jobs. Some say that

---

it does not matter which was more important; others argue that we need to know whether policies did what they were designed to do and that compassionate citizens will want to know what happened to former recipients.

While some benefited from economic independence and work, other former recipients, especially the most marginally employable, returned to welfare or remained impoverished off it. In earlier times, as many as one-half of former recipients returned to public assistance within two years of leaving it. And while employment is high at exit, family finances may not greatly improve. Although many left welfare to take jobs, their incomes often rose little because families must substitute earnings and other sources of income for welfare payments. Also, now off state aid, they may need to pay for the full amount of housing, child care, medical care expenses, and transportation, reducing their net earnings. Ex-recipients would need to earn a lot more to pay for these critical expenses, since their new jobs often do not provide such benefits.

Fortunately, information collected in the early to mid-1990s across the states permits us to follow public assistance recipients before and after leaving the welfare rolls, and link their fates to variations in state policies and economic conditions. While it is impossible to determine precisely the parts that policy and economy played separately, what we now know from a national study of women who were on welfare is that public policies were instrumental in encouraging women to leave Aid to Families with Dependent Children (AFDC) in the early 1990s. The economy played only a supporting role. We also know that a substantial proportion of families returned to welfare within two years, that the availability of jobs helped determine how soon they returned, and that many remained poor. High-risk families, such as those with young children, appear to be returning to public assistance faster than other former recipients. What we have learned about the effects of public policy on public assistance recipients and what it implies for the upcoming debate over reauthorization is the subject of this essay.

Welfare Reforms Before 1996

The Personal Responsibility and Work Opportunity Reconciliation Act of 1996 fundamentally altered the federal government's promise to maintain a safety net for low-income families. It did so by repealing the entitlement to cash assistance in the 60-year-old program of AFDC. Beginning no later than July 1, 1997, each state was required to assist needy families under the Temporary Assistance for Needy Families (TANF) block grant. Cash assistance could not be given to families in which an adult had received assistance for 60 months in his or her lifetime. Also, recipients could work after two years on assistance or even sooner, if the state preferred.

But welfare reform had started earlier. Most states had obtained waivers to federal requirements in the early 1990s. These state waivers established "natural experiments" in program administration that began considerably before the TANF program was passed. In essence, TANF formalized what was already in effect in many states prior to 1996. The substantial decline in the welfare rolls that predated the 1996 legislation—between 1994 (at its peak) and mid-1997 the decline was about 25 percent—is linked to these waivers. Variation from state to state in this waiver period permits researchers to examine which aspects of welfare reform have led to which consequences.

Of particular interest are the waivers that established:

- **Time limits**—Restricting total months on public assistance to 60 or fewer, depending on the state.
- **Work requirements**—Whether the state mandates that recipients work or look for work after a certain amount of time on public assistance.
- **Work exemption for having children under age 3**—Whether states require mothers of children under age three to work.
- **Earnings disregard**—Whether states allow recipients to disregard some of their earnings in calculating benefits.
- **Family cap**—Whether recipients who have additional children are prohibited from receiving additional benefits.
- **Sanctions**—Whether the state reduces recipients' benefits for failure to meet the work or other requirements.

In addition to changes in welfare policy in the early 1990s, other policy changes may have given recipients incentives to work. For example, the Earned Income Tax Credit (EITC) expanded beginning in 1993. This credit in the income tax code provides money to families in which there is at least one earner and in which earnings are below about $30,000, whether or not they owe income tax. In 1998 a working single mother with one child and an income of about $11,000 received a maximum benefit of $2,272, compared with a maximum of $950 in 1990. Since the earnings would be increased by the amount of the EITC to which they were entitled, it is possible that this credit also encouraged recipients to work. Other social insurance changes probably had little effect on the welfare rolls.

While it is still too soon to fully understand what happened after 1996, by examining how recipients behaved in states with different policies in the early 1990s under waivers, we can make an educated guess. I base my conclusions not just upon across-state variation, which was considerable, but also upon changes within states over time. States may differ in recipient behavior for many reasons having nothing to do with their public assistance policies, and I have adjusted for these differences.

Four questions arise: Did the new policies get recipients off welfare? Did they reduce how often ex-recipients returned to welfare? Did economic conditions affect leaving and returning? How well off were recipients in the two years after leaving welfare? Colleagues and I used a long-established survey of families, the Panel Study of Income Dynamics, which has followed thousands of families over many years, to answer these questions.

Did Public Policies Get Recipients Working?

The new welfare policies did what they were designed to do—they moved people off AFDC and into work. First, more families left public assistance in the mid-1990s after waivers were implemented than in the early 1990s. Second, waiver policies designed to get recipients working were associated with increased work. More recipients left welfare in those states that instituted key changes than in those that did not. And they left to work. For example, in the states that implemented a work requirement between 1993 and 1996, 2.4 percent left welfare within a month and began working, compared with fewer than 1 percent in states that did not do so. In work requirement states, 92 percent of those who left welfare left because they took a job. Fewer than one-half of 1 percent left welfare for other reasons, such as marriage or the loss of eligibility because the youngest child reached age 18. Similarly, recipients in states that implemented tightened work exemptions for mothers of young children also took jobs; leaving through work tripled. Some states, instead of simply requiring work, tried to encourage work by allowing recipients to keep more of their earnings and still get welfare. In these states, the rate of recipients leaving the rolls for jobs actually dropped to one-half the earlier rate.

Did Public Policies Keep Former Recipients Off Welfare?

Many recipients were unable to remain self-sufficient. One out of three former recipients returned to welfare within two years after leaving. Consistent with the increase in recipients leaving the rolls, fewer of them returned to welfare in the mid-1990s compared with the early 1990s. Surprisingly, however, welfare policies had little to do with keeping recipients off the rolls.

The one rule that affected returning was requiring mothers of very young children to work. In states that required work from such mothers, recipients were two and one-half times as likely to return to AFDC as were those mothers in other states, though the overall probability of returning was quite low. As described earlier, that rule also encouraged such mothers to leave welfare in the first place. It is likely that the costs of working were simply too high for these mothers and, unable to maintain self-sufficiency without considerable help, they soon reappeared at the welfare office. Former recipients who left welfare to take a job returned to welfare sooner than those who left for other reasons. Taking an initial job is still very difficult for public assistance recipients, particularly for those with young children, and does not guarantee continuous employment. Another route off welfare is finding a partner. However, forming a partnership with a male is also not, by itself, a ticket to self-sufficiency. The most successful at becoming self-sufficient were women who took both a job and a partner for a year or more.

How Much Did Good Times Help?

The overall level of prosperity and availability of jobs in the 1990s was an undeniably important context for the declines in welfare rolls. In more prosperous states, defined as those with higher family incomes, recipients were somewhat slower to leave AFDC. Such states had higher benefit levels, which encouraged recipients to stay. The research shows, however, that in states requiring work, recipients left AFDC more quickly if the state was prosperous than if it was not. Prosperity helped welfare reform work.

Higher unemployment in a state, while it should make getting a job more difficult, did not appear to hurt recipients' ability to get off AFDC. In fact, it did not affect whether or not welfare recipients left the rolls. I suspect that because overall levels of unemployment were low, many states assisted recipients in finding jobs, making that first job possible. However, the level of state unemployment substantially affected the chances of staying off welfare; former recipients in high unemployment states were more likely to return to public assistance than those in low unemployment states.

How Well Off Are Families After Leaving AFDC?

As the women described here moved off AFDC, they entered the workforce and their financial well-being typically improved. At exit, about one-half were employed; after two years, two-thirds of those still off welfare were employed (figure 1). For all leavers (including some who returned before 24 months), earnings rose 17 percent, and family income rose an average of 54 percent between the first and 24th month off AFDC (figure 2). For continuous leavers (those who remained off at 24 months), earnings increased 28 percent and family income increased 32 percent over the same two years. But many were still unable to escape poverty (figure 3). More than two-thirds were poor at exit. (Because not all income is counted in determining welfare benefits and because increases in income may result from combining households, not all families are poor at exit.) Three out of five families remained poor two years later.

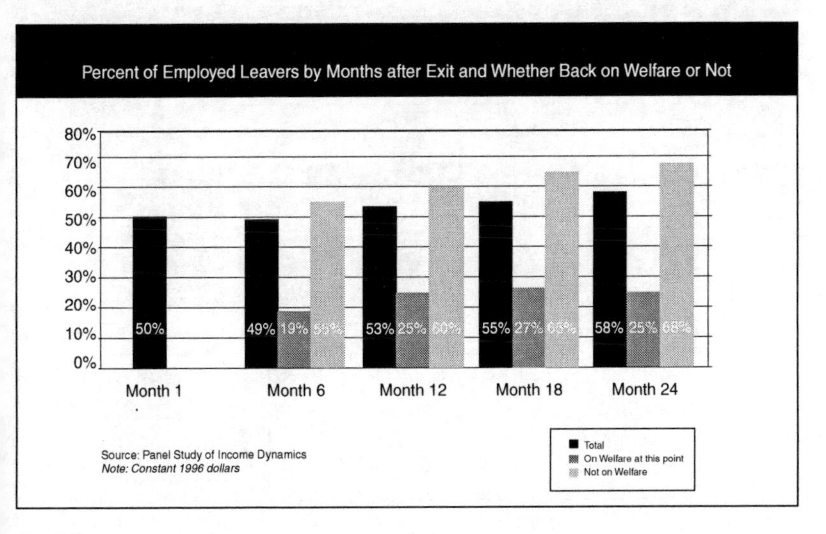

FIGURE 1

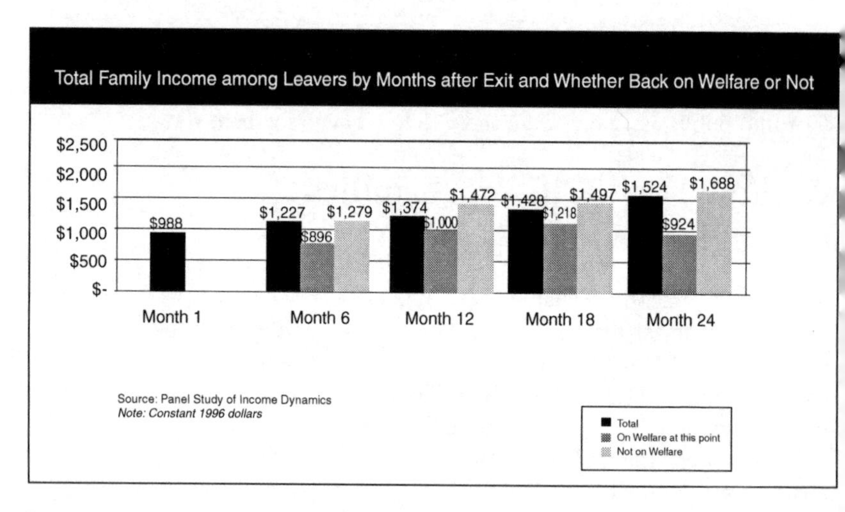

FIGURE 2

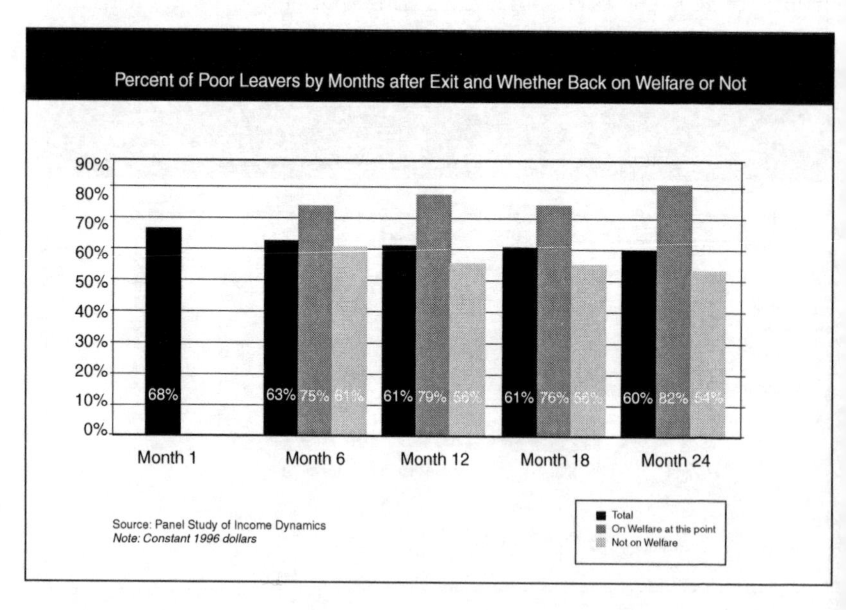

FIGURE 3

Of course, those who go back on welfare have less income and are highly likely to be poor (figures 2 and 3). How people leave AFDC is important for whether or not they return. Increases in family income and self-sufficiency can occur either through finding a partner or through work. Each one alone is not enough. Mothers who exited AFDC through a combination of work and a partnership had the highest incomes and the lowest rates of poverty.

The kinds of income families receive also affect their chances of returning to AFDC. Receiving child support and supplemental security income (SSI) is associated with staying off AFDC longer, while receiving food stamps and private transfers is associated with going back on sooner. Child support and SSI tend to be stable, long-term sources of income. Other research has found child support to be more important than many other sources of support for the well-being of children. Child support also provides a considerably larger share of income than do other sources. Personal gifts and loans tend to be small and probably not very consistent over time; thus they are not likely to assist a young mother in remaining off welfare. Instead, they may create a set of obligations that the young woman may have difficulty paying off. Receipt of private transfers and food stamps may also be an indicator of financial distress for some. For others off AFDC, the hassle of continuing to be certified to receive food stamps may outweigh the benefit to be gained. Or they may simply not realize that they remain eligible. The data we used lack information on child care and health insurance coverage—critical support services—so I can draw no conclusions about their likely contribution to self-sufficiency.

What Are the Effects of Work Programs on Families and Children?

In the late 1980s and early 1990s, Canada and states as diverse as Minnesota, Wisconsin, Michigan, California, and Georgia tested a variety of interventions to increase the earnings of welfare families. The results of these earlier projects shed light on what the long-term consequences of the work provisions in TANF may be for families and their children. Women enrolled in programs that included a substantial subsidy for work, that required work of 30 hours per week or more, and that provided substantial support services such as child care worked more, had higher earnings, and were less likely to be poor. The larger the subsidy, the larger the gains.

None of the programs significantly changed parents' emotional or physical health, the quality of parent-child interactions or the home environment. However, some studies found that children's achievements in school and their behavior improved when they were in the test programs. Studies in Minnesota and Canada suggest that the increased financial and emotional security, benefits such as health insurance, child care, and after-school activities provided by the programs account for these improvements. Adolescent children in program families, however, showed more problem behaviors such as staying out late, smoking, drinking and using drugs. Studies suggest that supervised after-school activities are important for keeping the children of newly employed welfare mothers out of trouble.

The conclusion from these early studies is that programs that provide substantial subsidies and services increase family self-sufficiency. Programs that are more modest, that are similar to those the states are now operating post-TANF, produce very small or no economic benefits for families. Numerous state studies of welfare leavers demonstrate that families subject to these minimal programs do leave welfare but that they do not significantly improve their economic well-being. Young children do not suffer any harm in these cases, although there is some evidence of potential behavioral and emotional adjustment problems, particularly for older children. The evidence to date is that absent large subsidies and support services, the goal of improving family self-sufficiency eludes us still.

Implications for the Next Decade

The research reported here describes how welfare policies under state waivers in the 1990s led more recipients to leave AFDC and go to work. Since TANF policies passed in 1996 are very similar to the more modest waiver policies, and since low unemployment played only a supporting role in leaving AFDC under the waiver experience, this movement to work should have continued through the late 1990s, under TANF.

This would be the end of the story except that many former recipients returned within two years, having failed to become independent. Given the states' experiences, it seems quite possible that absent substantial help for former recipients, returns to TANF may accelerate in the next few years. Few waiver policies affected returning, but the unemployment rate, which rose significantly after the events of September 11, 2001, strongly increased the rate of return to welfare. By our estimates, if unemployment goes up from 3 to 9 percent in a state, twice as many women will return to welfare. Since the economic boom of the 1990s seems to be over, with unemployment increasing welfare rolls could soon expand just as they once contracted. Or women could be left with nowhere to turn.

One group of mothers—women with children under age three—is at especially high risk. Public policies affect their risk both of leaving and of returning. Attention must be paid to their needs. In most states only a small fraction of eligible children receive child care subsidies. Children's health problems hinder mothers' ability to remain employed. Many mothers lack health insurance for their children, in spite of eligibility. With little job flexibility and accumulated leave time, mothers who have to choose between taking their child to see a doctor and their job are likely to choose the former. It is not surprising that turnover is high and many cycle on and off welfare.

While many former recipient families continue to improve after leaving AFDC, the mothers of very young children are at greater risk of failure because they face greater hurdles. Their children may also be at risk from poor-quality child care. We could return to a uniform standard exemption from work requirements for TANF mothers of children under age one. This would reduce the cost to mothers of caring for infants and the cost to the government of child care and other support services it provides to working mothers, as well as slow down what may be a revolving door. The problem is that unless the government ensured paid maternity leave for all mothers, such a subsidy would be inconsistent with national policies toward new mothers. Few working and nonpoor mothers in America receive paid leaves. The debate over this issue was not fully aired prior to the passage of welfare reform in 1996, and should be reconsidered based on the additional information available today.

Recipients who leave and stay off AFDC, on average, clearly lead better lives. More get married, find jobs and increase their household incomes. The bad news is that their own earnings increase by only about 30 percent, and 60 percent are still poor several years after leaving AFDC. These women may be in precarious situations if their partnerships dissolve. And the good outcomes do not come cheaply; former recipients' incomes do not increase without public subsidies. Supportive public policies can assist low-income families who have exited AFDC. We saw that mothers who had child support or SSI were less likely to return to AFDC. The next challenge will be to focus upon the highest-risk and most vulnerable group of former AFDC recipients and low-income mothers.

Working improved the well-being of women and their families as did having a partner. Neither work nor partnering alone substantially increases women's fortunes. The sticky issue here is what types of partnerships. Research suggests that long-term cohabitation, as well as marriage, may be good both for the economic stability of the family and for the children.

The waiver experiments of the mid-1990s tell us that welfare reform does encourage independence, at least within the context of a prosperity in which jobs are available for those willing and able to work. After the recent economic down-turn, the effects of welfare reform may be less rosy. In any case, when jobs are scarce the waiver experiments predict that there will be more returns to public assistance. Policies that would help both former recipients and their working-poor counterparts include stronger support services on and off the job. Finally, in the reauthorization debates more thought needs to be given to whether this country really believes that it is cost-effective and desirable to require mothers of infants to work outside the home.

Questions

1. What is TANF? What are its limitations?
2. Did public policies in the 1990s keep former recipients off welfare?
3. What effect did the economic conditions in the 1990s have on people leaving or returning to welfare?
4. Explain why mothers with children under the age of three are at especially high risk of returning to welfare. Devise a program that would help these women and their children.
5. If you were writing an editorial for your local newspaper in support of revising TANF, what would you say?

Women in the Global Factory

ANNETTE FUENTES AND BARBARA EHRENREICH

During the 1980s and 1990s, American business interests continually expanded overseas. The reasons for this expansion are clearly economic: Multinational firms face lower wages and less restrictive labor and environmental regulations. In this article, published in 1983, Annette Fuentes and Barbara Ehrenreich address the role of women in developing nations. While their study was done at the beginning of the global expansion, little has changed for women working in various manufacturing enterprises.

In Penang, Malaysia, Julie K. is up before the three other young women with whom she shares a room and starts heating the leftover rice from last night's supper. She looks good in the company's green-trimmed uniform and she's proud to work in a modern, U.S.-owned factory. Not quite so proud as when she started working three years ago, she thinks, as she squints out the door at a passing group of women. All day at work, she peers through a microscope, bonding hair-thin gold wires to silicon chips that will end up inside pocket calculators. At 21 years of age, she is afraid she can no longer see very clearly.

In the 1890s, farm girls in England and the northeastern United States filled the textile mills of the first Industrial Revolution.

Today, from Penang to Ciudad Juarez, young Third World women have become the new "factory girls," providing a vast pool of cheap labor for globetrotting corporations. Behind the labels "Made in Taiwan" and "assembled in Haiti" may be one of the most strategic blocs of womanpower of the 1980s. In the last 15 years, multinational corporations, such as Sears Roebuck and General Electric, have come to rely on women around the world to keep labor costs down and profits up. Women are the unseen assemblers of consumer goods such as toys and designer jeans, as well as the hardware of today's "Microprocessor Revolution."

Low wages are the main reason companies move to the Third World. A female assembly line worker in the U.S. is likely to earn between $3.10 and $5 an hour.* In many Third World countries a woman doing the same work will earn $3 to $5 a *day*. Corporate executives with their eyes glued to the bottom line, wonder why they should pay someone in Massachusetts on an hourly basis what someone in the Philippines will earn in a day. And, for that matter, why pay a male worker anywhere to do what a female worker can be hired to do for 40 to 60% less?

. . .

> We need female workers; older than 17, younger than 30; single and without children; minimum education primary school, maximum education one year of preparatory school [high school]; available for all shifts.
>
> Advertisement from a Mexican newspaper

> A nimble veteran seamstress, Miss Altagracia eventually began to earn as much as $5.75 a day . . . "I was exceeding my piecework quota by a lot." . . . But then, Altagracia said, her plant supervisor, a Cuban emigre, called her into his office. "He said I was doing a fine job, but that I and some

---

*Eds. Note–The wages are from 1983.

FIGURE 1 *Cheap Labor Wages Per Hour in U.S. Dollars*

	Wage	Wage & Fringe Benefits
Hong Kong	$1.15	$1.20
Singapore	.79	1.25
South Korea	.63	2.00
Taiwan	.53	.80
Malaysia	.48	.60
Philippines	.48	.50
Indonesia	.19	.35

Source: *Semiconductor International*, February 1982.

other of the women were making too much money, and he was being forced to lower what we earned for each piece we sewed." On the best days, she now can clear barely $3, she said. "I was earning less, so I started working six and seven days a week. But I was tired and I could not work as fast as before." Within a few months she was too ill to work at all.

Story of 23-year-old Basilia Altagracia, a seamstress in the Dominican Republic's La Romana free trade zone, in the *AFL-CIO American Federalist.*[1]

There are over one million people employed in industrial free trade zones in the Third World. Millions more work outside the zones in multinational-controlled plants and domestically-owned subtracting factories. Eighty to 90% of the light-assembly workers are women. This is a remarkable switch from earlier patterns of foreign-controlled industrialization. Until recently, economic development involved heavy industries such as mining and construction and usually meant more jobs for men and—compared to traditional agricultural society—a diminished economic status for women. But multinationals consider light-assembly work, whether the product is Barbie dolls or computer components, to be women's work.

Women everywhere are paid lower wages than men. Since multinationals go overseas to reduce labor costs, women are the natural choice for assembly jobs. Wage-earning opportunities for women are limited and women are considered only supplementary income earners for their families. Management uses this secondary status to pay women less than men and justify layoffs during slow periods, claiming that women don't need to work and will probably quit to get married.

Women are the preferred workforce for other reasons. Multinationals want a workforce that is docile, easily manipulated and willing to do boring, repetitive assembly work. Women, they claim, are the perfect employees, with their "natural patience" and "manual dexterity." As the personnel manager of an assembly plant in Taiwan says, "Young male workers are too restless and impatient to be doing monotonous work with no career value. If displeased they sabotage the machine and even threaten the foreman. But girls, at most they cry a little."[2]

Multinationals prefer single women with no children and no plans to have any. Pregnancy tests are routinely given to potential employees to avoid the issue of maternity benefits. In India, a woman textile worker reports that "they do take unmarried women but they prefer women who have had an operation," referring to her government's sterilization program.[3] In the Philippines' Bataan Export Processing Zone the Mattel toy company offers prizes to workers who undergo sterilization.[4]

Third World women haven't always been a ready workforce. Until two decades ago, young women were vital to the rural economy in many countries. They worked in the home, in agriculture, or in local cottage industries. But many Third World governments adopted development plans favoring large-scale industry and agribusiness as advocated by such agencies as the World Bank and the International Monetary Fund. Traditional farming systems and communities are now crumbling as many families lose their land and local enterprises collapse. As a result of the breakdown of the rural economy, many families now send their daughters to the cities or the free trade zones in an attempt to assure some income.

The majority of the new female workforce is young, between 16 and 25 years old. As one management consultant explains, "when seniority rises, wages rise"; so the companies prefer to train a fresh group of teenagers rather than give experienced women higher pay. Different industries have different age and skill standards. The youngest workers, usually under 23 years old, are found in electronics and textile factories where keen eyesight and dexterity are essential. A second, older group of women work in industries like food processing where nimble fingers and perfect vision aren't required. Conditions in these factories are partially bad. Multinationals can get away with more because the women generally can't find jobs elsewhere.

Not all companies want young women, although this is the exception rather than the rule. In Singapore, some companies had problems with young women workers who went "shopping for jobs from factory to factory." Management consultants suggested "housewives-only" assembly lines. Older and too responsible for "transient glamour jobs," housewives would make better candidates, they reasoned. One consultant recommended that "a brigade of housewives could run the factory from 8 a.m. to 1 p.m. and leave. Then a second brigade could come in [and] take over till 6 p.m. This way housewives need only work half a day. They will be able to earn and spend time with their families. The factories will get a full and longer day's work. Deadlines will be met."[5]

Corporate apologists are quick to insist that Third World women are absolutely thrilled with their newfound employment opportunities. "You should watch these kids going to work," said Bill Mitchell, an American who solicits U.S. business for the Burmudez Industrial Park in Ciudad Juarez. "You don't have any sullenness here. They smile." A top-level management consultant who advises U.S. companies on where to relocate their factories said, "The girls genuinely enjoy themselves. They're away from their families. They have spending money. They can buy motor bikes, whatever. Of course, it is a regulated experience, too—with dormitories to live in—so it's a healthful experience." Richard Meier, a professor of environment design believes that "earning power should do more for the women of these countries than any amount of organization, demonstration and protest. . . . The benefits and freedom to be gained by these women from their employment in these new industries are almost always preferred to the near slavery associated with the production of classical goods, such as batik."[6]

Liberation or virtual slavery? What is the real experience of Third World women? A study of Brazilian women working in a textile factory drew positive conclusions: work "represents the widening of horizons, a means of confronting life, a source of individualization. The majority of women . . . drew a significant part of their identity from being wage-workers."[7] By earning money and working outside the home, factory women may find a certain independence from their families. Meeting and working with other women lays the foundation for a collective spirit and, perhaps, collective action.

But at the same time, the factory system relies upon and reinforces the power of men in the traditional patriarchal family to control women. Cynthia Enloe, a sociologist who organized an international conference of women textile workers in 1982, says that in the Third World, "the emphasis on family is absolutely crucial to management strategy. Both old-time firms and multinationals use the family to reproduce and control workers. Even recruitment is a family process. Women don't just go out independently to find jobs: it's a matter of fathers, brothers and husbands making women available after getting reassurances from the companies. Discipline becomes a family matter since, in most cases, women turn their paychecks over to their parents. Factory life is, in general, constrained and defined by the family life cycle."

One thing is certain: when multinational corporate-style development meets traditional patriarchal culture, women's lives are bound to change.

Endnotes

[1]Flannery, M. (1978, May). America's sweatshops in the sun. *AFL-CIO American Federationist,* 16.

[2]Cantwell, B., Luce, D., & Weinglass, L. (1978). *Made in Taiwan.* New York: Asia Center, 14.

[3]Chhachhi, A. (1981). The experiences of retrenchment: Women textile workers in India. Paper presented at textile worker conference of the Transnational Institute, Amsterdam, October 1981, p. 7.

[4]From a slide show on women in the Philippines by the Philippine Solidarity Network, San Francisco, California.

[5]Our fussy factory workers. (1978, June 18). *New Straits Times* (Singapore).

[6]Meier, R. L. (1977, November). Multinationals as agents of social development. *Bulletin of the Atomic Scientists*, 32.

[7]Saffioti, H. I. B. (1981). The impact of industrialization on the structure of female employment. Paper presented at textile workers conference of the Transnational Institute, Amsterdam.

Questions

1. Why do multinational manufacturing firms prefer to employ women? Are the reasons simply economic? If not, what else affects this trend?

2. To what degree does age also play a role in the work conditions described in the article?

3. Do you agree with the "corporate apologists" that employment for women in the Third World is liberating?

4. In 1982, the minimum wage in the United States was $3.10 per hour. What is the minimum wage now? If you look up today's standard wages for the countries listed in Table 1, how do they compare to the standard wages in 1982? Has the gap (i.e., profit) between U.S. labor rates and labor rates in various Asian nations

increased or decreased? What does this change imply for multinational companies?

The Feminization of Poverty in Africa

DAPHNE TOPOUZIS

Poverty is a major problem in most nations. However, it is particularly striking in Africa because of the alarming rate with which it is becoming feminized. More and more women are falling into poverty on that continent. In the reading below, Topouzis addresses why this is happening and what can be done about it. As you will see, the reasons behind the increasing feminization of poverty are complex and the solutions formidable. Finding an enduring solution is likely to be difficult.

An alarming trend with potentially devastating economic, social, and environmental consequences is developing across Africa, with evidence showing that nearly two-thirds of Africa's fast-growing, poverty-stricken population consists of women. The picture becomes bleaker considering that between 1970 and 1985, the number of Africans living in abject poverty rose by 75% to about 270 million, or half the population of the continent, according to the International Labor Organization.

Poor shelter, malnutrition, disease, illiteracy, overwork, a short life expectancy, and high maternal and infant mortality rates mark the lives of the poorest of poor women and their dependent families. Poverty is growing faster in Africa than in any other part of the world. Even more alarming, perhaps, is the fact that the feminization of poverty is becoming increasingly structural, advancing well beyond the reach of policy-makers and development projects. As a result, it

"The Feminization of Poverty in Africa," by Daphne Topouzis, reprinted from *Africa Report*, July/August 1990. pp. 60–63.

is becoming virtually impossible for women to escape the cycle of crushing poverty in which they are entrenched.

If this trend is not reversed, however, about 400 million Africans will be living in absolute poverty by 1995, argues the newly released UNDP *1990 Human Development Report*, and up to 260 million could be women.

The feminization of poverty is only beginning to be recognized as a pressing problem in Africa and elsewhere in the world, and there are as yet no statistical indicators or figures available to help identify the magnitude of the crisis. At best, studies on poverty refer to it in passing, but more often, they fail to appreciate the ramifications of this shift in the pattern of poverty on overall economic development.

The reasons behind the increasing concentration of poverty among women in Africa are as varied as they are complex. A combination of prolonged drought and the debt crisis have triggered large-scale male migrations to the cities, leaving one-third of all rural households headed by women. In some regions of sub-Saharan Africa, up to 43% of all households are headed by women, according to the UN *1989 World Survey on Women in Development.*

This phenomenon is transforming the family structure and socioeconomic fabric of African societies across the continent, placing additional financial burdens on already poor and overworked women. Women heads of households tend to have more dependents, fewer breadwinning family members, and restricted access to productive resources. "Female members of a poor household are often worse off than male members because of gender-based differences in the distribution of food and other entitlements within the family," adds the *1990 Human Development Report.*

The poverty crisis has been further aggravated by ill-fated agricultural policies or a neglect of agriculture by national governments, rapid population growth, and pressure on land available for cultivation—all of which have contributed to declining productivity and food consumption in many African countries. Between 1980 and 1985, per capita income in Africa declined by 30%, taking into account the negative terms of trade. The first victims of food shortages and famine tend to be women with young children. . . .

The adverse effects of the economic recession and remedial structural adjustment programs should be added to the list of factors that have contributed to the impoverishment of women. Structural adjustment has in many cases increased unemployment in the cities, and women are again the first to be laid off in the formal sector. Austerity measures have also decreased women's purchasing power and removed subsidies on basic foodstuffs. Thus, already overworked women have no choice but to work even longer hours to keep their families afloat, often at the expense of caring for their children and their own health. According to the UN Fund for Population Activity's *State of the World Population 1990*, rural African women tend to have more children in order to lighten their load with food production.

And last but not least, armed conflicts in Sudan, Ethiopia, Angola, Mozambique, and civil unrest in several other countries have left thousands of women widowed, displaced, or abandoned to a life of permanent emergency as refugees: An estimated two-thirds of the 5 million adult refugee population on the continent are women. "When armies march, there is no harvest," reads one African saying. As a result, women refugees often become almost totally dependent on relief from international organizations whose resources for them are currently on the decline.

The Plight of Rural Women

From near food self-sufficiency in 1970, Africa over the past two decades has witnessed a marked decline in food production and consumption per person, while real per capita access to resources has decreased accordingly. African women, who produce, process, and market over 75% of the food, suffer greater deprivations than men and continue to be ignored by national policy-makers and international aid organizations.

Thus, even though the past two years have seen bumper crops in many Sahelian countries, women farmers have not benefited from this, and the poorest among them are still unable to grow enough food to sustain their families. One of the reasons is that, as a whole, they remain excluded from access to improved technology, credit, extension services, and land. Landless, unskilled, and illiterate rural women often live precarious lives on the edge of impoverishment, regardless of how hard they work.

Women in developing countries work twice as many hours as men for one-tenth of the income. In East Africa, women spend up to 16 hours every day growing, processing, and preparing food, gathering fuel and water, and performing other household chores, in addition to caring for their children and the extended family. In Malawi, women put in twice as many hours as men cultivating maize, the main cash crop, and the same number of hours in cotton, in addition to doing all the housework. . . .

Urban Women in "Pink Collar Jobs"

Women are still a minority in the public sector in Africa: In Benin and Togo, 21% of public sector employees are women, while in Tanzania, their share in formal employment was 15.6% in 1983. Poor urban women have little professional training. As a result, they are reduced to low-wage, low-status, or "pink collar" jobs, which include clerical, teaching, and social services. In Kenya, 78.9% of the female work force in the service sector is employed in pink collar jobs, while only 6.1% is employed in high-paying jobs. The economic crisis has had a profound effect on these women, with unemployment rising by 10% annually in the period 1980–1985. In Botswana and Nigeria, the rate of unemployment among young women under 20 was 44% and 42% respectively in 1987, as opposed to males of the same age group, at 23.5 and 22.2%. For those who retained their jobs, wages were often slashed by one-third.

The vast majority of urban women work in the informal sector where earnings are meager, and there is no legal protection or job security: In Ghana, 85% of all employment in trade in 1970 was accounted for by women; in Nigeria, 94% of the street food vendors are women. These women earn substantially less than their male counterparts and often live on the edge of poverty, so that a slight deterioration in economic conditions, such as price rises of essential foodstuffs, can directly threaten their survival, as well as that of their families. In Dar es Salaam, argues the *1990 Human Development Report*, poor women had to cut back from three meals a day to two. In extreme cases, poor urban women have resorted to begging, prostitution, and other illicit activities in order to survive.

Structural Adjustment

Structural adjustment programs prescribed by international financial institutions have largely failed to integrate women into economic development and have imposed drastic cuts in education and health services, thereby exacerbating existing inequalities and marginalizing women further. A recent study conducted by a group of experts set up by the Commonwealth Ministers Responsible for Women, entitled *Engendering Adjustment for the 1990s*, argues that women in developing countries "have been at the epicenter of the crisis and have borne the brunt of the adjustment efforts."

Particularly alarming is the fact that for the first time in many years, maternal and infant mortality rates are beginning to rise and girls' school enrollments are starting to fall. "If you educate a man, you simply educate an individual, but if you educate a woman, you educate a family," said J. E. Aggrey, a Ghanaian educator. Few, however, have taken this message seriously. Illiteracy in Africa is four times as high among women as among men, and the higher the level of education, the lower the percentage of girls. . . .

Women's health has also suffered severe setbacks as a result of structural adjustment programs. In Nigeria, where health fees and social service subsidies were slashed, health care and food costs have spiralled by 400 to 600%, according to a recent report in *West Africa*. About 75,000 women die each year from causes related to pregnancy or childbirth in Nigeria alone—that is, one woman every seven minutes, according to the same source. In Benin, Cameroon, Nigeria, Malawi, Mali, and Mozambique, one out of five 15-year-old women dies before she reaches 45 years of age for reasons related to pregnancy and childbirth.

Women in Development

Between 1965 and 1986, women were neglected by development planners largely due to misconceptions and misdirected efforts and as a result, hardly benefited from development aid, argued a 1988 World Bank report. Thus, it was taken for granted that all households are male-headed, that women do not work, and that by increasing the income of a household, everyone will benefit. Rural development projects geared toward women tended to emphasize training and health, hygiene, nutrition, and child care, neglecting to help women improve their capabilities as farmers. Women were barred from access to credit and improved technology because it was the men who were addressed as the real producers. . . .

The devastating drought, famines, and the economic crisis of the 1980s pressured African governments and development organizations into recognizing the vital role women play in economic development. Most African governments now have a ministry bureau, or department dealing with women's affairs and some legislative adjustments have been made to improve the socio-economic status of women. These initiatives, however, have not reached the most vulnerable and impoverished of women, not least because their needs are multi-sectoral and are unlikely to be met by a single government department, while being ignored or given token recognition by other ministries.

In essence, women's economic contributions remain largely overlooked an equitable development strategies have yet to be translated into the effective plans of action. In many countries, African women still cannot own the land they cultivate or get access to credit. In Lesotho, women lack the most basic legal and social rights: They cannot sign contracts, borrow money, or slaughter cattle without their husbands' consent.

Sustainable development has to become synonymous and equitable development, and economic recovery will only come about if the feminization of poverty is tackled as an economic and social program rather than as a purely developmental or exclusively a women's problem. There are some encouraging initiatives in Ghana, Tanzania, and Nigeria, where farmers' cooperatives are obtaining loans for poor women from local banks.

However, a formidable task awaits national governments and development workers: Access to productive resources such as land, capital, and technology, fair wages, training, and education and basic health care are essential conditions if African women are to break out of the vicious circle of poverty and underdevelopment. Equally pressing, however, are policy-making and legislative reforms to combat discrimination against women and change male attitudes regarding women's contributions to social and economic life.

Questions

1. What "marks the lives" of poor women in Africa?
2. Why does Topouzis claim that the reasons for the feminization of poverty are becoming increasingly structural?
3. What types of problems and circumstances have contributed to the increased poverty rate among women in Africa?
4. How are the experiences of poor women in rural areas similar to those in urban areas? How are they different?
5. What type(s) of reforms are needed to help combat poverty? What is the likelihood that these programs will be successful?

Of Our Spiritual Strivings

W.E.B. Du Bois

W.E.B. Du Bois's classic manuscript, The Souls of Black Folk, *is often viewed as one of the earliest and most insightful works examining the plight of Black people in the United States. In this selection, Du Bois traces major developments between the emancipation proclamation and the early 1900s and discusses the concept of "double-consciousness" that Black people experience while trying to balance the notions of being "American" and "colored."*

Double Consciousness

Between me and the other world there is ever an unasked question: unasked by some through feelings of delicacy; by others through the difficulty of rightly framing it. All, nevertheless, flutter round it. They approach me in a half-hesitant sort of way, eye me curiously or compassionately, and then, instead of saying directly, How does it feel to be a problem? they say, I know an excellent colored man in my town; or, I fought at Mechanicsville; or, Do not these Southern outrages make your blood boil? At these I smile, or am interested, or reduce the boiling to a simmer, as the occasion may require. To the real question, How does it feel to be a problem? I answer seldom a word.

And yet, being a problem is a strange experience—peculiar even for one who has never been anything else, save perhaps in babyhood and in Europe. It is in the early days of rollicking boyhood that the revelation first bursts upon one, all in a day, as it were. I remember well when the shadow swept across me. I was a little thing, away up in the hills of New England, where the dark Housatonic winds between Hoosac and Taghkanic to the sea. In a wee wooden schoolhouse, something put it into the boys' and girls' heads to buy gorgeous visiting-cards—ten cents a package—and exchange. The exchange was merry, till one girl, a tall newcomer, refused my card—refused it peremptorily, with a glance. Then it dawned upon me with a certain sud-

---

"Double Consciousness" by W.E.B. Dubois, from *The Souls of Black Folk*, 1905.

denness that I was different from the others; or like, mayhap, in heart and life and longing, but shut out from their world by a vast veil. I had thereafter no desire to tear down that veil, to creep through; I held all beyond it in common contempt, and lived above it in a region of blue sky and great wandering shadows. That sky was bluest when I could beat my mates at examination time, or beat them at a foot race, or even beat their stringy heads. Alas, with the years all this fine contempt began to fade; for the worlds I longed for, and all their dazzling opportunities, were theirs, not mine. But they should not keep these prizes, I said; some, all, I would wrest from them. Just how I would do it I could never decide: by reading law, by healing the sick, by telling the wonderful tales that swam in my head—some way. With other black boys the strife was not so fiercely sunny: their youth shrunk into tasteless sycophancy, or into silent hatred of the pale world about them and mocking distrust of everything white; or wasted itself in a bitter cry, Why did God make me an outcast and a stranger in mine own house? The shades of the prison-house closed round about us all: walls strait and stubborn to the whitest, but relentlessly narrow, tall, and unscalable to sons of night who must plod darkly on in resignation, or beat unavailing palms against the stone, or steadily, half hopelessly, watch the streak of blue above.

After the Egyptian and Indian, the Greek and Roman, the Teuton and Mongolian, the Negro is a sort of seventh son, born with a veil, and gifted with second sight in this American world—a world which yields him no true self-consciousness, but lets him see himself through the revelation of the other world. It is a peculiar sensation, this double-consciousness, this sense of always looking at one's self through the eyes of others, of measuring one's soul by the tape of a world that looks on in amused contempt and pity. One ever feels his two-ness—an American, a Negro; two souls, two thoughts, two unreconciled strivings; two warring ideals in one dark body, whose dogged strength alone keeps it from being torn asunder.

The history of the American Negro is the history of this strife—this longing to attain self-conscious manhood, to merge his double self into a better and truer self. In this merging he wishes neither of the older selves to be lost. He would not Africanize America, for America has too much to teach the world and Africa. He would not bleach his Negro soul in a flood of white Americanism, “for he knows that Negro blood has a message for the world. He simply wishes to make it possible for a man to be both a Negro and an American, without being cursed and spit upon by his fellows, without having the doors of opportunity closed roughly in his face.

This, then, is the end of his striving: to be a coworker in the kingdom of culture, to escape both death and isolation, to husband and use his best powers and his latent genius. These powers of body and mind have in the past been strangely wasted, dispersed, or forgotten. The shadow of a mighty Negro past flits through the tale of Ethiopia the Shadowy and of Egypt the Sphinx. Throughout history, the powers of single black men flash here and there like falling stars, and die sometimes before the world has rightly gauged their brightness. Here in America, in the few days since Emancipation, the black man's turning hither and thither in hesitant and doubtful striving has often made his very strength to lose effectiveness, to seem like absence of power, like weakness. And yet it is not weakness—it is the contradiction of double aims. The double-aimed struggle of the black artisan—on the one hand to escape white contempt for a nation of mere hewers of wood and drawers of water, and on the other hand to plough and nail and dig for a poverty-stricken horde—could only result in making him a poor craftsman, for he had but half a heart in either cause. By the poverty and ignorance of his people, the Negro minister or doctor was tempted toward quackery and demagogy; and by the criticism of the other world, toward ideals that made him ashamed of his lowly tasks. The would-be black *savant* was confronted by the paradox that the knowledge his people needed was a twice-told tale to his white neighbors, while the knowledge which would teach the white world was Greek to his own flesh and blood. The innate love of harmony and beauty that set the ruder souls of his people a-dancing and a-singing raised but confusion and doubt in the soul of the black artist; for the beauty revealed to him was the soul-beauty of a race which his larger audience despised, and he could not articulate the message of another people. This waste of double aims, this seeking to satisfy two unreconciled ideals, has wrought sad havoc with the courage and faith and deeds of ten thousand thousand people—has sent them often wooing false gods and invoking false means of salvation, and at times has even seemed about to make them ashamed of themselves.

Away back in the days of bondage they thought to see in one divine event the end of all doubt and disappointment; few men ever worshipped freedom with half such unquestioning faith as did the American Negro for two centuries. To him, so far as he thought and dreamed, slavery was indeed the sum of all villainies, the cause of all sorrow, the root of all prejudice; Emancipation was the key to a promised land of sweeter beauty than ever stretched before the eyes of wearied Israelites. In song and exhortation swelled one refrain—liberty; in his tears and curses, the God he implored had freedom in his right hand. At last it came—suddenly, fearfully, like a dream. With one wild carnival of blood and passion came the message in his own plaintive cadences:

> Shout, O children!
> Shout, you're free!
> For God has bought your liberty!

Years have passed away since then—ten, twenty, forty; forty years of national life, forty years of renewal and development, and yet the swarthy specter sits in its accustomed seat at the nation's feast. In vain do we cry to this our vastest social problem.

> Take any shape but that, and my firm nerves
> Shall never tremble!

The nation has not yet found peace from its sins; the freedman has not yet found in freedom his promised land. Whatever of good may have come in these years of change, the shadow of a deep disappointment rests upon the Negro people—a disappointment all the more bitter because the unattained ideal was unbounded save by the simple ignorance of a lowly people.

The first decade was merely a prolongation of the vain search for freedom, the boon that seemed ever barely to elude their grasp—like a tantalizing will-o'-the-wisp, maddening and misleading the headless host. The holocaust of war, the terrors of the Ku Klux Klan, the lies of carpetbaggers, the disorganization of industry, and the contradictory advice of friends and foes, left the bewildered serf with no new watchword beyond the old cry for freedom. As the time flew, however, he began to grasp a new idea. The ideal of liberty demanded for its attainment powerful means, and these the Fifteenth Amendment gave him. The ballot, which before he had looked upon as a visible sign of freedom, he now regarded as the chief means of gaining and perfecting the liberty with which war had partially endowed him. And why not? Had not votes made war and emancipated millions? Had not votes enfranchised the freedmen? Was anything impossible to a power that had done all this? A million black men started with renewed zeal to vote themselves into the kingdom. So the decade flew away, the revolution of 1876 came, and left the half-free serf weary, wondering, but still inspired. Slowly but steadily, in the following years, a new vision began gradually to replace the dream of political power—a powerful movement, the rise of another ideal to guide the unguided, another pillar of fire by night after a clouded day. It was the ideal of *book-learning:* the curiosity, born of compulsory ignorance to know and test the power of the cabalistic letters of the white man, the longing to know.

Here at last seemed to have been discovered the mountain path to Canaan; longer than the highway of Emancipation and law, steep and rugged, but straight, leading to heights high enough to overlook life.

Up the new path the advance guard toiled, slowly, heavily, doggedly; only those who have watched and guided the faltering feet, the misty minds, the dull understandings of the dark pupils of these schools know how faithfully, how piteously, this people strove to learn. It was weary work. The cold statistician wrote down the inches of progress here and there, noted also where here and there a foot had slipped or someone had fallen. To the tired climbers, the horizon was ever dark, the mists were often cold, the Canaan was always dim and far away. If, however, the vistas disclosed as yet no goal, no resting-place, little but flattery and criticism, the journey at least gave leisure for reflection and self-examination; it changed the child of Emancipation to the youth with dawning self-consciousness, self-realization, self-respect. In those somber forests of his striving his own soul rose before him, and he saw himself—darkly as through a veil; and yet he saw in himself some faint revelation of his power, of his mission. He began to have a dim feeling that, to attain his place in the world, he must be himself, and not another. For the first time he sought to analyze the burden he bore upon his back, that dead weight of social degradation partially masked behind a half-named Negro problem. He felt his poverty; without a cent, without a home, without land, tools, or savings, he had entered into competition with rich, landed, skilled neighbors. To be a poor man is hard, but to be a poor race in a land of dollars is the very bottom of hardships. He felt the weight of his ignorance—not simply of letters, but of life, of business, of the humanities; the accumulated sloth and shirking and awkwardness of decades and centuries shackled his hands and feet. Nor was his burden all poverty and ignorance. The red stain of bastardy which two centuries of systematic legal defilement of Negro women had stamped upon his race, meant not only the loss of ancient African chastity, but also the hereditary weight of a mass of corruption from white adulterers, threatening almost the obliteration of the Negro home.

A people thus handicapped ought not to be asked to race with the world, but rather a allowed to give all its time and thought to its own social problems. But alas! While sociologists gleefully count his bastards and his prostitutes, the very soul of the toiling, sweating black man is darkened by the shadow of a vast despair. Men call the shadow prejudice, and learnedly explain it as the natural defense of culture against barbarism, learning against ignorance, purity against crime, the "higher" against the "lower" races. To which the Negro cries *Amen!* and swears that to so much of this strange prejudice as is founded on just homage to civilization, culture, righteousness, and progress, he humbly bows and meekly does obeisance. But before that nameless prejudice that leaps beyond all this he stands helpless, dismayed, and well-nigh speechless; before that personal disrespect and mockery, the ridicule and systematic humiliation, the distortion of fact and wanton license of fancy, the cynical ignoring of the better and the boisterous welcoming of the worse, the all-pervading desire to inculcate disdain for everything black, from Toussaint to the Devil—before this there rises a sickening despair that would disarm and discourage any nation save that black host to whom *discouragement* is an unwritten word.

But the facing of so vast a prejudice could not but bring the inevitable self-questioning, self-disparagement, and lowering of ideals which ever accompany repression and breed in an atmosphere of contempt and hate. Whisperings and portents came borne upon the four winds. Lo! We are diseased and dying, cried the dark hosts; we cannot write, our voting is vain; what need of education, since we must always cook and serve? And the nation echoed and enforced this self-criticism, saying: Be content to be servants, and nothing more; what need of higher culture for half-men? Away with the black man's ballot, by force or fraud—and behold the suicide of a race! Nevertheless, out of the evil came something of good—the more careful adjustment of education to real life, the clearer perception of the Negroes' social responsibilities, and the sobering realization of the meaning of progress.

So dawned the time of *Sturm und Drang:* storm and stress today rocks our little boat on the mad waters of the world-sea; there is within and without the sound of conflict, the burning of body and rending of soul; inspiration strives with doubt, and faith with vain questionings. The bright ideals of the past—physical freedom, political power, the training of brains and the training of hands—all these in turn have waxed and waned, until even the last grows dim and overcast. Are they all wrong, all false? No, not that, but each alone was over-simple and incomplete—the dreams of a credulous race-childhood, or the fond imaginings of the other world which does not know and does not want to know our power. To be really true, all these ideals must be melted and welded into one. The training of the schools we need today more than ever—the training of deft hands, quick eyes and ears, and above all the broader, deeper, higher culture of gifted minds and pure hearts. The power of the ballot we need in sheer self-defense—else what shall save us from a second slavery? Freedom, too, the long-sought, we still seek the freedom of life and limb, the freedom to work and think, the freedom to love and aspire. Work, culture, liberty—all these we need, not singly but together, not successively but together, each growing and aiding each, and all striving toward that vaster ideal that swims before the Negro people, the ideal of human brotherhood, gained through the unifying ideal of race; the ideal of fostering and developing the traits and talents of the Negro, not in opposition to or contempt for other races, but rather in large conformity to the greater ideals of the American Republic, in order that some day on American soil two world-races may give each to each those characteristics both so sadly lack. We the darker ones come even now not altogether empty-handed: there are today no truer exponents of the pure human spirit of the Declaration of Independence than the American Negroes; there is no true American music but the wild sweet melodies of the Negro slave; the American fairy tales and folklore are Indian and African; and, all in all, we black men seem the sole oasis of simple faith and reverence in a dusty desert of dollars and smartness. Will America be poorer if she replaces her brutal dyspeptic blundering with light-hearted but determined Negro humility? Or her coarse and cruel wit with loving jovial good-humor? Or her vulgar music with the soul of the Sorrow Songs?

Merely a concrete test of the underlying principles of the great republic is the Negro Problem, and the spiritual striving of the freedmen's sons is the travail of souls whose burden is almost beyond the measure of their strength, but who bear it in the name of an historic race, in the name of this, the land of their fathers' fathers, and in the name of human opportunity.

Questions

1. What does Du Bois mean by "double consciousness"?
2. Can double consciousness apply to other groups in the United States, historically or contemporarily?
3. Of the four major stages reviewed by Du Bois (i.e. physical freedom, political power, education, technical training), which do you think is currently most developed in contemporary America? Which is the least developed? Explain.
4. To what degree is it possible to apply Du Bois' transitions or stages to other minority groups in the United States? In other nations?

Race Matters

Cornel West

In the article below, Cornel West concludes that, despite recent beliefs otherwise, race still matters in many aspects of American life. He contends that some of the most pressing issues facing blacks include feelings of worthlessness and despair, and a lack of clear leadership. This selection is from the introduction to West's book, Race Matters. *In it, the author sets forth possible strategies for easing racial tension and fostering equality.*

...

What happened in Los Angeles in April of 1992 was neither a race riot nor a class rebellion. Rather, this monumental upheaval was a multiracial, trans-class, and largely male display of justified social rage. For all its ugly, xenophobic resentment, its air of adolescent carnival, and its downright barbaric behavior, it signified the sense of powerlessness in American society. Glib attempts to reduce its meaning to the pathologies of the black underclass, the criminal actions of hoodlums, or the political revolt of the oppressed urban masses miss the mark. Of those arrested, only 36 percent were black, more than a third had full-time jobs, and most claimed to shun political affiliation. What we witnessed in Los Angeles was the consequence of a lethal linkage of economic decline, cultural decay, and political lethargy in American life. Race was the visible catalyst, not the underlying cause.

The meaning of the earthshaking events in Los Angeles is difficult to grasp because most of us remain trapped in the narrow framework of the dominant liberal and conservative views of race in America,

---

"Race Matters," by Cornel West, reprinted from *Race Matters*, pp. 1–8, 1994, Beacon Press.

which with its worn-out vocabulary leaves us intellectually debilitated, morally disempowered, and personally depressed. The astonishing disappearance of the event from public dialogue is testimony to just how painful and distressing a serious engagement with race is. Our truncated public discussions of race suppress the best of who and what we are as a people because they fail to confront the complexity of the issue in a candid and critical manner. The predictable pitting of liberals against conservatives, Great Society Democrats against self-help Republicans, reinforces intellectual parochialism and political paralysis.

The liberal notion that more government programs can solve racial problems is simplistic—precisely because it focuses *solely* on the economic dimension. And the conservative idea that what is needed is a change in the moral behavior of poor black urban dwellers (especially poor black men, who, they say, should stay married, support their children, and stop committing so much crime) highlights immoral actions while ignoring public responsibility for the immoral circumstances that haunt our fellow citizens.

The common denominator of these views of race is that each still sees black people as a "problem people," in the words of Dorothy I. Height, president of the National Council of Negro Women, rather than as fellow American citizens with problems. Her words echo the poignant "unasked question" of W. E. B. Du Bois, who, in *The Souls of Black Folk (1903)*, wrote:

> They approach me in a half-hesitant sort of way, eye me curiously or compassionately, and then instead of saying directly, How does it feel to be a problem? they say, I know an excellent colored man in my town. . . . Do not these Southern outrages make your blood boil? At these I smile, or am interested, or reduce the boiling to a simmer, as the occasion may require. To the real question, How does it feel to be a problem? I answer seldom a word.

Nearly a century later, we confine discussions about race in America to the "problems" black people pose for whites rather than consider what this way of viewing black people reveals about us as a nation.

This paralyzing framework encourages liberals to relieve their guilty consciences by supporting public funds directed at "the problems"; but at the same time, reluctant to exercise principled criticism of black people, liberals deny them the freedom to err. Similarly, conservatives blame the "problems" on black people themselves—and thereby render black social misery invisible or unworthy of public attention.

Hence, for liberals, black people are to be "included" and "integrated" into "one" society and culture, while for conservatives they are to be "well behaved" and "worthy of acceptance" by "our" way of life. Both fail to see that the presence and predicaments of black people are neither additions to nor defections from American life, but rather *constitutive elements of that life.*

To engage in a serious discussion of race in America, we must begin not with the problems of black people but with the flaws of American society—flaws rooted in historic inequalities and long-standing cultural stereotypes. How we set up the terms for discussing racial issues shapes our perception and response to these issues. As long as black people are viewed as a "them," the burden falls on blacks to do all the "cultural" and "moral" work necessary for healthy race relations. The implication is that only certain Americans can define what it means to be American—and the rest must simply "fit in."

The emergence of strong black-nationalist sentiments among blacks, especially among young people, is a revolt against this sense of having to "fit in." The variety of black-nationalist ideologies, from the moderate views of Supreme Court Justice Clarence Thomas in his youth to those of Louis Farrakhan today, rest upon a fundamental truth: white America has been historically weak-willed in ensuring racial justice and has continued to resist fully accepting the humanity of blacks. As long as double standards and differential treatment abound—as long as the rap performer Ice-T is harshly condemned while former Los Angeles Police Chief Daryl F. Gates's antiblack comments are received in polite silence, as long as Dr. Leonard Jeffries's anti-Semitic statements are met with vitriolic outrage while presidential candidate Patrick J. Buchanan's anti-Semitism receives a genteel response—black nationalisms will thrive.

Afrocentrism, a contemporary species of black nationalism, is a gallant yet misguided attempt to define an African identity in a white society perceived to be hostile. It is gallant because it puts black doings and sufferings, not white anxieties and fears, at the center of discussion. It is misguided because—out of fear of cultural hybridization and through silence on the issue of class, retrograde views on black women, gay men, and lesbians, and a reluctance to link race to the common good—it reinforces the narrow discussions about race.

To establish a new framework, we need to begin with a frank acknowledgment of the basic humanness and Americanness of each of us. And we must acknowledge that as a people—*E Pluribus Unum*—we are on a slippery slope toward economic strife, social turmoil, and cultural chaos. If we go down, we go down together. The Los Angeles upheaval forced us to see not only that we are not connected in ways we would like to be but also, in a more profound sense, that this failure to connect binds us even more tightly together. The paradox of race in America is that our common destiny is more pronounced and imperiled precisely when our divisions are deeper. The Civil War and its legacy speak loudly here. And our divisions are growing deeper. Today, eighty-six percent of white suburban Americans live in neighborhoods that are less than 1 percent black, meaning that the prospects for the country depend largely on how its cities fare in the hands of a suburban electorate. There is no escape from our interracial interdependence, yet enforced racial hierarchy dooms us as a nation to collective paranoia and hysteria—the unmaking of any democratic order.

The verdict in the Rodney King case which sparked the incidents in Los Angeles was perceived to be wrong by the vast majority of Americans. But whites have often failed to acknowledge the widespread mistreatment of black people, especially black men, by law enforcement agencies, which helped ignite the spark. The verdict was merely the occasion for deep-seated rage to come to the surface. This rage is fed by the "silent" depression ravaging the country—in which real weekly wages of all American workers since 1973 have declined nearly 20 percent, while at the same time wealth has been upwardly distributed.

The exodus of stable industrial jobs from urban centers to cheaper labor markets here and abroad, housing policies that have created "chocolate cities and vanilla suburbs" (to use the popular musical artist George Clinton's memorable phrase), white fear of black crime, and the urban influx of poor Spanish-speaking and Asian immigrants—all have helped erode the tax base of American cities just as the federal government has cut its supports and programs. The result is unemployment, hunger, homelessness, and sickness for millions.

And a pervasive spiritual impoverishment grows. The collapse of meaning in life—the eclipse of hope and absence of love of self and others, the breakdown of family and neighborhood bonds—leads to the social deracination and cultural denudement of urban dwellers, especially children. We have created rootless, dangling people with little link to the supportive networks—family, friends, school—that sustain some sense of purpose in life. We have witnessed the collapse of the spiritual communities that in the past helped Americans face despair, disease, and death and that transmit through the generations dignity and decency, excellence and elegance.

The result is lives of what we might call "random nows," of fortuitous and fleeting moments preoccupied with "getting over"—with acquiring pleasure, property, and power by any means necessary. (This is not what Malcolm X meant by this famous phrase.) Post-modern culture is more and more a market culture dominated by gangster mentalities and self-destructive wantonness. This culture engulfs all of us—yet its impact on the disadvantaged is devastating, resulting in extreme violence in everyday life. Sexual violence against women and homicidal assaults by young black men on one another are only the most obvious signs of this empty quest for pleasure, property, and power.

Last, this rage is fueled by a political atmosphere in which images, not ideas, dominate, where politicians spend more time raising money than debating issues. The functions of parties have been displaced by public polls, and politicians behave less as thermostats that determine the climate of opinion than as thermometers registering the public mood. American politics has been rocked by an unleashing of greed among opportunistic public officials—who have followed the lead of their counterparts in the private sphere, where, as of 1989, 1 percent of the population owned 37 percent of the wealth and 10 percent of the population owned 86 percent of the wealth—leading to a profound cynicism and pessimism among the citizenry.

And given the way in which the Republican Party since 1968 has appealed to popular xenophobic images—playing the black, female, and homophobic cards to realign the electorate along race, sex, and sexual-orientation lines—it is no surprise that the notion that we are all part of one garment of destiny is discredited. Appeals to special interests rather than to public interests reinforce this polarization. The Los Angeles upheaval was an expression of utter fragmentation by a powerless citizenry that includes not just the poor but all of us.

What is to be done? How do we capture a new spirit and vision to meet the challenges of the post-industrial city, post-modern culture, and post-party politics?

First, we must admit that the most valuable sources for help, hope, and power consist of ourselves and our common history. As in the ages of Lincoln, Roosevelt, and King, we must look to new frameworks and languages to understand our multilayered crisis and overcome our deep malaise.

Second, we must focus our attention on the public square—the common good that undergirds our national and global destinies. The vitality of any public square ultimately depends on how much we *care* about the quality of our lives together. The neglect of our public infrastructure, for example—our water and sewage systems, bridges, tunnels, highways, subways, and streets—reflects not only our myopic economic policies, which impede productivity, but also the low priority we place on our common life.

The tragic plight of our children clearly reveals our deep disregard for public well-being. About one out of every five children in this country lives in poverty, including one out of every two black children and two out of every five Hispanic children. Most of our children—neglected by overburdened parents and bombarded by the market values of profit-hungry corporations—are ill-equipped to live lives of spiritual and cultural quality. Faced with these facts, how do we expect ever to constitute a vibrant society?

One essential step is some form of large-scale public intervention to ensure access to basic social goods—housing, food, health care, education, child care, and jobs. We must invigorate the common good with a mixture of government, business, and labor that does not follow any existing blueprint. After a period in which the private sphere has been sacralized and the public square gutted, the temptation is to make a fetish of the public square. We need to resist such dogmatic swings.

Last, the major challenge is to meet the need to generate new leadership. The paucity of courageous leaders—so apparent in the response to the events in Los Angeles—requires that we look beyond the same elites and voices that recycle the older frameworks. We need leaders—neither saints nor sparkling television personalities—who can situate themselves within a larger historical narrative of this country and our world, who can grasp the complex dynamics of our peoplehood and imagine a future grounded in the best of our past, yet who are attuned to the frightening obstacles that now perplex us. Our ideals of freedom, democracy, and equality must be invoked to invigorate all of us, especially the landless, propertyless, and luckless. Only a visionary leadership that can motivate "the better angels of our nature," as Lincoln said, and activate possibilities for a freer, more efficient, and stable America—only that leadership deserves cultivation and support.

This new leadership must be grounded in grass-roots organizing that highlights democratic accountability. Whoever our leaders will be as we approach the twenty-first century, their challenge will be to help Americans determine whether a genuine multiracial democracy can be created and sustained in an era of global economy and a moment of xenophobic frenzy.

Let us hope and pray that the vast intelligence, imagination, humor, and courage of Americans will not fail us. Either we learn a new language of empathy and compassion, or the fire this time will consume us all.

Questions

1. According to West, what underlying conditions lead to violence by blacks? Why does West contend that the violence is a *symptom* of a problem, not the problem itself?

2. What must be done to combat the problem of growing racial tension?

3. Of West's recommendations, which do you think hold the most promise of being implemented? Which hold the most promise of being effective, regardless of the likelihood of their being implemented? Why?

4. Think of examples of racially based violence that you have personally experienced, witnessed in your school or community, or seen reported on television. What were the *purported* causes of the violence? What do you think the *underlying* causes of the violence might have been? Do these causes align with West's conceptualization? Explain.

The Monochrome Society

AMITAI ETZIONI

American society is becoming increasingly nonwhite. By most demographic estimates, in the next forty to fifty years, the majority of the American population will be minorities—in other words, while whites may continue to be the largest single ethnic group, the sum of the separate racial and ethnic minority groups will be greater. Some estimates predict that in the next century whites will lose their status to Hispanics as the single largest group. This so-called "browning" of America has many white Americans (conservatives and liberals alike) concerned that "traditional" American values will be lost as racial and ethnic minorities become the numeric majority. In this selection, Amitai Etzioni attempts to alleviate this concern by demonstrating that minorities and whites are much more alike than many may recognize—especially when it comes to values and beliefs that are at the core of American society. He contends that while American society may become more diverse in its skin color and language, it will continue to be homogenous in its "traditional" American attitudes, values, and beliefs.

Various demographers and social scientists have been predicting for years that the end of the white majority in the United States is near, and that there will be a majority of minorities. The issue has moved to the center of American political discourse: CNN has broadcasted a special program on the subject; President Clinton has called attention to it in his national dialogue on race relations; and numerous books and articles in recent years have addressed America's changing demography from vastly different—and frequently antagonistic—perspectives.

Some have reacted to the expected demise of the white majority with alarm or distress. Dale Maharidge, author of The Coming White Minority: California's Eruptions and America's Future, claims that by the year 2000, California's population will be less than 50 percent white. As he explains, "'Minorities' will be in the majority, a precursor to the 2050 state of racial composition nationwide, when the nation will be almost half nonwhite." According to Maharidge, "whites are scared," especially in California:

The depth of white fear is underestimated and misunderstood by progressive thinkers and the media. Whites dread the unknown and not-so-distant tomorrow when a statistical turning point will be reached that could have very bad consequences for them. They fear the change that seems to be transforming their state into something different from the rest of the United States. They fear losing not only their jobs but also their culture. Some feel that California will become a version of South Africa, in which whites will lose power when minorities are the majority.

Fearing the "browning" of America, many whites have already formed residential islands surrounded by vast ethnic communities, foreshadowing, Maharidge claims, what the rest of America might become. Whites and non-whites alike recently passed the anti-immigrant Proposition 187, which Maharidge links to these same fears about the end of the white majority. "There is ample evidence," he concludes, "that white tension could escalate."

In contrast, John Isbister, a professor of economics at the University of California at Santa Cruz, asks us to ponder whether America is too white. He contends that the decline in the white proportion of the population is a healthy development for the country, because it will gradually replace a majority-minority confrontation with interactions between groups of more equal size and influence. He further notes that "the principal case for a falling white proportion is simply this: it will be easier for us to transform a society of hostility and oppression into one of cooperation if we are dealing not with a majority versus several small minorities, but with groups of roughly equivalent size."

One People

As I see it, both views, that of alarm and celebration, are fundamentally wrong because these positions are implicitly and inadvertently racist: They assume that people's pigmentation or other racial attributes determine their opinions, values, and votes. In fact, very often the opposite is true. America is blessed with an economic and political system, as well as culture and core values, that while far from flawless, are embraced by most Americans of all races and ethnic groups. (To save breath, from here on, race is used to encompass ethnicity.) It is a grievous error to suggest that as America's racial mix changes so will its core values. Of course, nobody can predict what people will believe 50 years from now. But it is clear that today the races share the same basic aspirations and principles. Moreover, current trends in attitudes that are concomitant with increases in the proportion of the nonwhite population further support the thesis that while American society may well change, whites and nonwhites will largely change together.

A 1992 survey finds that most black and Hispanic Americans (86 percent and 85 percent, respectively) seek "fair treatment for all, without prejudice or discrimination." One may expect that this principle is of special concern to minorities, but white Americans feel the same way. As a result, the proportion of all Americans who agree with the quoted statement about fairness is 79 percent.

A poll of New York residents shows that the vast majority of respondents consider it very important to teach our common heritage and values. One may expect this statement to reflect a white, majoritarian view. However, minorities endorse this position more strongly than whites: 88 percent of Hispanics and 89 percent of blacks—compared to 70 percent of whites. A nationwide poll finds that equal proportions of blacks and whites, 93 percent, concur that they would vote for a black presidential candidate. Another national poll finds that over 80 percent of all respondents in every category—age, gender, race, location, education, and income—agree with the statement that freedom must be tempered by personal responsibility. Far from favoring a multicultural curriculum, approximately 85 percent of all parents, 83 percent of African-American parents, 89 percent of Hispanic parents, and 88 percent of foreign-born parents agree that "to graduate from high school, students should be required to understand the common history and ideas that tie all Americans together."

Even in response to a deliberately loaded question, a 1997 poll shows that similarities between the races are much larger than differences. Asked, "Will race relations in this country ever get better?" 43 percent of blacks and 60 percent of whites reply in the affirmative. (Pollsters tend to focus on the 17 percent who strike a different position rather than on the 43 percent who embrace the same one. The difference between 57 percent of blacks and 40 percent of whites who do not believe that race relations are going to get better is also 17 percent.)

Not Black and White

While Americans hold widely ranging opinions on what should be done about various matters of social policy, people across racial and ethnic categories identify the same issues as important to them and to the country. For instance, in a 1996 survey, whites, African Americans, Latinos, and Asian Americans concurred that education is "the most important issue facing [their] community today." Similarly, more than 80 percent of blacks, Latinos, and whites share the belief that "it is 'extremely important' to spend tax dollars on 'educational opportunities for children.'" In another survey, 54 percent of blacks and 61 percent of whites rank "increased economic opportunity" as the most important goal for blacks. And 97 percent of blacks and 92 percent of whites rate violent crime a "very serious or most serious problem."

Other problems that trouble America's communities highlight points of convergence among members of various racial and ethnic groups. "Between 80 and 90 percent of black, white, and 'other' Americans agree that it is 'extremely important' to spend tax dollars on 'reducing crime' and 'reducing illegal drug use' among youth." In addition, some shared public-policy preferences emerge. Among whites, African Americans, Latinos, and Asian Americans surveyed by the Washington Post/Kaiser Foundation/Harvard Survey Project, between 75 percent and 82 percent of each group feel "strongly" that Congress should balance the budget. Between 30 percent and 41 percent are convinced that Congress should instate limited tax breaks for business; between 46 percent and 55 percent concur that Congress should cut personal income taxes; between 53 percent and 58 percent agree that Congress should reform Medicare. 67 percent of all parents, 68 percent of African-American parents, 66 percent of Hispanic parents, and 75 percent of foreign-born parents—close to 70 percent of each group—tell Public Agenda that the most important thing for public schools to do for new immigrant children is "to teach them English as quickly as possible, even if this means they fall behind in other subjects."

All this is not to suggest that there are no significant differences of opinion along racial and ethnic lines, especially when the subject directly concerns race. For instance, many whites and many blacks (although by no means all of either group) take different views of whether O.J. Simpson was guilty. In one survey, 62 percent of whites believed Simpson was guilty, in contrast to 55 percent of African Americans who believed he was not guilty. Likewise, concerning affirmative action, 51 percent of blacks in a 1997 poll "favor programs which give preferential treatment to racial minorities," a much higher percentage than the 21 percent of whites who favor such programs. And a very large difference appears when one examines voting patterns. For instance, in 1998, 55 percent of whites versus 11 percent of African Americans voted for Republican Congressional candidates.

Still, if one considers attitudes toward the basic tenets of the American creed, the majority of blacks accept them. A Public Perspective poll from

1998 finds that 54 percent of blacks and 66 percent of whites agree with the following statement: "In the United States today, anyone who works hard enough can make it economically." Most blacks (77 percent) say they prefer equality of opportunity to equality of results (compared to 89 percent of whites). On the question, "Do you see yourself as traditional or old fashioned on things such as sex, morality, family life, and religion, or not," the difference between blacks and whites is only 5 percent, and when asked whether values in America are seriously declining, the difference is down to one point.

A question from an extensive national survey conducted at the University of Virginia by James Davison Hunter and Carl Bowman asks: "How strong would you say the U.S. decline or improvement is in its moral and ethical standards?" Twentythree percent of blacks and 33 percent of whites said there was a strong decline, but 29 percent of blacks and 24 percent of whites said the standards were holding steady, and 40 percent of blacks and 38 percent of whites said there was a moderate decline. When asked "How strong would you say the U.S. decline or improvement is in the area of family life?" 18 percent of blacks and 26 percent of whites said there was a strong decline while 42 percent of blacks and 40 percent of whites saw a moderate decline and 131 percent of blacks and 25 percent of whites said family life was holding steady. Roughly the same percentages of blacks and whites strongly advocate balancing the budget, cutting personal income taxes, reforming the welfare system, and reforming Medicare. Percentages are also nearly even in responses to questions on abortion and marijuana.

Pollsters and commentators tend to play up small differences and downplay large similarities. In most of the figures cited above, the differences among the races are much smaller than the similarities. On most issues, there are no findings that could be considered, even by a farfetched interpretation, to show a "white" versus a "black" position, nor a single position of any other ethnic group. Race simply does not determine a person's views.

Class Trumps Race

Most interestingly, differences within a racial group are often larger than those among races. For instance, sociologist Janet Saltzman Chafetz concludes in a recent study that "in any dimension one wishes to examine—income, education, occupation, political and social attitudes, etc.—the range of difference within one race or gender group is almost as great as that between various groups." A 1994 Kansas City study shows that income differences between age groups in a given race are greater than income differences between entire races.

Indeed, though African Americans are the least mainstreamed group in America, the black middle class is growing, and many of its members have adopted life styles and aspirations similar to those of other middle-class Americans and distinct from those of other black Americans. A 1998 Wall Street Journal public-opinion poll shows that differences within distinct classes of a single race are greater than differences among those races, on several, though not on all, key issues. Eighty-two percent of middle-class whites and 70 percent of non-middleclass whites report satisfaction with their personal finances (a disparity of 12 percent), while 74 percent of middle-class blacks and 56 percent of non-middle-class blacks report such satisfaction (a difference of 18 percent). The differences, 12 percent and 18 percent respectively, are higher than the differences in opinion between the races (an 8 percent difference between middle-class whites and blacks, and a 14 percent difference between non-middle-class whites and blacks).

On numerous issues, the differences within various minority groups are as big or bigger than those between these groups and "Anglo" Americans. For instance, while fewer Cuban Americans agree with the statement that U.S. citizens should be hired over noncitizens than Anglos (42 percent of Cubans compared to 51 percent of Anglos), other Hispanic groups agree more strongly with the statement than Anglos (55 percent of Puerto Ricans and 54 percent of Mexican Americans). Quotas for jobs and college admissions are favored only by a minority of any of these four groups, but Cubans differ from Mexicans and Puerto Ricans more (by 14 percent) than from Anglos (by 12 percent).

The fact that various minorities do not share a uniform view, which could lead them to march lock-step with other minorities to a new "multicultural" America (as some on the left fantasize), is also reflected in elections. Cuban Americans tend to vote Republican while other Americans of Hispanic origin are more likely to vote Democratic. Americans of Asian origin cannot be counted on to vote one way or another. First-generation Vietnamese Americans tend to be strong antiCommunists and favor the Republican party, while older Japanese and Chinese Americans are more often Democrats, and Filipino Americans are more or less equally divided between the parties. Of the Filipino Americans registered to vote, 40 percent list themselves as Democrats, 38 percent as Republicans, and 17 percent as independent.

I am not suggesting that race makes no difference in a person's position, feelings, or thinking. One can find polls, especially in response to single questions, that show a strong racial influence. However, race does not determine a person's response, and often, on the most important matters, Americans of different racial backgrounds share many convictions, hopes, and goals—even in recent years, as we see the beginning of the decline of the white majority.

The Social Construction of Race

Many social scientists call into question the very category of race drawn on by those who foresee increasing racial diversity and conflict. Alain Corcos, author of several books on genetics, race, and racism, notes that "race" has no single definition.

Race is a slippery word because it is a biological term, but we use it every day as a social term. . . . Social, political, and religious views are added to what are seen as biological differences. . . . Race also has been equated with national origin . . . with religion . . . with language.

The different definitions of race indicate that it is not a very reliable way to categorize human beings. Even anthropological and genetic definitions of race prove inadequate, because while each describes divisions among the human population, each fails to provide reliable criteria for making such divisions. As Corcos notes, such definitions "do not tell us how large divisions between populations must be in order to label them races, nor do they tell us how many there are." They are, he notes, "all matters of choice for the classifier."

Corcos also notes that strict biological divisions by race do not hold up. "Geographical and social barriers have never been great enough to prevent members of one population from breeding with members of another. Therefore, any characteristic which may have arisen in one population at one time will be transferred later to other populations through mating." Corcos further chronicles the failure of scientists and social scientists to categorize humans into definite races by such sundry methods as craniology, skin coloring, nose size and shape, and blood type or other genetic markers.

Social anthropologist Audrey Smedley shares these observations. She admits there are apparent biophysical differences among humans but reminds us that "race originated as the imposition of an arbitrary value system on the facts of biological (phenotypic) variations in the human species." She argues that race "was the cultural invention of arbitrary meanings applied to what appeared to be natural divisions within the human species. The meanings had social value but no intrinsic relationship to the biological diversity itself."

In other words, at first it may seem obvious that there are black, brown, yellow, and white people. But upon closer examination, we realize that there are great differences within each group, even if we choose to focus on, for example, skin color rather than on, say, manners. And these differences do not perfectly correlate with one another. That is, not all persons with darker skin are necessarily short (or tall), and so on. Race, which has been magnified in recent decades by identity politics, is but one imprecise social category, one that does not determine human conduct any more than numerous other social attributes, and often to a much lesser extent.

"Asian Americans" and "Latinos"

Such social groupings as "Asian American" or "Latino" are really statistical artifacts reflecting the way social data are coded and reported. Many ethnic leaders favor these labels, and the media finds them a convenient shorthand. Most socalled "Asian Americans" do not see themselves as such, and many resent being labeled this way. Many Japanese Americans do not feel a particular affinity to Filipino or Pakistani Americans—or even to Korean Americans. And the feeling is reciprocal. As Paul Watanabe, an expert on Asian Americans and himself an American of Japanese descent, puts it: "There's this concept that all Asians are alike, that they have the same history, the same language, the same background. Nothing could be more incorrect."

The same holds for so-called Latinos, including three of my sons. Hispanic Americans trace their origins to many different countries and cultures. According to Eduardo Diaz, a social service administrator, "There is no place called Hispanica. I think it's degrading to be called something that doesn't exist." Many Americans from Central America think of themselves as "mestizo," a term that refers to a mixture of Indian and European ancestry. Among those surveyed in the National Latino Political Survey in 1989, the greatest number of respondents choose to be labeled by their country of origin, as opposed to "pan-ethnic" terms like "hispanic" or "latino."

The significance of such data is that far from seeing a country divided into two or three hardened minority camps, we are witnessing an extension of a traditional American picture: Americans of different origins identifying with groups of other Americans from the same country, at least for a while, but not with any large or more lasting group. Far from there being a new coalition of nonwhite minorities soon to gain majority status (something President Clinton points to and Jesse Jackson calls a rainbow, one that contains all colors but white), racial groups differ greatly from each other—and within themselves.

"Nonwhite" States and Cities

We can learn about the future, in which nonwhite majorities will prevail, by examining election results in the states and cities in which minorities already comprise the majority. They show that people of a given racial background often do not vote for a candidate of their color—and above all, that nonwhite groups often do not jointly support any one candidate of any one color or racial background. Any suggestion that race or ethnicity determines voting patterns is belied by the facts. For example, Peter Skerry, author of Mexican Americans: The Ambivalent Minority, notes that "when first elected to the San Antonio City Council in 1975, [the popular Henry] Cisneros was the candidate of the Anglo establishment and received a higher proportion of Anglo than Mexican votes cast."

We often encounter the future first in California. In a 1991 Los Angeles election for the California State Assembly, Korean-American, Filipino-American, and Japanese-American groups each ran their own candidate, thus splitting the socalled Asian-American vote, not deterred by the fact that they thereby ensured the election of a white candidate.

In some nonwhite-majority cities, the mayor's office is held in succession by whites, blacks, and Hispanics, despite only relatively small changes in the composition of the city population. For instance, in Los Angeles, which is roughly 64 percent nonwhite, Tom Bradley, an African American, served as mayor for 20 years, until 1993, when residents elected Richard Riordan, a white politician. New York City and San Francisco also have alternated in recent years between white and black mayors without witnessing any dramatic changes in the racial and ethnic makeup of those cities.

New York City, which is approximately 29 percent black, 24 percent Hispanic, and 7 percent Asian and Pacific Islander, elected for mayor the white Ed Koch, then chose the African American David Dinkins, followed by Rudolph Giuliani. The roughly 55 percent minority city San Francisco was served by three white mayors from 1976 through 1995, but elected the

African American Willie Brown in 1996. Dallas, which is about 30 percent black, 21 percent Hispanic, and 2 percent Asian, had no African-American mayor until 1995. Philadelphia, long served by white mayors, elected Wilson Goode to serve between 1984 and 1992, the city's first African-American mayor. Goode was followed by the white Edward Rendell in this city of nearly 40 percent blacks, 6 percent Hispanics, and 3 percent Asians. The fact that cities like D.C. (nearly 66 percent black) and Detroit (nearly 76 percent black) tend to elect black mayors is beside the point, because neither comprises a coalition of minorities but one minority. (Blacks, in some respects, exhibit more racial cohesion than other minorities.)

Virginia, in which whites outnumber minorities significantly (1.5 million minorities and 4.8 million whites), elected a black governor, L. Douglas Wilder, who served from 1989 to 1994. In the rural and conservative Second District of Georgia, a two-thirds white voter majority reelected Sanford D. Bishop, Jr., an African-American Democrat. Washington state, comprising only 4.5 percent Asian Americans, elected Gary Locke in 1996, putting in office the first Asian-American governor in the mainland United States. While one can find counter examples, the ones listed here indicate that the majority of minorities do not necessarily elect people of color, nor does the white majority necessarily elect white officials.

Intermarriage and the Rise of "Others"

Last but not least, the figures used by those who project a majority of minorities, or the end of a white majority, are misleading. These figures are based on a simplistic projection of past trends, ignoring the rapidly rising category of racially mixed Americans, the result of the rising number of crossracial marriages. One out of 12 marriages in 1995 (8.4 percent) were interracial or interethnic marriages. Intermarriages between Asian Americans and whites are particularly common; marriages between Hispanic Americans and whites are also rather frequent, while such marriages with African Americans are the least common. About half of third-generation Mexican Americans marry non-Hispanic whites; even higher numbers of Asian Americans do the same.

Intermarriage between black and other Americans is less common but rising. "In 1990, 84 percent of all married black people over the age of 65 were in both-black marriages, but only 53 percent of married blacks under 25 were," according to the Statistical Assessment Service. The Census Bureau finds that over the past 20 years, the number of marriages between blacks and whites has more than quadrupled, increasing from 65,000 in 1970 to 296,000 in 1994.

All together, since 1970, the proportion of marriages among people of different racial or ethnic origin increased by 72 percent. The 1990 Census notes 1.5 million interracial marriages. Some put the number of children of mixed-race parents at 3 million, not including Hispanic mestizos and black Americans who have European or Indian ancestry.

Another indication of the declining salience of race in American society can be gleaned from the fact that in the 1990 Census, 4 percent of Americans (9.8 million) chose to classify themselves as "others," i.e., not members of any particular racial group. Even if the trends already cited do not accelerate and continue only at the present pace, the figures for 2050 may read something like the following: 51 percent white, 14 percent multiracial, 35 percent minorities. Far from dividing the country still further, the rise of the "others," along with the fact that more and more Americans will be of mixed heritage, will serve to blur the racial lines. While there may well be more Americans of non-European origin, a growing number of the American white majority will have an Hispanic daughter-or son-in-law, an Asian stepfather or mother, and a whole rainbow of cousins. If one must find a simple image for the future of America, Tiger Woods seems more appropriate than Louis Farrakahn or David Duke.

Regrettably, identity politics led the U.S. Census Bureau to drop the category of "other" from its 2000 Census. This in turn makes it more difficult for Americans of mixed background, or those who wish to forgo racial labels, to declare themselves what I would call "All Americans." Because the Census's categories influence other institutions—for example, colleges and universities which employ quotas—the "other" category of multiracial Americans is spreading more slowly than it otherwise would. In effect, at least 10 million Americans are forced into racial categories they seek to shed or modify, and American society appears more divided along racial lines than it actually is.

Multiculturalism vs. the American Creed

In sum, foreseeable changes in America's demography do not imply that the American creed is being, or will be, replaced by something called "multiculturalism." Roberto Suro, author of Strangers Among Us: How Latino Immigration is Transforming America, reminds us that we do not need to divest ourselves of plurality in order to achieve harmony.

Americans have never thought of themselves as a single people as, for example, the Germans do. Although white, English-speaking Christians of European ancestry have set most of the norms for American society, there is still no deep sense of a Volk (a group that shares a common ancestry and culture and that embodies the national identity.) Ideas, not biology, are what generate oneness and homogeneity in the United States, and so long as the faith in those ideas has remained strong, the country has shown an extraordinary capacity to absorb people of many nationalities.

The American creed has always had room for a pluralism of subcultures, of people upholding some of the traditions and values of their countries of origin, from praying to sports to senses of humor. But American pluralism is bound by a shared moral and political framework. Otherwise, America would suffer the kind of ethnic tribalism that—when driven to extremes—tears apart countries as different as Yugoslavia and Rwanda, and has even split apart well-established democracies such as Canada and the United Kingdom (where Scottish separatism is on the rise).

The social, cultural, and legal elements that hold America together are well known. They include a shared commitment to the democratic way of life, to the Constitution and its Bill of Rights, and to mutual tolerance. The common culture that underlies America's racial and ethnic pluralism is further fortified by a strong conviction that one's station in life is determined by hard work, saving, and taking responsibility for one's self and one's family. And most Americans still believe that while we are different in some respects, we are joined by the shared responsibilities of providing a good society for our children and ourselves—one free of racial and ethnic strife, a model of the thriving political order.

Questions

1. Given the information presented by Etzioni, should the audience, be alarmed or celebratory regarding the "browning" of America?

2. What kinds of things do all Americans seem to value?

3. In what ways do minorities and whites seem to differ in their values, attitudes, or beliefs?

4. Is there greater variation in attitudes and values *within* racial and ethnic groups or *between* racial and ethnic groups and whites? Explain.
5. According to Etzioni, what role will intermarriage play in the transformation of American society?

Why Sexist Language Matters

SHERRYL KLEINMAN

In everyday language, people often will address a group as "you guys"—even if the group is all women. This and other expressions that similarly disregard women are commonly accepted. While some contend that the use of such male-based generic expressions is minor in the constellation of social problems that we face, Sherryl Kleinman explains why it merits our attention. After reading this essay, you might agree.

For eleven years I've been teaching a sociology course at the University of North Carolina on gender inequality. I cover such topics as the wage gap, the "second shift" (the disproportionate amount of housework and child care that heterosexual women do at home), the equation of women's worth with physical attractiveness, the sexualizing of women in the media, lack of reproductive rights for women (especially poor women), sexual harassment, and men's violence against women. But the issue that both female and male students have the most trouble understanding—or, as I see it, share a strong unwillingness to understand—is sexist language.

I'm not referring to such words as "bitch," "whore," and "slut." What I focus on instead are words that most people consider just fine: male (so-called) generics. Some of these words refer to persons occupying a position: postman, chairman, freshman, congressman, fireman. Other words refer to the entire universe of human beings: "mankind" or "he." Then we've got manpower, man-made lakes, and "Oh, man, where did I leave my keys?" There's "manning" the tables in a country where we learn that "all men are created equal."

The most insidious, from my observations, is the popular expression "you guys." People like to tell me it's a regional term. But I've heard it in Chapel Hill, New York, Chicago, San Francisco, and Montreal. I've seen it in print in national magazines, newsletters, and books. I've heard it on television and in films. And even if it were regional, that doesn't make it right. I bet we can all think of a lot of practices in our home regions we'd like to get rid of.

Try making up a female-based generic, such as "freshwoman," and using it with a group of male students, or calling your male boss "chairwoman." Then again, don't. There could be serious consequences for referring to a man as a woman—a term that still means "lesser" in our society. If not, why do men get so upset at the idea of being called women?

What's the big deal? Why does all this "man-ning" and "guys-ing" deserve a place on my list of items of gender inequality?

The answer is because male-based generics are another indicator—and, more importantly, a *reinforcer*—of a system in which "man" in the abstract and men in the flesh are privileged over women. Some say that language merely reflects reality and so we should ignore our words and work on changing the unequal gender arrangements that are reflected in our language. Well, yes, in part.

It's no accident that "man" is the anchor in our language and "woman" is not. And of course we should make social change all over the place. But the words we use can also reinforce current realities when they are sexist (or racist or heterosexist). Words are the tools of thought. We can use words to maintain the status quo or to think in new ways—which in turn creates the possibility of a new *reality*. It makes a difference if I think of myself as a "girl" or a "woman"; it makes a difference if we talk about "Negroes" or "African Americans." Do we want a truly inclusive language or one that just pretends?

For a moment, imagine a world—as the philosopher Douglas R. Hofstadter did in his 1986 satire on sexist language—where people used generics based on race rather than gender. In that world, people would use "freshwhite," "chairwhite," and, yes, "you whiteys." People of color would hear "all whites are created equal"—and be expected to feel included. In an addendum to his article, Hofstadter says that he wrote "A Person Paper on Purity in Language" to shock readers: Only by substituting "white" for "man" does it become easy to see the pervasiveness of male-based generics and to recognize that using "man" for all human beings is wrong. Yet, women are expected to feel flattered by "freshman," "chairman," and "you guys."

And why do so many women cling to "freshman," "chairman," and "you guys?"

I think it's because women want to be included in the term that refers to the higher-status group: men. But while being labeled "one of the guys" might make women *feel* included, it's only a guise of inclusion, not the reality. If women were really included we wouldn't have to disappear into the word "guys."

At the same time that women in my classes throw around "you guys"—even here in the southern United States, where "y'all" is an alternative—they call themselves "girls." I'm not sure if this has gotten worse over the years or I've just noticed it more. When I was an undergraduate in the early to mid 1970s, we wanted to be women. Who would take us seriously at college or at work if we were "girls?" To many of my students today, "woman" is old enough to be "over the hill." A "girl" is youthful and thus more attractive to men than a "woman." Since they like the term so much, I suggest that we rename Women's Studies "Girls' Studies." And since the Women's Center on campus provides services for them, why not call it "The Girls' Center." They laugh. "Girls" sounds ridiculous, they say. The students begin to see that "girl"—as a label for twenty-one-year-olds—is infantilizing, not flattering.

"Girl" and "you guys" aren't the only linguistic problems on campus. A few years ago Bob, a student in my class, said that his fraternity is now open to women as well as men and that a controversy had erupted over whether to continue to use the term "brother" to refer to all fraternity members, or to use "sister" for female members. Almost all the women in his fraternity, he said, voted to be called brother rather than sister. As with "you guys," the women wanted to take on the word that has more value. Yet the practice of using "brother" reinforces the idea that a real member of the group is a brother (i.e., a man). I asked what would happen if he had suggested that all fraternity members be called sisters rather than brothers, or that they rename the fraternity a sorority. Everyone laughed at the absurdity of this suggestion. Exactly. Yet it is not absurd, but acceptable, to call women by the term "guys" or "brothers."

Since the "fraternity" Bob referred to is no longer exclusively male, and since gender is no longer a criterion for membership, I asked him how he thought others might react if he suggested they substitute "association" or "society" for "fraternity." Perhaps they could call both men and women "members," or, if students preferred a more informal term, "friends?"

"Yes, that makes sense," Bob told us. "But, I just don't think they'll go for it." He paused. "I'm not sure why."

We talked as a class about why this simple solution might meet with resistance. We concluded that many men would resist losing these linguistic signifiers of male superiority, and many women would resist losing the valued maleness implied by "brother" and "fraternity." "Member" would feel like a drop in status for both women and men!

The students, like most people who use male "generics," don't have bad intentions. But as sociologists, we know that it's important to look at the *consequences*. All those "man" words—said many times a day—cumulatively reinforce the message that men are the standard and that women should be subsumed by the male category.

I worry about what people with the best of intentions are teaching our children. A colleague's five-year-old daughter recently left her classroom crying after a teacher said, "What do you guys think?" She thought the teacher didn't care about what *she* thought. When the teacher told her that of course she was included, her tears stopped. But what was the lesson? She learned that her opinion as a girl mattered only when she's a guy. She learned that men are the norm.

A friend's six-year-old son refused to believe that the female firefighter who came to his school to talk to the class—dressed in uniform—actually fought fires. The firefighter repeatedly referred to herself as a "fireman." Despite the protests of the teacher and the firefighter, the boy would not be convinced. "A fire*man* can't be a woman," he said. His mother, who is fastidious in her use of nonsexist language, had a tough time doing damage control.

So, is it any surprise that the worst insult a boy can hurl at another boy is "girl?"

We know from history that making a group invisible makes it easier for the powerful to do what they want with members of that group. Perhaps that's why linguists use the strong language of "symbolic annihilation" to refer to the disappearance of women into male-based terms. And we know, from too many past and current studies, that far too many men are doing "what they want" with women. Most of us can see a link between calling women "sluts" and "whores" and men's sexual violence against women. We need to recognize that making women linguistically a subset of man/men through terms like "mankind" and "guys" also makes women into objects. If we, as women, aren't worthy of such true generics as "first-year," "chair," or "you all," then how can we expect to be paid a "man's wage," be respected as people rather than objects (sexual or otherwise) on the job and at home, be treated as equals rather than servers or caretakers of others, be considered responsible enough to make our own decisions about reproduction, and define who and what we want as sexual beings? If we aren't even deserving of our place in humanity in language, why should we expect to be treated as decent human beings otherwise?

Some people tell me that making English nonsexist is a slippery slope. As one colleague said to me, "Soon we'll have to say 'waitperson,' which sounds awful. We won't be able to 'man' the table at Orientation. And we'll become 'fellowpersons' at the Institute!" I told him that "server" works well. We can "staff" the table. And why not use "scholars" instead of "fellows?" We've got a big language to roam in. Let's have fun figuring out how to speak and write without making "man" the center. If sliding down that slope takes us to a place where we speak nonsexist English, I'm ready for the ride.

And this doesn't mean that every word with "m-e-n" in it is a problem. Menstruation and mending are fine. Making amends is good, too. There's only a problem when "men," as part of a word, is meant to refer to everyone (freshmen, chairmen, and so on).

Now and then someone says that I should work on more important issues—like men's violence against women—rather than on "trivial" issues like language. Well, I work on lots of issues. But that's not the point. Working against sexist language *is* working against men's violence against women. It's one step. If we cringe at "freshwhite" and "you whiteys" and would protest such terms with loud voices, then why don't we work as hard at changing "freshman" and "you guys?" Don't women deserve it? That women primarily exist in language as "girls" (children), "sluts" (sex objects) and "guys" (a subset of men) makes it less of a surprise that we still have a long list of gendered inequalities to fix.

We've got to work on *every* item on the list. Language is one we can work on right now, if we're willing. It's easier to start saying "you all," "y'all" or "you folks" instead of "you guys" than to change the wage gap tomorrow.

And what might help us make changes in our language? About a year ago I was complaining, as usual, about the "you guys" problem. "What we need is a card that explains why we don't want to be called guys!" Smita Varia, a veteran of my gender course, said. "Let's write one."

And so we did. Smita enlisted T. Christian Helms, another former student, to design a graphic for the card. You can access the layout of this business-sized card from our website: www.youall.freeservers.com. Make lots of copies. Give the cards to friends and ask them to think about sexist language. Leave one with a big tip after you've been "you guysed" during a meal. The card explains the problem and offers alternatives.

And institutional change is also possible. Some universities have adopted "first-year student" (instead of "freshman") because some students and faculty got angry about the male-based generics embedded in university documents. The American Psychological Association has a policy of using only inclusive language in their publications. Wherever you work or play, get together with other progressive people and suggest that your organization use "chair" instead of "chairman," "Ms." instead of "Mrs." or "Miss," "humankind" instead of "mankind," and "she or he" instead of "he." In my experience, members of some activist groups think sexist language is less important than other issues. But if we're going to work on social change, shouldn't we start by practicing nonsexist English among ourselves? Let's begin creating *now* the kind of society we want to live in later.

Nonsexist English is a resource we have at the tip of our tongues. Let's start using it.

Reference

Hofstadter, D. R. (1986). A person paper on purity in language. In D. R. Hofstadter, *Metamagical themas: A questing for the essence of mind and pattern* (pp. 159–167). New York: Bantam.

Questions

1. Why does Kleinman consider the use of male-based generics a problem?
2. Why do many women embrace male-based generics? Why do men resist female-based generics?
3. Kleinman argues that it is dangerous to make a group invisible through language. Does she convince you of this? Why, or why not?
4. After reading this article and thinking about the effects of using male-based generics in everyday life, are you likely to change the language you use? Why, or why not?

Perceptons of Aging in America

W. ANDREW ACHENBAUM

Historian W. Andrew Achenbaum helps us understand why Americans perceive aging the way they do. He begins by describing three universals of aging that transcend time and place. He then explains how Americans' views of old age have changed since the 18th century, when old age was equated with wisdom and experience. Now, Americans, if they think about old age at all, tend to equate old age with senility and disability. Achenbaum suggests that the importance of issues affecting older people will grow as baby boomer Americans reach old age.

"So, you want to be an historian," my father (then age fifty-one) said to me, his eldest son (then aged twenty-four). His eyes conveyed the disappointment that he did not dare utter—Dad hoped that one of his boys would be a lawyer. "What will you write about?" "Old age," I smartly replied. "No one has written a history of aging in America. I think that I can create a niche for myself in the profession." "What do you know about old age, boy?" Dad snapped back. "Hell, I don't know much. And you—you have not even begun to experience life."

In this dialogue, still vivid in my memory, lie the central themes of this essay. Most of us really do not know much about growing older. Unless we are quite advanced in years, old age always looms as a gray stage of life to be experienced sometime down the road. Its contours are ill defined. The lack of clarity scares us—almost as much as when we contemplate the alternative.

Many of our ideas about what aging means, as a consequence, are mainly projections (including fears and hopes) about our future selves. We would like to be spared the aches and woes of older men and women whom we know—or at least we try to deny that a similar fate awaits us. Most of us want to live long, fruitful lives surrounded by kin and good friends. If we are fortunate enough to pass along the wisdom of experience to rising generations, so much the better.

My father and I wanted pretty much the same things for me—happiness, well-being, security. But as the dialogue indicates, we had different notions of how I should aim to achieve them. Generational differences were a factor: he was a child of the Depression, while I was born amidst postwar affluence. Our perspectives on where I was likely to end up were grounded in past events that were shared, but not fully. Assumptions we made at the time were in any case shattered by decade's end.

Dad died suddenly a few years after our conversation about my career—before he retired, before I published my first book on historical gerontology. His withering sarcasm notwithstanding, I did learn some things about old age by poring over dusty magazines and books. I discovered that there are certain enduring universals of aging.

But my father was also on the mark. Only by coming to terms with who I am, by raising children with my wife, by enjoying good times with friends, by grappling with chronic pains and other maladies, and by suffering disappointments personal and professional, have I really come to comprehend the multifaceted dimensions of aging. And now that I am fifty, past continuities and changes in perceptions of old age in the United States appear different—but only somewhat—from the way that they did to me two decades ago. What surprises me is how much that I did not anticipate about aging in the proximate future.

The Three Universals of Aging

Many aspects of aging in America today resemble conditions in times past. Ideas about old age in classical texts, ranging from books of the Bible and Greek mythology to Eastern medical guides, resonate with our current perceptions of senescence. Physical changes embody decline. Invariably writers then and now seize on the telltale signs of age thinning, graying hair; slowing gait; stooped shoulders; and wrinkles. There are at least three other universals of aging that transcend particular times and places.

First, old age has always been considered the last stage of existence before death. None of us "knows" the precise moment of our dying, and very few of us live as long as theoretically possible. Gerontologists generally agree that the maximum human life span is one hundred to one hundred twenty-five years; life expectancy at birth currently is around eighty years. Wear and tear occur decades earlier, as our bodies succumb to the cumulative adverse effects of genetics, bad habits, or an unhealthy environment.

But when do we fall apart? Should most of the deterioration take place at the end of life? That there is no "right" answer to such queries invites disagreement among experts and ordinary people about when old age begins. (Aging, in my view, is a lifelong process, commencing at the moment of conception.) Many age-related decrements develop gradually, insidiously with the passage of time. Some ailments prevalent among those over seventy, such as asthma or arthritis, strike before the onset of puberty.

Old age, of course, is a social phenomenon, not just a physical state. Yet the stage lacks rites of passage comparable to those we celebrate in youth. We make a big deal out of Sweet Sixteen parties, turning twenty-one, and birthdays that end with zero or five. In contrast, there are few rituals to signify that we have grown old. The American Association of Retired Persons, the second largest social institution in the nation after the Roman Catholic Church, sends out plastic cards to prospective members when they reach fifty. A few corporate executives still get gold watches when they retire. Card companies and confectioners promote "Grandparents Day" in this country, but it is hardly the equivalent of the Japanese observance. In any case, not all senior citizens have grandchildren—some lost them in their offsprings' divorce cases, or became grandparents in their forties.

For convention's sake, even allowing for radical differences over the centuries in life expectancy at birth, sixty-five has become a convenient if arbitrary benchmark for acknowledging old age. Picking any single birth year, however, illustrates an important contrast between the ends of the life course. No expectant mother is going to say that she is five months pregnant, give or take a dozen or so years. If I tell you that my nephew in third grade shaves, you are going to think all sorts of (nasty) things about him. Old age's boundaries, however, are broader than those that delineate earlier stages. Claiming that the second half of life begins at fifty is reasonable. Equally plausible are 55, 57, 60, 62, 64, 65, 70, 72, and 75. It takes a lot of money and luck for men and women still to look youthful at eighty, but most are going to look, feel, and act more vital at that age than did their parents or parents' friends.

Recognizing that the last stage of human existence is potentially the longest in terms of duration prompts a second universal: older people are more diverse than any other age group. This generalization holds true in virtually every domain. Some octogenarians are running marathons, while some of their peers have been confined to beds for years. We all know elderly men and women who are kind and generous; most of us have also encountered people who probably were just as obnoxious in youth as they are in their dotage. Many grow intellectually, while others' fields of interest diminish precipitously. Although salaries tend to peak in the fifth decade, many of the country's most affluent persons are senior citizens. Yet wealth is not evenly distributed. Without monthly Social Security checks, the incomes of roughly two-thirds of current beneficiaries would fall below the official poverty line.

The third universal of aging reflects the diverse composition of elders and their varied physical, behavioral, and socioeconomic characteristics. Attitudes toward age and aging are very mixed. We respect older people who have accomplished good and productive things in their lives. We salute those who overcame handicaps and do not belabor their losses. Nonetheless, young and old alike fear decline and dependency. Some try to deny the finitude of their lives. Depression immobilizes a large portion of the elderly population; suicide rates are highest among the aged. Prospects for the later years look different to men and women in their sixties than in their thirties. People who achieve success earlier in life worry about encores, whereas those who have not made their mark at fifty wonder whether they ever will.

These three universals of aging probably account for roughly 80 percent of what needs to be said about perceptions of old age. Some features never change. But within these historical and cultural similarities is room for a great deal of variation.

The elderly as a group thus far have never constituted more than a fifth of any country's population, yet they have always represented one of its most diverse constituencies. The very heterogeneity of conditions in later years provokes a wide range of emotions and attitudes. Nonetheless, like a kaleidoscope's variegated spectrum, important shifts in societal attitudes have occurred about the elderly's status and about the relative value of growing older. The history of old age in America can be divided into three periods.

Three Eras

In the early years of the Republic, Americans by and large thought that they could rely on most older men and women to contribute to the nation's well-being. Experience, it was said, had seasoned the elderly's judgment about practical matters. So, in the absence of agronomists, old farmers were living almanacs who gave good advice about where and when to plant seeds. Senior partners knew how to negotiate deals; widows understood the ways of the heart. Old folks' remedies were considered as efficacious in treating wounds and illnesses as nostrums sold by quacks and prescriptions written by physicians.

Above all, the aged were deemed guardians of morality. Attaining a ripe old age presupposed a moderate, sober lifestyle. Those who did not live virtuously epitomized the dire consequences: preachers and orators invoked the images of fallen women and slovenly drunks in their later years as warnings to those tempted to stray too far from the paths of righteousness.

By the middle of the nineteenth century, different cultural beliefs and institutions were challenging the value that earlier generations of Americans had ascribed to late life. Captains of industry and commerce put a premium on the efficiency and speed with which young employees worked. They shunted the old and disabled aside, promising (but not always delivering) pensions based on age and years of service.

Whereas old age was portrayed in the Revolutionary era as a period of natural decline, medical researchers in 1900 were describing physical and psychological aspects of senility in pathological terms. Lesions in the intestines and the brain, experts claimed, caused elderly people to slow down. Some "geezers" (a term coined in the 1880s) lost their grasp on reality. That there was no known cure for the vicissitudes of age contributed to people's dread of growing older.

The passage of the Social Security Act in 1935 ushered in the modern era of old age in the United States. For the first time in our nation's history, needy men and women over the age of sixty-five had the right to ask for a monthly pension. The federal government joined private foundations in underwriting research into biomedical and psychosocial aspects of aging. Senior citizens became eligible after World War II for other age-based entitlements, including Medicare and Medicaid (1965), discounts on public transportation and meals, tax breaks, and special housing.

There is no question that the current generation of older people has benefited in this age of entitlements. Some propose that white, middle-class senior citizens actually have profited too much. Policy analysts seize on the paradox of allocating resources on the basis of years when research on gerontology shows that chronological age per se has become a less robust predictor of a person's physical and economic condition. Advocates on the right and left argue that current arrangements hurt the children of minorities. Magazines excoriate "greedy geezers" on their covers. Baby Boomers worry, as do members of Generation X, that they will be shortchanged when they turn sixty-five. Prominent ethicists wonder whether those over a certain age should be denied health care and/or encouraged to die. A new animus against age competes with efforts by experts and the aged themselves to portray the golden years in glowing light.

Three Predictions

Historians make better Monday-morning quarterbacks than social forecasters. Nevertheless, at least three predictions are bound to prove correct, because they build on trends already underway:

- Perceptions of age increasingly will be colored by women's experiences. Men slightly outnumbered women in the population over sixty-five in 1900; now the female:male ratio has reversed, especially among persons over the age of eighty. This does not mean that feminists will become the major voice in the gray lobby, for political positions are also conditioned by matters of class, race, occupation, education, and geography.
- Insofar as Spanish-speaking people constitute the nation's fastest growing segment of the population, we can expect Hispanic attitudes about age and aging to be a larger determining factor in overall perceptions. Once again, there will be variations: Filipino views are not exactly the same as Mexican views.
- Because of the malleability of age boundaries, it is likely that an increasing array of partnerships will arise across public and private sectors. The gray lobby will work with children's groups. I bet that organizations that represent the disabled will collaborate with senior-citizen groups under the banner of fighting (prejudice against) chronic disease, but that may be wishful thinking.

Whatever happens, perceptions of aging will remain diverse. Changes are likely to be subtle, not revolutionary in scope. And if demography is destiny, then life-and-death issues that affect older people's choices and conditions are bound to grow in importance.

Questions

1. Briefly describe the three universals of aging.
2. What does Achenbaum mean when he says old age is a social phenomenon?
3. How have Americans' views of old age changed over time? During which period would you have preferred to be old, and why?
4. What are Achenbaum's three predictions for aging in America? Which of these is most likely to affect you, and why?

Never Too Late

KRIS BULCROFT, St.Olaf College

MARGARET O'CONNER-RODEN, University of Minnesota

Take a moment, and imagine a couple who are in love. Did you think of a handsome young man and a beautiful young woman who can't take their eyes off one another? If so, the image in your mind is consistent with a cultural message that love is for the young and attractive. The reality is that people experience love at all ages. As you read this article, you'll discover that you have a lot more in common with senior citizens than you might have imagined.

What is the age of love? The star-crossed lovers Romeo and Juliet were teenagers; Anthony and Cleopatra's torrid affair occurred at the prime of their health and beauty; Lady Diana Spencer was barely 20 when she married her Prince Charming. How old is too old for the sparkle in the eye and the blush in the cheek?

The message our culture often gives us is that love is only for the young and the beautiful—people over 65 are no longer interested in or suited for things such as romance and passion. Few of us imagine older couples taking an interest in the opposite sex other than for companionship—maybe a game of bridge or conversation out on the porch. But, in fact, there are quite a few older single people who not only date but are involved sexually with someone.

Statistically there are good reasons for older people to be dating. At the turn of the century only about 4 percent of the total American population was 65 years of age or older. Today that number has soared to approximately 11 percent, with the total expected to increase to about 20 percent by the year 2050. In addition, older people are living longer and staying healthier, and they are less likely than before to have children living at home. And an increasing number of divorces among the elderly is casting many of these older people back into the singles' pool. All of these factors create an expanded life stage, made up of healthy and active people looking for meaningful ways to spend their leisure.

The question of whether older people date, fall in love and behave romantically, just as the young do, occurred to us while we were observing singles' dances for older people at a senior center. We noticed a sense of anticipation, festive dress and flirtatious behavior that were strikingly familiar to us as women recently involved in the dating scene. Although our observations indicated that older people dated, when we looked for empirical research on the topic we found there was none. We concluded this was due partly to the difficulty in finding representative samples of older daters and partly to the underlying stereotype of asexual elders. So we decided to go out and talk to older daters ourselves. Once we began looking, we were surprised at the numbers of dating elders who came forward to talk to us. We compared their responses to those from earlier studies on romance and dating, in which the people were much younger.

Dating, as defined by our sample of older people, meant a committed, long-term, monogamous relationship, similar to going steady at younger ages. The vast majority of elderly daters did not approach dating with the more casual attitude of many younger single people who are "playing the field." All respondents clearly saw dating as quite distinct from friendship, although companionship was an important characteristic of over-60 dating.

Who's Who in the Sample

For our study we interviewed 45 older people in a Midwestern metropolitan area who were widowed or divorced and had been actively dating during the past year. Fifty-four percent were men and 46 percent were women; all were white. The age of the subjects ranged from 60 to 92; the average age was 68. Although most of the group was middle-class, some were affluent and others lived solely on Social Security. Names were obtained through a variety of methods, including a membership list of a singles' club for older persons, senior citizens' centers, newspaper ads and word of mouth. The face-to-face interviews were, for the most part, conducted in the home of the older person. We asked people questions about how they met, what they did on a date, how important sexuality was in their relationship and what family and friends' reactions were to their dating.

One of our major findings was the similarity between how older and younger daters feel when they fall in love—what we've come to call the "sweaty palm syndrome." This includes all the physiological and psychological somersaults, such as a heightened sense of reality, perspiring hands, a feeling of awkwardness, inability to concentrate, anxiety when away from the loved one and heart palpitations. A 65-year-old man told us, "Love is when you look across the room at someone and your heart goes pitty-pat." A widow, aged 72, said, "You know you're in love when the one you love is away and you feel empty." Or as a 68-year-old divorcée said, "When you fall in love at my age there's initially a kind of 'oh, gee!' feeling . . . and it's just a little scary."

We also found a similarity in how both older and younger daters defined romance. Older people were just as likely to want to participate in romantic displays such as candlelight dinners, long walks in the park and giving flowers and candy. Older men, just like younger ones, tended to equate romance with sexuality. As a 71-year-old widower told us, "You can talk about candlelight dinners and sitting in front of the fireplace, but I still think the most romantic thing I've ever done is to go to bed with her."

A major question for us was "What do older people do on dates?" The popular image may suggest a prim, card-playing couple perhaps holding hands at some senior center. We found that not only do older couples' dates include the same activities as those of younger people, but they are often far more varied and creative. In addition to traditional dates such as going to the movies, out for pizza and to dances, older couples said they went camping, enjoyed the opera and flew to Hawaii for the weekend.

Not only was the dating behavior more varied, but the pace of the relationship was greatly accelerated in later life. People told us that there simply was "not much time for playing the field." They favored the direct, no-game-playing approach in building a relationship with a member of the opposite sex. As one elderly dater commented, "Touching people is important, and I know from watching my father and mother that you might just as well say when lunch is ready . . . and I don't mean that literally."

Sexuality was an important part of the dating relationship for most of those we spoke to, and sexual involvement tended to develop rapidly. While sexuality for these couples included intercourse, the stronger emphasis was on the nuances of sexual behavior such as hugging, kissing and touching. This physical closeness helped fulfill the intimacy needs of older people, needs that were especially important to those living alone whose sole source of human touch was often the dating partner. The intimacy provided through sex also contributed to self-esteem by making people feel desired and needed. As one 77-year-old woman said, "Sex isn't as important when you're older, but in a way you need it more."

A major distinction we found between older and younger daters was in their attitudes toward passionate love, or what the Greeks called "the madness from the gods." Psychologists Elaine Hatfield, of the University of Hawaii in Manoa, and G. William Walster, of Los Gatos, California, have similarly defined passionate love as explosive, filled with fervor and short-lived. According to their theory of love, young people tend to equate passionate love with being in love. Once the first, intense love experience has faded, young lovers often seek a new partner.

For older daters, it is different. They have learned from experience that passionate love cannot be sustained with the same early level of intensity. But since most of them have been in marriages that lasted for decades, they also know the value of companionate love, that "steady burning fire" that not only endures but tends to grow deeper over time. As one older man put it, "Yeah, passion is nice . . . it's the frosting on the cake. But it's her personality that's really important. The first time I was in love it was only the excitement that mattered, but now it's the friendship . . . the ways we spend our time together that count."

Nonetheless, the pursuit of intimacy caused special problems for older people. Unlike younger daters, older people are faced with a lack of social cues indicating whether sexual behavior is appropriate in the dating relationship. Choosing to have a sexual relationship outside of marriage often goes against the system of values that they have followed during their entire lives.

Older couples also felt the need to hide the intimate aspects of their dating relationship because of a fear of social disapproval, creating a variety of covert behaviors. As one 63-year-old retiree said, "Yeah, my girlfriend (age 64) lives just down the hall from me . . . when she spends the night she usually brings her cordless phone . . . just in case her daughter calls." One 61-year-old woman told us that even though her 68-year-old boyfriend has been spending three or four nights a week at her house for the past year, she has not been able to tell her family. "I have a tendency to hide his shoes when my grandchildren are coming over."

Despite the fact that marriage would solve the problem of how to deal with the sexual aspects of the relationship, very few of these couples were interested in marriage. Some had assumed when they began dating that they would eventually marry but discovered as time went on that they weren't willing to give up their independence. For women especially, their divorce or widowhood marked the first time in their lives that they had been on their own. Although it was often difficult in the beginning, many discovered that they enjoyed their independence. Older people also said they didn't have the same reasons for marriage that younger people do: beginning a life together and starting a family. Another reason some elders were reluctant to marry was the possibility of deteriorating health. Many said they would not want to become a caretaker for an ill spouse.

Contrary to the popular belief that family would be protective and jealous of the dating relative, family members tended to be supportive of older couples' dating and often included the dating partner in family gatherings. The attitude that individuals have the right to personal happiness may be partially responsible for families' positive attitudes. But more importantly, many families realize that a significant other for an older person places fewer social demands on family members.

Peers also tended to be supportive, although many women reported sensing jealousy among their female friends, who were possibly unhappy because of their inability to find dating partners themselves and hurt because the dating woman didn't have as much time to spend with them.

Our interviews with older daters revealed that the dating relationship is a critical, central part of elders' lives that provides something that cannot be supplied by family or friends. As one 65-year-old man told us, "I'm very happy with life right now. I'd be lost without my dating partner. I really would."

Our initial question, "What is the age of love?" is best answered in the words of one 64-year-old woman: "I suppose that hope does spring eternal in the human breast as far as love is concerned. People are always looking for the ultimate, perfect relationship. No matter how old they are, they are looking for this thing called love."

Questions

1. What is the sweaty palm syndrome?
2. How are dating experiences of older people similar to those of younger people? In what ways are they different?

3. The authors note that older couples often hide the "intimate aspects of their dating relationships" from family. Why do you think this is the case?

4. Do you think that you will be sexually active when you are in your 70s? Why, or why not?

5. How would you feel if your widowed grandmother moved in with her new boyfriend? Explain.

The Way We Weren't: The Myth and Reality of the "Traditional" Family

STEPHANIE COONTZ

Many politicians and religious leaders have urged a return to the "traditional" family. However, historian Stephanie Coontz argues that this supposed "traditional" family is actually mythological. In this article, she provides snapshots of family life from colonial to present times. By doing so, she reveals that none of these family structures protected people from inequalities based on race, class, gender, or interpersonal conflict.

. . .

Colonial Families

American families always have been diverse, and the male breadwinner-female homemaker, nuclear ideal that most people associate with "the" traditional family has predominated for only a small portion of our history. In colonial America, several types of families coexisted or competed. Native American kinship systems subordinated the nuclear family to a much larger network of marital alliances and kin obligations, ensuring that no single family was forced to go it alone.

"The Way We Weren't: The Myth and Reality of the 'Traditional' Family," by Stephanie Coontz, reprinted from *National Forum: The Phi Kappa Phi Journal*, Summer 1995, pp. 11-14.

Wealthy settler families from Europe, by contrast, formed independent households that pulled in labor from poorer neighbors and relatives, building their extended family solidarities on the backs of truncated families among indentured servants, slaves, and the poor. Even wealthy families, though, often were disrupted by death; a majority of colonial Americans probably spent some time in a stepfamily. Meanwhile, African Americans, denied the legal protection of marriage and parenthood, built extensive kinship networks and obligations through fictive kin ties, ritual co-parenting or godparenting, adoption of orphans, and complex naming patterns designed to preserve family links across space and time.

The dominant family values of colonial days left no room for sentimentalizing childhood. Colonial mothers, for example, spent far less time doing child care than do modern working women, typically delegating this task to servants or older siblings. Among white families, patriarchal authority was so absolute that disobedience by wife or child was seen as a small form of treason, theoretically punishable by death, and family relations were based on power, not love.

The Nineteenth-Century Family

With the emergence of a wage-labor system and a national market in the first third of the nineteenth century, white middle-class families became less patriarchal and more child-centered. The ideal of the male breadwinner and the nurturing mother now appeared. But the emergence of domesticity for middle-class women and children depended on its absence among the immigrant, working class, and African American women or children who worked as servants, grew the cotton, or toiled in the textile mills to free middle-class wives from the chores that had occupied their time previously.

Even in the minority of nineteenth-century families who could afford domesticity, though, emotional arrangements were quite different from nostalgic images of "traditional" families. Rigid insistence on separate spheres for men and women made male-female relations extremely stilted, so that women commonly turned to other women, not their husbands, for their most intimate relations. The idea that all of one's passionate feelings should go toward a member of the opposite sex was a twentieth-century invention—closely associated with the emergence of a mass consumer society and promulgated by the very film industry that "traditionalists" now blame for undermining such values.

Early Twentieth-Century Families

Throughout the nineteenth century, at least as much divergence and disruption in the experience of family life existed as does today, even though divorce and unwed motherhood were less common. Indeed, couples who marry today have a better chance of celebrating a fortieth wedding anniversary than at any previous time in history. The life cycles of nineteenth-century youth (in job entry, completion of schooling, age at marriage, and establishment of separate residence) were far more diverse than they became in the early twentieth-century. At the turn of the century a higher proportion of people remained single for their entire lives than at any period since. Not until the 1920s did a bare majority of children come to live in a male breadwinner-female homemaker family, and even at the height of this family form in the 1950s, only 60% of American children spent their entire childhoods in such a family.

From about 1900 to the 1920s, the growth of mass production and emergence of a public policy aimed at establishing a family wage led to new ideas about family self-sufficiency, especially in the white middle class and a privileged sector of the working class. The resulting families lost their organic connection to intermediary units in society such as local shops, neighborhood work cultures and churches, ethnic associations, and mutual-aid organizations.

As families related more directly to the state, the market, and the mass media, they also developed a new cult of privacy, along with heightened expectations about the family's role in fostering individual fulfillment. New family values stressed the early independence of children and the romantic coupling of husband and wife, repudiating the intense same-sex ties and mother-infant bonding of earlier years as unhealthy. From this family we get the idea that women are sexual, that youth is attractive, and that marriage should be the center of our emotional fulfillment.

Even aside from its lack of relevance to the lives of most immigrants, Mexican Americans, African Americans, rural families, and the urban poor, big contradictions existed between image and reality in the middle-class family ideal of the early twentieth century. This is the period when many Americans first accepted the idea that the family should be sacred from outside intervention; yet the development of the private, self-sufficient family depended on state intervention in the economy, government regulation of parent-child relations, and state-directed destruction of class and community institutions that hindered the development of family privacy. Acceptance of a youth and leisure culture sanctioned early marriage and raised expectations about the quality of married life, but also introduced new tensions between the generations and new conflicts between husband and wife over what were adequate levels of financial and emotional support.

The nineteenth-century middle-class ideal of the family as a refuge from the world of work was surprisingly modest compared with emerging twentieth-century demands that the family provide a whole alternative world of satisfaction and intimacy to that of work and neighborhood. Where a family succeeded in doing so, people might find pleasures in the home never before imagined. But the new ideals also increased the possibilities for failure: America has had the highest divorce rate in the world since the turn of the century.

In the 1920s, these contradictions created a sense of foreboding about "the future of the family" that was every bit as widespread and intense as today's. Social scientists and popular commentators of the time hearkened back to the "good old days," bemoaning the sexual revolution, the fragility of nuclear family ties, the cult of youthful romance, the decline of respect for grandparents, and the threat of the

"New Woman." But such criticism was sidetracked by the stock-market crash, the Great Depression of the 1930s, and the advent of World War II.

Domestic violence escalated during the Depression, while murder rates were as high in the 1930s as in the 1980s. Divorce rates fell, but desertion increased and fertility plummeted. The war stimulated a marriage boom, but by the late 1940s one in every three marriages was ending in divorce.

The 1950s Family

At the end of the 1940s, after the hardships of the Depression and war, many Americans revived the nuclear family ideals that had so disturbed commentators during the 1920s. The unprecedented postwar prosperity allowed young families to achieve consumer satisfactions and socioeconomic mobility that would have been inconceivable in earlier days. The 1950s family that resulted from these economic and cultural trends, however, was hardly "traditional." Indeed it is best seen as a historical aberration. For the first time in 100 years, divorce rates dropped, fertility soared, the gap between men's and women's job and educational prospects widened (making middle-class women more dependent on marriage), and the age of marriage fell—to the point that teenage birth rates were almost double what they are today.

Admirers of these very *nontraditional* 1950s family forms and values point out that household arrangements and gender roles were less diverse in the 1950s than today, and marriages more stable. But this was partly because diversity was ruthlessly suppressed and partly because economic and political support systems for socially-sanctioned families were far more generous than they are today. Real wages rose more in any single year of the 1950s than they did in the entire decade of the 1980s; the average thirty-year-old man could buy a median-priced home on 15 to 18% of his income. The government funded public investment, home ownership, and job creation at a rate more than triple that of the past two decades, while 40% of young men were eligible for veteran's benefits. Forming and maintaining families was far easier than it is today.

Yet the stability of these 1950s families did not guarantee good outcomes for their members. Even though most births occurred within wedlock, almost a third of American children lived in poverty during the 1950s, a higher figure than today. More than 50% of black married-couple families were poor. Women were often refused the right to serve on juries, sign contracts, take out credit cards in their own names, or establish legal residence. Wife-battering rates were low, but that was because wife-beating was seldom counted as a crime. Most victims of incest, such as Miss America of 1958, kept the secret of their fathers' abuse until the 1970s or 1980s, when the women's movement became powerful enough to offer them the support denied them in the 1950s.

The Post-1950s Family

In the 1960s, the civil rights, antiwar, and women's liberation movements exposed the racial, economic, and sexual injustices that had been papered over by the Ozzie and Harriet images on television. Their activism made older kinds of public and private oppression unacceptable and helped create the incomplete, flawed, but much-needed reforms of the Great Society. Contrary to the big lie of the past decade that such programs caused our current family dilemmas, those antipoverty and social justice reforms helped overcome many of the family problems that prevailed in the 1950s.

In 1964, after 14 years of unrivaled family stability and economic prosperity, the poverty rate was still 19%; in 1969, after five years of civil rights activism, the rebirth of feminism, and the institution of nontraditional if relatively modest government welfare programs, it was down to 12%, a low that has not been seen again since the social welfare cutbacks began in the late 1970s. In 1965, 20% of American children still lived in poverty; within five years, that had fallen to 15%. Infant mortality was cut in half between 1965 and 1980. The gap in nutrition between low-income Americans and other

Americans narrowed significantly, as a direct result of food stamp and school lunch programs. In 1963, 20% of Americans living below the poverty line had *never* been examined by a physician; by 1970 this was true of only 8% of the poor.

Since 1973, however, real wages have been falling for most Americans. Attempts to counter this through tax revolts and spending freezes have led to drastic cutbacks in government investment programs. Corporations also spend far less on research and job creation than they did in the 1950s and 1960s, though the average compensation to executives has soared. The gap between rich and poor, according to the April 17, 1995, *New York Times,* is higher in the United States than in any other industrial nation.

Family Stress

These inequities are not driven by changes in family forms, contrary to ideologues who persist in confusing correlations with causes; but they certainly exacerbate such changes, and they tend to bring out the worst in *all* families. The result has been an accumulation of stresses on families, alongside some important expansions of personal options. Working couples with children try to balance three full-time jobs, as employers and schools cling to policies that assume every employee has a "wife" at home to take care of family matters. Divorce and remarriage have allowed many adults and children to escape from toxic family environments, yet our lack of social support networks and failure to forge new values for sustaining intergenerational obligations have let many children fall through the cracks in the process.

Meanwhile, young people find it harder and harder to form or sustain families. According to an Associated Press report of April 25, 1995, the median income of men aged 25 to 34 fell by 26% between 1972 and 1994, while the proportion of such men with earnings below the poverty level for a family of four more than doubled to 32%. The figures are even worse for African American and Latino men. Poor individuals are twice as likely to divorce as more affluent ones, three to four times less likely to marry in the first place, and five to seven times more likely to have a child out of wedlock.

As conservatives insist, there is a moral crisis as well as an economic one in modern America: a pervasive sense of social alienation, new levels of violence, and a decreasing willingness to make sacrifices for others. But romanticizing "traditional" families and gender roles will not produce the changes in job structures, work policies, child care, medical practice, educational preparation, political discourse, and gender inequities that would permit families to develop moral and ethical systems relevant to 1990s realities.

America needs more than a revival of the narrow family obligations of the 1950s, whose (greatly exaggerated) protection for white, middle-class children was achieved only at tremendous cost to the women in those families and to all those who could not or would not aspire to the Ozzie and Harriet ideal. We need a concern for children that goes beyond the question of whether a mother is waiting with cookies when her kids come home from school. We need a moral language that allows us to address something besides people's sexual habits. We need to build values and social institutions that can reconcile people's needs for independence with their equally important rights to dependence, and surely we must reject older solutions that involved balancing these needs on the backs of women. We will not find our answers in nostalgia for a mythical "traditional family."

Questions

1. Describe how children and childhood were perceived in colonial times. How does this perception compare to our view of children today? What changes in society caused us to change our perspective?

2. If you were a white female, in which historical period would you choose to live? Which historical period would you select if you were African American? Explain why you made these choices.

3. According to Coontz, what puts stress on families today? What can we do to relieve some of this stress?

4. Suppose that an editorial appearing in your local newspaper called for a return to the traditional family values of the 1950s as a way to save the family. Write a letter to the editor explaining why this plea is neither feasible nor desirable.

African American Families: A Legacy of Vulnerability and Resilience

BEVERLY GREENE

Many people think of African American families as dysfunctional. Beverly Greene refutes this image. As she sees it, such families are amazingly resilient despite the historical and contemporary racism that they have suffered. As you read this piece, compare the images that you have of African American families with those presented in the article.

...

African Americans are one of the oldest and largest groups of persons of color in the United States. The first census in 1790 counted 760,000 African Americans. By 1990, over 30,000,000 were counted. African Americans are descendants of people who belonged to the tribes of the West African coast and were the primary objects of the U.S. slave trade. Many African Americans have Native American and European ancestry as well.

They are perhaps the only ethnic group in the United States whose immigration was wholly involuntary. Entry into the United States was not, as it was for members of white ethnic groups and

---

"African American Families: A Legacy of Vulnerability and Resilience," by Beverly Greene, reprinted from *National Forum: The Phi Kappa Phi Journal*, Summer 1995, pp. 29-32.

other groups of persons of color, the result of an effort to better their circumstances or find a more advantageous political climate than their homeland could offer. Instead of bettering their circumstances, their forced departure from the West African coast resulted in pervasive losses. Aside from the loss of life for many, there was a loss of community, the loss of original languages, and the loss of status as human beings for those who survived the Atlantic Passage.

As slaves, literally deprived of all human rights, they were to provide free labor and were bought and sold as any other commodity. Their children were salable commodities as well. In this system, family attachments were routinely ignored as slaves were transported, sold, and regarded as livestock with no regard for their family or important emotional ties. In this context, slave families came to place less emphasis on the role of biological parents because most children were separated from and not raised by them. Rather, children were informally "adopted" and raised by other people in their immediate community in extended rather than nuclear family arrangements. These extended family arrangements are still a prominent feature of contemporary African American families and may be considered a major survival tool.

The struggles of African Americans are often viewed as if they ended with emancipation. This belief ignores over a century more of legal racial discrimination that led to the civil rights struggles which reached a peak in the 1950s and 1960s. Even in the wake of legislation designed to make racial discrimination illegal, discrimination in more subtle, institutionalized forms still operates to this day in ways that continue to challenge the optimal physical, psychological, and economic well-being of African Americans.

Characteristics of African American Families

Characteristics of contemporary African American families represent an interaction of African cultural derivatives, the need to adapt to a racially antagonistic environment, and the influence of American cultural imperatives. They include extended networks of kinship between family members and persons who are not blood-related in complex networks of obligation and support. African Americans as a group are geographically and socioeconomically diverse. However, they share both cultural origins and the need to manage the anxieties and prejudices of a dominant group that is culturally different and that discriminates against African Americans both actively and passively on the basis of race. In some form, all African Americans must make psychological sense out of their disparaged condition, deflect hostility from the dominant group, and negotiate racial barriers under a wide range of circumstances. If the group is to survive, the members must teach their children to do so as well.

In this regard, African American parents have a special task and a unique stressor that are not shared by their white counterparts. These consist of the special things they must do to prepare their children to function in an adaptive fashion without internalizing the dominant culture's negative messages about African American people. In *Children of Color,* Allen and Majidi-Ahi note that teaching African American children how to cope with racism represents a socialization issue that exemplifies all that is distinct about the African American experience in America. A major component of this experience entails the task of communicating to African American children the racial realities and dangers of the world, how to correctly identify and cope with the resulting barriers, and how to seek support for the feelings evoked when confronting these barriers.

Succeeding Against Odds

Despite many historical and contemporary obstacles, African Americans have succeeded against many overwhelming odds in every generation. African American families are an important source of socialization and support for their members and can be an important translator of the dominant culture for African American children. At its best, this system teaches African American children to imitate and function in the dominant culture without believing that its demeaning images of African Americans are true.

Another role of the family is to pass along different kinds of successful coping strategies against racism. One strategy, the heightened sensitivity to the potential for exploitation by white persons, has been referred to by Grier and Cobbs in *Black Rage* as cultural paranoia. While this heightened sensitivity often has been pathologized by the dominant culture, it is a realistic and adaptive way of approaching situations that have frequently been antagonistic. Hopson and Hopson in *Different and Wonderful* suggest that another important coping strategy and a major source of psychological resilience is reflected in the sharing of African cultural derivatives with children while encouraging them to take pride in their ancestry. In *Long Memory*, Mary Berry and John Blassingame note that each generation of African Americans prepares the next for survival in a society that devalues them by passing along "searing vignettes" about what has preceded them. They view this process as a long collective memory that is in and of itself an instrument of survival.

African American families must do all of these things in addition to providing the normal range of basic necessities that all families must provide for their children. In the context of a racist society, however, African American families' ability to do this may be compromised by the institutional barriers that providers in the family invariably confront. In these scenarios there may be a drain on the family's emotional and material resources, making the extended family structure an important resource in this regard. Sharing the burden of child care and child rearing helps to ease this burden in many families and can be seen as an example of resilience.

Multiple Mothering

In *Black Families*, Nancy Boyd-Franklin gives one example of this in what she describes as "multiple mothering." "Multiple mothers" refers to grandmothers, aunts, cousins, close friends, or people considered "kin" to a child's mother. They need not be biologically related. These multiple mothers provide emotional safety valves, sounding boards, and alternative role models to children while often providing their real mothers with important tangible support in the form of child care. These arrangements also emphasize the important role for elder members of the family and the importance of their connection to members of the next generation. It is important to remember this extended family structure when viewing "single-parent families." The fact that African American families may deviate in structure from the White Anglo Saxon Protestant norm does not warrant pathologizing them or presuming that this deviation accounts for family problems.

In what appear to be many single-parent families, extensive networks of other family members, family friends, neighbors, and others are routinely involved in the caretaking of children. Hence, the unmarried status of the mother does not automatically tell us what the rest of the family structure is like. The single-parent family as a large and diverse group among African Americans is not synonymous with teenaged or underaged mothers. Becoming a parent before one is biologically and emotionally mature, or when it interferes with important developmental tasks of the parent, is certainly not what is recommended. Rather, I suggest that African American family structures be viewed as perhaps having a wider range of flexibility in what is available to its members, reflected in a wider range of persons, in addition to biological parents, involved in parenting roles.

Gender Role Flexibility

Robert Hill, in *The Strengths of Black Families*, identifies major characteristics of African American families: strong kinship bonds, a strong achievement motivation, a strong religious and spiritual orientation, and a strong work orientation. Hill views these characteristics as strengths that have helped African Americans survive and function under difficult circumstances. He further cites gender role flexibility as an important and adaptive characteristic of African American families. This flexibility in gender roles is explained in part as a derivative of the value of interdependence among group members, typical of Western African precolonial cultures, that is unlike the value of rugged individualism of the West. It is also a function of the need to adapt to racism in the United States in many different ways.

One of the features that distinguished African American women from their white counterparts was their role as workers. Aside from being brought into the country as slaves whose primary function was to work, the status of African American women as slaves superseded their status as women. Hence they were not given the courtesies of femininity that were routinely accorded white women. Conventions of femininity considered many forms of labor that were routine for white males inappropriate for white females. Slavery deprived African American women of this protection, and as such their roles as workers did not differ from those of African American males. Hence at the very outset, rigid gender-role stratification among African Americans was not permitted. Later, because African American men faced significant racial barriers in the workplace and could not fit the idealized image of the Western male provider, women were forced to work to help support the home. Thus, the dominant cultural norm of women remaining in the home while men worked outside the home was never a practical reality for African American families.

This does not mean that there is no sexism within African American families. Tensions are often produced when African American men internalize the dominant culture's value of male domination and female subordination. Working women become the targets of African American male frustration rather than institutional racism. Despite such occurrences, flexibility in gender roles represents another example of an adaptive strategy that has contributed to the survival of African American families.

Summary

African American families have functioned under a legacy of challenges to their survival, beginning with slavery when families were not allowed to exist and when they were continually disrupted by abrupt and permanent separations. Surviving these disruptions,

African American families have continued to demonstrate their flexibility and resilience under many adverse circumstances. It is not surprising that many African American families would be in crisis, given the range of routine assaults they face. What is more surprising is that many of these families display a remarkable legacy of adaptive strengths. James Comer, in *Maggie's American Dream*, reminds us that what we learn from survivors will tell us more about the circumvention of problems than will an exclusive focus on victims. African Americans are, if anything, survivors of historical and contemporary circumstances that may increase their vulnerability. However, as survivors, they have much to teach us about resilience.

Questions

1. What are some coping strategies used by African American families?
2. What are multiple mothers? What important functions do they provide?
3. What does Greene mean when she says that African American families have been pathologized? How does pathologizing affect African American families?
4. Watch two prime-time television shows that feature African American families. How are these families depicted? Are these depictions accurate? Do you think that these programs encourage or deter an accurate understanding of African American family life? Explain your answer.

If the French Can Do It, Why Can't We?

STEVEN GREENHOUSE

Finding quality, affordable daycare is a problem for many working parents. Some people just don't have the money to pay for good daycare, while others live in communities where demand for care far exceeds the slots available. In this article, Steven Greenhouse describes the French child-care system, which is open to all infants regardless of their parents' ability to pay.

Pascal Favre-Rochex is in the midst of that morning tightrope walk parents know so well—settling his son in preschool. His knees are scrunched up against the pint-size table as he hams it up, reading "Monsieur Rigolo" to 3-year-old Clément. A moment later he gives his son a hug and is out the door. The teacher, Maryse Corne, invites Clément, Antoine, Inès, Mehdi, Stanislas and 16 other toddlers to sit on the gray rug at her feet. First they recite rhymes about escargots and bumblebees and then they sing "Frère Jacques," pumping their right arms up and down to ring imaginary church bells.

By French standards it's just another day in preschool. But through American eyes what's going on in this Parisian preschool is extraordinary. This class is part of a free, full-day, public preschool, or école maternelle. Many New Yorkers, Washingtonians and Californians pay $8,000 to $14,000 a year to send a child to preschool or a day-care center, if they are lucky enough to find a place. In France, 99 percent of 3-, 4- and 5-year-olds attend preschool at no or minimal charge.

In sharp contrast, just one-third of American 3- and 4-year-olds attend preschools or day-care centers, and in many communities, the nonaffluent need not apply. But with the strong backing of left and right, the French spend $7 billion a year to make sure every child—rich, middle class or poor—gets off to a good start. They feel the benefits outweigh the cost.

Comparing the French system with the American system—if that word can be used to describe a jigsaw puzzle missing half its pieces—is like comparing a vintage bottle of Château Margaux with a $4 bottle of American wine. The first child-care centers were built in the early 1800's to protect the children of women who took jobs in rapidly industrializing Paris. But it was only after World War II that the system exploded in size as the battle-scarred nation sought to protect its young from starvation and disease. Today, for France's 4.5 million children under the age of 6, the constellation of child-care offerings is vast and all of them are linked to health care. The three major categories are day-care centers and day-care homes, for children 3 months to 3 years of age, and preschools, for children 2 1/2 to 5 years old. Day-care centers, or crèches and day-care homes charge fees on a sliding scale. Public preschools, or écoles maternelles, are free; parochial preschools are heavily subsidized.

"Our objective is to be both a place of learning and a place that stimulates children," says Josiane Mattei, the director of the preschool Clément attends, off Avenue du Général Leclerc. Mattei coordinates the curriculum for 210 children and, since this is France, sees to it that the children use proper table manners.

"We don't want parents to feel that they're leaving their kids at a baggage claim," she says.

Preschools run from 8:30 A.M. to 4:30 P.M.; parents can pay $300 a year for wraparound programs that provide supervised activities from 7:30 to 8:30 A.M. and 4:30 to 6 P.M.

Local government supports the day-care centers, which are normally open from 7 A.M. to 7 P.M. The overall cost of sending a child to a Parisian day-care center is $10,000. Poor families pay $390 per year, middle-class families pay about $3,200, and the rich pay $5,300. When we lived in France, our son, Jeremy, attended a crèche in the Latin Quarter. The fee was $3,850 a year.

The staff of 19 was responsible for 72 children. The director, Odile Caplier, is a registered nurse who spent two years studying child development. Like all municipal crèche directors, she has an apartment in the same building, enabling her to keep a child past 7 P.M. in an emergency. The staff includes a deputy director (also a registered nurse) and two teachers (each with the equivalent of four years of college). The 12 child-care aides are high-school graduates who have taken a one-year course in child development.

What wowed my wife, Miriam, was the food. She often mailed copies of the crèche's weekly menu to friends in the United States so they could salivate over the poached fish, cauliflower mousse, parsleyed potatoes and Camembert cheese—not bad compared with the peanut butter sandwiches served at so many American preschools.

Concluding that our daughter, Emily, would do better in a more intimate situation, we sent her not to a day-care center but to a day-care *home*. France has 30,000 such homes—what amounts to a network of full-time government-licensed baby sitters who look after 57,000 children under the age of 3. Baby sitters must pass medical and psychological exams, and their homes are inspected for safety.

Once a month, Danièle Naudin, the matronly director of a municipal day-care center in western Paris, goes on her rounds. She pushes open the door of a turn-of-the-century brown brick building, walks up two flights of stairs and presses the doorbell of one of the eight baby sitters under her supervision.

"Bonjour, Mme. Naudin," Malika Akdim says, as she opens the door to her apartment, where she is looking after two girls, 11 months and 19 months old.

Naudin organizes monthly training sessions for the baby sitters, teaching them how to cope with emergencies, keep children clean and prepare healthful meals. One morning a week, the baby sitters take their charges to the center, where they play with other children and are examined by doctors.

Eager to encourage baby sitters to work within the system instead of in an off-the-books limbo, the French are trying to make the job more respectable and lucrative. Akdim, who emigrated from Morocco 15 years ago, has three school-age children and earns about $1,000 a month as a baby sitter. The local government provides bedding, bottles, toys and strollers for the children she cares for. The national Government has created an incentive for parents to use licensed sitters by refunding the Social Security taxes they pay (about $800 a year). . . .

France also offers parent-run day-care cooperatives and short-term drop-in programs. Municipalities put up money to build the cooperatives and provide a child development specialist to work with parents. Government-run "garderies," which are akin to indoor playgrounds, offer a few hours' respite for parents. Paris is experimenting with a center for children in "difficult" family situations that provides special care night and day supervised by a psychologist and social worker. Called Enfant Présent, it works with the court system and social service agencies.

Small wonder that many American educators and child-care experts—including Hillary Rodham Clinton—have looked to France as a model. Four years ago, as chairwoman of the Children's Defense Fund, she was one of 14 American experts who took part in a study of French child care sponsored by the French-American Foundation. "We found that most programs in France looked as good as the best American programs," says Gail Richardson, director of the foundation study. "What you see for everybody in France is what you see for just a small percentage of people in the United States."

French child care is not perfect, Richardson concedes. Though the ratio of children to teachers in French preschools, sometimes more than 25 to 1, is high by American standards, it is offset by the use of teachers' aides and by extensive teacher training. Most French preschool teachers have the equivalent of a master's degree. But don't expect the First Lady to make a big push for a French-style system anytime soon. The simple reason is cost.

Even if the White House were to unfurl a grand plan for child care, Federal, state and local governments would no doubt squabble over how to finance and control it. American and French taxpayers' attitudes toward spending on social services are very different. Almost half of France's gross domestic product goes to taxes, compared with less than a third in the United States. Even after the conservatives ousted the Socialists in the April elections, and amid signs of growing worry about France's budget deficit and high payroll taxes, the French are clamoring for more, not less, spending on child care.

In Paris over the last decade, crèche enrollment has doubled to 22,000. But in some neighborhoods, there still aren't enough places for all the children that need them. And in this year of deep recession throughout France, local officials say they are feeling intense pressure to hold down the cost to the taxpayer. The solution: continue building day-care centers while charging parents, especially the rich ones, more.

During the 70's, most middle-class and rich French parents preferred to use nannies. But attitudes changed radically after research demonstrated that socialization is important and that children who had been in crèches and écoles maternelles did better in the first years of elementary school.

"Nowadays, most parents want collective care, which is exactly the opposite of 20 years ago," says Sylvie Rayna, a researcher for the Ministry of National Education. "Now everybody seems to be demanding a place at a crèche."

Questions

1. Explain how the French and American daycare systems differ.
2. What are "garderies"? What is their function?
3. Describe the problems with the French child-care system. Do these problems outweigh the benefits? Explain your answer.
4. Could a system like the one embraced by the French be put in place in the United States? Why or why not? How might implementing this system change family life?

Sometimes the Perfect Mate Is Someone You Hardly Know

ANDY STEINER

If you are like most Americans, you will marry at least once in your lifetime. And, as with most American marriages, the person you marry will be someone with whom you have fallen in love. However, in some parts of the world, marriages are not formed on the basis of romantic love. In this article, Andy Steiner interviews Aslam Abullah, an Indian man whose marriage was arranged by a matchmaker.

How was your marriage arranged?

First, my sister and my mother and other family members talked to me. They asked what I was looking for in a wife. Then they looked around, found a family they felt was suitable, and sent a formal proposal to the parents. Through the parents, the proposal went to the girl. But I think that she learned about the proposal before her parents told her, through other girls.

"Sometimes Your Perfect Mate Is Someone You Hardly Know," by Andy Steiner, reprinted from *Utne Reader*, Vol. 93, May–June 1999. pp. 68–69.

Did Amtul know who you were before she accepted your proposal?

In a way, yes. I was involved in the student movement in India, so my photo had appeared in newspapers, and I had been interviewed on television. Also, my family was well known in India. So she knew this, and I think she agreed to marry me after she was briefed by her friends and family. Usually you trust the judgment of your parents and other members of your family because you trust they are acting in your best interest.

At the time of your betrothal, arranged marriage was already on the decline in India. What did your friends think when you told them your match would be arranged?

At my university, almost everyone was getting married in the modern style. I was really one of the only people I knew who chose to follow the old marriage traditions. My friends were mostly following the mood of the age, the way they felt modern romance should develop: dating or talking with one another, falling in love, deciding to marry, and then at last involving their parents and family.

My friends asked me, "Why, when you are living in such a modern age, would you want to do something like this?" I said, "I believe in traditional values. Families ought to have a say in these things. Marriage is not just a union of two individuals. It is a union of two families."

You saw your bride just a few times before you married. What was your state of mind at your wedding?

I was excited and quite nervous. This is the kind of moment that most of us would feel excited about. Here you are meeting a new person, and you have the opportunity to win over that person. If you are successful, together you will embark on a wonderful journey that will last a lifetime. It is both thrilling and romantic.

What advantages do arranged marriages have over those based entirely on love?

In an arranged marriage, you start with the presumption that you will live your entire life with this person. Because of this, you accept that you have to change and adjust yourself according to the mood and the character of your spouse, because you expect that this partnership will certainly continue until your death.

Other kinds of marriages can be like shopping at a market, where you go by yourself and try on the clothes and select whatever fits you best at that moment. Maybe the next day you pick up what you've bought and realize that you've gained weight overnight. Then you throw that garment out and buy a new one. In an arranged marriage, your family has selected your mate according to your interests, and you accept that they know your heart the same way as you do.

Why do Westerners discount arranged marriage?

I'm not certain, because if you look at Western civilization you find that until the nineteenth century, arranged marriages of a fashion were quite common in Europe. Then came the First World War and the Second World War, when people went far away from home and a different standard of family involvement in romantic relationships came to be accepted. Even now in the West, marriages are still somewhat arranged in certain social classes. Families make connections between their children, and parents may try to influence their children's decisions. They'll say, "Look at that girl. She's compatible to you." So it's the same, only less blatant.

Will you expect to play the same role in your children's marriages as your parents played in yours?

We live in modern times, so I cannot force this sort of decision on my children. Because my older children were born in India, they are still more influenced by Indian culture. The younger ones are much more American.

When it comes time for our children to marry, we will help identify people for them—if they ask us for help. We would like to be part of their decision-making process, not because we've forced them to comply with our wishes, but because we have that kind of relationship with our children. This culture is very different from the one my wife and I were raised in. As long as they respect the values of their faith, their decisions will be fine.

Questions

1. Through what process was Aslam's and Amtul's marriage arranged?
2. What are some advantages of arranged marriage? What are some advantages of selecting your own mate?
3. Aslam's argues that members of Western societies engage in a form of arranged marriage. Refute or support his argument.
4. Ask six people how they would feel if their mate were selected for them by their parents through a matchmaker. Compare the six responses to your own answer to this question. What does this exercise suggest about the role of culture in setting our expectations for marriage?

Did You Really Go to Church This Week? Behind the Poll Data

C. KIRK HADAWAY AND PENNY LONG MARLER

Many public opinion polls have shown that American church attendance has remained relatively stable (around 40 percent of the population), for a number of years. Some observers have suggested that this number provides further evidence that religion remains vibrant and important to most people in the United States today. In this selection, C. Kirk Hadaway and Penny Long Marler discuss the accuracy of self-reported church-attendance polls and explore reasons why some people may not accurately report their attendance.

Church attendance in the U.S. is, apparently, stable and strong. Year after year 40 percent of Americans tell pollsters that they attended church or synagogue in the last seven days. From this evidence, American religion seems quite hardy, especially compared to the statistics from European nations. If the poll data can be believed, three decades of otherwise corrosive social and cultural change has left American church attendance virtually untouched.

Public opinion polls, which measure everything from church attendance to confidence in the president, provide many of the "hard facts" that social scientists (and the general public) use to understand the social world. But how much trust should we put in the polls, particularly in the accounts people give of their own behavior?

"Did You Really Go to Church This Week? Behind the Poll Data," by C. Kirk Hadaway and Penny Long Marler, reprinted from *The Christian Century*, May 6, 1998. pp. 472-475.

Numerous studies show that people do not accurately report their behavior to pollsters. Americans misreport how often they vote, how much they give to charity and how frequently they use illegal drugs. Their misreporting is in the expected direction: people report higher than actual figures for voting and charitable giving, lower for illegal drug use. People are not entirely accurate in their self-reports about other areas as well. Males exaggerate their number of sexual partners; university workers are not very honest about reporting how many photocopies they make. Actual attendance at museums, symphonies and operas does not match survey results.

We should not expect religious behavior to be immune to such misreporting. Several years ago we teamed up with sociologist Mark Chaves to test the 40 percent figure for church attendance. Our initial study, based on attendance counts in Protestant churches in one Ohio county and Catholic churches in 18 dioceses, indicated a much lower rate of religious participation than the polls report. Instead of 40 percent of Protestants attending church, we found 20 percent. Instead of 50 percent of Catholics attending church, we found 28 percent. In other words, actual church attendance was about half the rate indicated by national public opinion polls.

Gerald Marwell, then editor of *American Sociological Review,* said our research raised questions about "stylized facts" that are passed around "as if they were the truth." Of course, much depends on whose experience does or does not match the presumed "truth" about American church attendance.

Many people, and particularly local church pastors, did not seem surprised by our findings. In fact, a story in the *Cleveland Plain Dealer* reported that "plenty of religious leaders express private doubts about polls that find almost half of American adults say they worship God each week." Less congratulatory, although still confirming, were the reactions of some of our colleagues, friends and family which tended to go something like, "So you discovered what everybody else already knew," or "Well, I could have told you that church attendance wasn't that high without doing a study about it."

Others saw the truth about American church attendance quite differently. While very few laypersons or clergy seemed troubled by our findings, one active laywoman did call to protest that her suburban church was "packed" at every service.

The greatest outcry, however, came from survey organizations who produce the polls, social scientists who utilize poll findings to bolster arguments about the vitality of American religion, and a number of Roman Catholic researchers who argued that we exaggerated the overreporting in their constituency. One prominent sociologist, who represents all three groups, said our research was "a sloppy piece of work" and added, "I doubt if the subject was anything but religion that a serious science journal would publish it."

Rather than attack the research directly, the Gallup Organization tried to explain the positive (and, in its eyes, erroneous) response to it. In *Emerging Trends* Gallup suggested that those who doubt the validity of the 40 percent figure may be reacting to their own experience in places (such as large cities) where attendance is likely to be low.

We did not begin our research with the assumption that the Gallup figures were "wrong." Like other social scientists who use survey data, we trusted Gallup poll results because we knew they employed sound sampling methods. Doubts emerged, however, when we compared statistics on church membership from American denominations to Gallup's reports on church attendance. If the percentage of Americans attending church is stable, aggregate church membership should have increased as the American population grew. But after adding together denominational membership statistics (including estimates of membership for independent congregations) we found that the aggregate membership total has been virtually static since the late 1960s. This contradiction led us to wonder if Americans were reporting the same level of attendance to pollsters while their actual church participation was dropping. Our first study provided an initial test of this dynamic. Subsequent research confirmed it in important ways.

We returned to Ashtabula County, Ohio, to add a Roman Catholic attendance count to our previous count of Protestants. Because Catholic parishes did not regularly record attendance, we counted Catholic mass attendance ourselves by attending each scheduled mass at every Catholic parish in the county. We attended a total of 38 masses in 13 parishes over several months, counting attendance at each mass. Our counts showed that 24 percent of Catholics attended mass during an average week. In a poll of Ashtabula county residents, however, 51 percent of Roman Catholic respondents said they attended church during the past week. The gap between what people say and do in this rural county is roughly the same as that found in the original study among Catholics in 18 metropolitan dioceses.

We also conducted a study of church attendance in a county in Canada (Oxford County in southern Ontario) using the same methods employed in Ashtabula (using a survey of county residents, attendance reports from Protestant churches and personal counts of Catholic attendance). The results confirm that a large church attendance gap also exists north of the border. The same is true for Great Britain. In the U.S., Canada and Great Britain, the number of people who say they attend church is much higher than the number who actually attend. The proportion of residents who say they attend church is lower in Canada and Britain, of course, but the proportionate size of the discrepancy is remarkably similar.

These studies increased our confidence that church attendance is overreported and that it is not a uniquely American phenomenon. But we also wanted to know *why* people overreport. Although some colleagues have (somewhat) jokingly accused us of calling decent Americans "liars," we have never argued that people "lie" about their church attendance. Follow-up questions about what people meant by "attending church" revealed that a few were counting things other than attending worship—such as going to weddings, funerals, committee meetings, Sunday school and choir practice. One individual in Ashtabula County even said his attendance consisted of mowing the church lawn on the previous Saturday. Being at church for reasons other than worship "counts" as church attendance for some people who answer poll questions. But these cases represent less than 2 percent of all persons polled, and a large attendance gap remains when they are removed. Why do other people misreport attendance?

A few years ago a longtime staff member of the national Council of Churches and an active church member responded to our findings by admitting that if Gallup called her to inquire about her attendance in the last seven days, she would say she attended even if she had not done so, and she would not consider her response to be a lie. Her reasoning? Saying yes was an affirmation of her involvement in and support of the church. Not attending was atypical, so to count her as a "nonattender" would be inaccurate and misleading.

Most overreporting occurs among those who consider themselves to be regular church attenders. In another study, conducted among members of a large evangelical church in the South, we were able to determine exactly who misreported their attendance. Most of those who said they attended and who, in fact, did not were people who report that they normally attend church "every week." People who attend less often—particularly those who say they normally attend once a month or less—accurately reported that they did not attend church in the previous week.

Researchers who study how people answer survey questions have long known that responses to behavioral questions represent more (or less) than "just the facts." When asked how many times they ate out last week, how frequently they have sex, and whether or not they voted in the last election, most people report what they usually do, what they would like to do or what they think someone like them *ought* to do. The question that Gallup asks, "Did you, yourself, happen to attend church or synagogue in the last seven days?" provokes similar, often less than factual responses.

Active church members who did not happen to attend church last Saturday or Sunday are expected to say no in response to Gallup's questions. But this creates problems for people who see themselves as committed church members and "weekly attenders." Many have an internal rule that says, "I am a person who attends church every week." Saying "No, I did not attend church" violates that internal rule and identifies them, symbolically, as nonchurchgoers. On the other hand, saying, "Yes, I went" is consistent with their internal rule, counts them on the side of active churchgoers, is in line with their usual behavior (including what they hope to do next week) and affirms their support of the church.

It is possible to reduce the gap between poll-based estimates of church attendance and actual attendance by using questions that do not make the respondent symbolically choose between being churched and unchurched. This is illustrated by the different rates of church attendance produced by different kinds of questions. In Great Britain, for instance, Gallup asks people what they did the previous weekend and presents a list of likely possibilities. Going to church is listed alongside watching television, taking a walk, reading a newspaper and a number of other options. This question produces a weekly attendance rate of about 14 percent.

When the U.S. version of the question is asked in Great Britain, the weekly attendance rate rises to 21 percent. How many people in Great Britain really attend church in a typical week? Peter Brierley's figures from the 1989 English Church Census and additional attendance data from the 1996–97 *UK Christian Handbook* indicate that only around 10 percent attend worship services each week. Typically, these lower figures are used when religious activity in Britain is compared to the U.S., which means that churchgoing in America appears to be three or four times greater than in Britain. When the same poll question is used in both countries, however, attendance in the U.S. is only twice as high as it is in Great Britain.

An Australian wording of the church attendance question also produces a lower rate. When asked, "How long is it since you last went to church, apart from weddings, funerals and similar occasions?" 15 percent of Australians said they attended church in the previous week. But when the U.S. version of the question was asked on a national poll in Australia, attendance claims rose to slightly over 20 percent.

Clearly, poll data should not be taken at face value. Moreover, it appears that poll results are not equal: different wording produces significantly different results. Why does it matter? Because the image of religion in America as exceptionally strong and stable has been at least partially supported by poll data. Our research raises doubts about that image.

If the portrait of American religion painted by poll data is not as strong as once thought, does it necessarily follow that it is less stable? Has a large gap always existed between what people say about attendance and what they actually do, or have consistent responses to the polls masked declines in actual church attendance?

The San Francisco Bay area provides the ingredients for testing the possibility of a changing attendance gap. We have accurate attendance counts along with poll-based estimates of church attendance in the region for several decades. Although the Bay area may seem atypical, it does reflect clear trends in the western region of the U.S. and, to a lesser degree, the rest of the country. Mainline Protestants have declined, whereas nontraditional groups, including once-marginal Protestant churches, smaller sects and non-Western religions, have increased. At the same time, a growing number of people have shed their particular religious affiliations, saying they are just "religious," "spiritual" or have no religion at all. The Archdiocese of San Francisco has collected attendance data from all its parishes since 1961. In the subsequent 35 years mass attendance fell by almost half, dropping from 205,000 to 107,000. Yet two surveys of community residents in the three-county archdiocese area (one in 1972 and one in 1996) reveal a very stable Roman Catholic population and a stable proportion of Catholics who say they attended church. The net result is an increasing gap between saying and doing. Actual mass attendance dropped while self-reported attendance remained the same.

An increasing attendance gap also was found in Great Britain. When identical survey questions are compared, poll-based rates of church and synagogue attendance are static from 1970 to the mid-1990s. At the same time, actual attendance counts in churches and synagogues dropped by more than a third.

What does a growing gap between saying and doing mean? The issue is one of self-identity at a couple of levels. First, a "churched" identity, once established, seems remarkably resilient and long-standing. Second, whereas "churched" behavior might be important for establishing such an identity, continued frequent attendance does not seem necessary for people to maintain it.

A middle-aged woman we interviewed in Connecticut—let's call her Carol—is typical of many people who continue to see themselves as "regular" churchgoers despite increasingly irregular attendance. She was raised in the 1950s and 1960s by parents who were United Church of Christ members and active churchgoers. Carol went to church or church-related youth events almost weekly through her teens but dropped out during college and the early years of marriage, childbearing and raising children. In their early 30s, Carl and her husband returned "for the sake of the children" to a Presbyterian church (a compromise between his Episcopal background and her own Congregational one).

Before long, however, Carol's kids lost interest in church school and the youth group to which few of their best friends belonged. Neither she nor her husband was inclined to fight their children's (or their own) competing interests. Carol, however, retains a lingering commitment to the church and likes to see herself as a "regular" member. She continues to go when she can, and she has managed to stay connected by donating her silk-screening services for youth retreats and other church events. Now the family attends church together only at Christmas or Easter or for other special services, and even then they may opt for the local Methodist or Episcopal church, depending on service times, the preacher, the music or which family members are going.

Carol and her family don't know the current minister or many active church members very well. There is less and less pressure to attend. Still, the church seems welcoming and familiar whenever they do go. And if a pollster calls? Well, depending on the time, circumstances or the question, Carol will either say she's Congregationalist or Presbyterian. And if asked about her church attendance?

Considering her volunteer work, her own solo attendance and participation with family members for special observances, she may easily reason that she's pretty active. She may even, if pushed, say she went "last Sunday." After all, she went the week before and made quite an effort to do so—and there was that memorial service at midweek at the Episcopal church, and she was expecting her daughter to visit this weekend and certainly they would try to go together. . . .

Regular church attendance is increasingly difficult, even for those committed to it. Sunday morning is no longer "sacred" time; job responsibilities, sports leagues, family outings, housework and many other things get in the way of traveling to a church building for worship at a scheduled time. And if you happen to miss church next weekend, will anyone know if you slept in, comforted a sick child, left home on business, or decided to have brunch at the Hyatt? Church attendance is increasingly a private matter, and it is correspondingly easier for each of us to maintain an idealized image of ourselves as regular attenders when in fact we may only manage to attend church two or three times a month at the most.

As long as the proportion of Americans who see themselves as regular, fairly active churchgoers is stable, the proportion of Americans who say they attend church each week will remain about the same—regardless of the actual level of attendance. Change in self-reported attendance will occur only when it becomes less important for Americans to see themselves as regular churchgoers or when the definition of "regular churchgoer" changes.

An identity transformation of this type occurred among many Roman Catholics in the U.S. following Vatican II, and it may happen to the next generation of Protestants if lower levels of childhood involvement in the church result in a different interpretation of what it means to be a Christian and an "active church member." Similar changes are happening now in Australia, where an increasing number of people are shedding their nominal church identities and saying they have "no religion."

Too much trust in survey data has produced a distorted image of religion in America by masking declines in church participation.

Church attendance is less strong and stable than poll data show. Still, many Americans continue to hold the church in great esteem and define themselves in traditional religious terms. The increasing gap between doing and saying reflects these countertrends.

But we do not think that this pattern can continue indefinitely. Enduring church-related identities are a legacy of involvement in the church. When experience is diminished over many years, church identity is likely to erode, and with it the need to say you went to church when you did not. The challenge for American churches is to help reconnect the doing and the saying, before all is said and done.

Questions

1. In general, do people accurately report their behavior to pollsters?
2. Most public opinion polls have shown about a 40-percent church-attendance rate for Protestants and a 50-percent church-attendance rate for Catholics. What did the authors find when they conducted their study? Do their findings support or refute previous findings?
3. According to the authors, why do people over-report church attendance?
4. What do the authors mean when they state that a "churched identity, once established, seems remarkably resilient and long-lasting"? How does this statement relate to the way in which people report their church attendance?
5. Is continued and frequent church attendance necessary for people to maintain a "churched" identity, according to the authors? Why or why not?
6. How might other people affect the way people choose to report their church attendance?

Making School Reform Work

CHESTER E. FINN JR.

America's public school students are consistently outperformed on standardized tests by students from other industrialized nations. Parents demand that something be done to improve public education and threaten to pursue private schooling for their children; politicians promise improvements and pass legislation that ties funding to measurable increases; educators ask that parents and politicians let them do their job. Chester E. Finn Jr. describes three competing reform schemes that place accountability for improvement with each interest group: "trust the customers" (parents); "trust, but verify" (politicians); and "trust the experts" (educators). On which of these approaches should society rely? Finn summarizes the demand for school accountability, the three current conceptualizations of how public schools can be reformed, and the hurdles each reform effort faces.

Accountability may be the hottest word in primary and secondary education nowadays, but it is a recent arrival on the scene. As long as we trusted the existing public school system to do a satisfactory job of educating children, accountability was not an issue. One was more likely to speak of the system's "governance," assuming that conventional public-sector mechanisms—a bureaucracy answerable to elected officials, thence to voters and taxpayers—would furnish whatever oversight and quality-control were needed. One seldom hears talk of accountability in the highway department or the water and sewer agency. The demand for accountability arises when something goes wrong, when people are discontented with an enterprise's operations or a system's results—and when they believe that it could work notably better.

In 1983, the National Commission on Excellence in Education declared us a "nation at risk" due to the poor performance of our schools. For two decades, we have sought to rectify that situation. We have asked who is responsible, and who should take the necessary steps to solve the problem.

But the demand for accountability in education is driven by more than discontent. First, a body of research dating back to James Coleman's pathbreaking studies has found that there is no direct relationship between the amount of resources a school receives and its level of academic performance. This realization has led education reformers to emphasize results rather than inputs and has made us more attentive to the systems by which those results are prescribed, fostered, and measured.

Second, between press accounts of highly successful schools and more formal "school effectiveness" studies, there is ample evidence that at least some children are getting a solid education. This proves that the situation is not hopeless and also encourages further questions. of accountability. Who, we want to know, can be held responsible for the fact that some schools succeed while others do not? Despair may not fan the flames of accountability, but envy does.

Lastly, increased efficiency and accountability in the business world has led some to believe that similar reforms could be made to work in the public school system. Thanks to keener management, better ideas, and stiffer competition, many faltering industries have been successfully overhauled. Large, rigidly structured companies have learned new strategies for boosting efficiency and productivity. If it can happen in those sectors, why not in K–12 education? Such comparisons intensify the demand for accountability in our public school system.

Three Ideas of Accountability

Several different reform schemes have been tried, driven by competing ideas about how to achieve improvement in K12 education and boost pupil and school performance. Those ideas in turn reflect distinct understandings of accountability.

Some education reformers would have us "trust the experts." This within-the-system approach goes beyond simply placing confidence in the local superintendent and school board and looks to national educational bodies for advice. As in medicine, law, or the clergy, it is characterized by habitual deference to what leaders of the profession deem the best way to do things, and by the craving for peer approval among its members. Thus we find educators pushing for schools to teach math in the manner propounded by the National Council of Teachers of Mathematics (NCTM)—less drill, more conceptual understanding—for having all colleges of education vetted by the National Council on Accreditation of Teacher Education (NCATE), and for rewarding superior teachers, as selected by the National Board for Professional Teaching Standards (NBPTS). We find enthusiasm for "school wide" reform designs developed by such education gurus as Theodore Sizer and James Coiner, and for schools shaped by the "multiple intelligences" theory of learning propounded by Harvard professor Howard Gardner.

Though government funding may be involved, and some of the national groups may wheedle their way into state policy and thus become virtual arms of the regulatory system, the basic dynamic of this approach is nongovernmental. Its major source of influence is found in the creeds, belief structures, and status hierarchies of the education profession. Indeed, embracing professional accountability is not unlike joining a religious sect and upholding its tenets. Like other true believers, those who feel primarily accountable to their peers are apt to pay only grudging attention to outside voices, to policies set by elected officials, or to bureaucratic control systems. They'll look for ways to surmount the hurdles that "know-nothing" laymen have placed in the path of true professionalism.

Other reformers would have us "trust, but verify." This standards approach is the most popular form of education accountability in government and business circles. It was the inspiration behind George W. Bush's recently enacted "No Child Left Behind" bill, as well as Bill Clinton's "Goals 2000" program and the former Bush administration's "America 2000" program. It commands the spotlight at national "summits," in governors' addresses and in legislative corridors. The standards approach is a top-down, externally mandated strategy for inducing change in education. The government will stipulate what children are supposed to learn, test to see whether they've learned it, and impose consequences on students, educators, and schools depending on the outcome. The essential mechanisms are easy to describe, though hard to do well: A higher level of political authority—usually a legislature or state board of education, outside the education profession itself—prescribes the skills and knowledge that a child, classroom , school, school system, or entire state is supposed to master. That same authority imposes tests or other measures by which to determine whether and how well its standards are being met. A fully wrought accountability system then dispenses rewards and sanctions meant to change behavior and yield improved results. It is a nakedly behaviorist theory, intended to alter individual actions and institutional norms through an array of external incentives.

Finally, there are those who believe we should "trust the customers." This free-market reform strategy first arose among schools that already answered to their clients through market dynamics. Private schools must satisfy their "customers" or they risk losing enrollment and revenue. Charter schools face a similar situation. They must attract and retain students in order to maintain income. What could be a better incentive?

Such market-style accountability has spread in recent years, not just from private to charter schools but also to sundry forms of public school choice, "virtual" schooling, "magnet" schools, and public and private vouchers. It remains, however, the most controversial of the three strategies, for it employs a flexible definition of public education and—in some versions—allows tax dollars to go to schools that are not directly controlled by governmental bodies.

These three approaches to reform are matched by three notions of who is accountable for improving the K-12 system: the professionals, the elected officials, or the "customers." While they might appear mutually exclusive, in the real world they often coexist, as do their constituencies. Indeed, it's rare to find a school where only one of these theories of reform is at work and common to find states and communities where elements of all three are working at the same time. That leads to confusion, to be sure, but it's hard to prevent, considering that these strategies tap into different loyalties and political bases. Each is extremely popular with its own believers and advocates.

Elements of all three are apt to be with us for a long time. But where should we place our hopes for achieving better education results for states and communities? We might usefully ask which of these strategies best advances achievement, and which is most amenable to implementation. Moreover, we must ascertain which carries the most negative baggage.

Political Obstacles

Standards-based reform (the "trust but verify approach") addresses the problem of academic achievement most directly. Old-fashioned regulatory compliance clearly hasn't done the job. If education experts had a record of producing better results, they might have been entrusted with the job of reform. As for market-style accountability, it focuses on achievement only insofar as academics is the foremost concern of parents. If parents are more concerned about the school's proximity to their homes, the football team, or average class size, the marketplace will not improve academic performance.

All of these reform strategies are difficult to put into operation. Each faces huge systemic inertia, political resistance, and mistrust, as well as competition from rival reforms. The "experts" have long encountered difficulty in putting their ideas into practice in public education. Though Americans often grow misty about the nobility and selflessness of teachers, this is not a field whose leaders enjoy the confidence of the broader public, and teachers seldom have complete control over key decisions and resources. Moreover, the profession is split into innumerable interests that vie to enlarge their resources and influence. This makes for politically embarrassing situations—and even less public trust. The curriculum experts, for example, may embrace the NCTM math standards, but that does not mean that the state math test will reflect these standards. NCATE may succeed in getting its accreditation required for all teacher-training programs in the state even as the legislature creates an alternative teacher certification scheme that bypasses those programs altogether. Moreover, a new school board or administrator may sweep away years of effort by their predecessors to restructure their schools around new "expert" notions.

Standards-based reform will have another opportunity as President Bush's "No Child Left Behind" law gains traction, but we know from earlier efforts that this kind of reform frequently fails. It is difficult to reach agreement on standards, tricky to develop the tests to match those standards, and politically painful to impose consequences on students, teachers, and schools. Where these challenges have been substantially met (in Texas and North Carolina, for instance), standards-based reform does appear to boost achievement, particularly for poor and minority youngsters. But many states are finding this approach difficult to put into operation. They succumb to the temptation to ease or delay their academic standards, and once the standards are set, problems arise in designing tests that accurately track academic progress. Even when a state holds firm in its standards and has suitable assessments, it may back away from the delicate task of attaching rewards and sanctions to pupil, school, and teacher performan ce. Most often, it is the students who are held accountable (i.e., held back or required to take summer school) while little happens to the teachers or school administration. Their jobs and salaries, for example, are almost never at stake. School children don't employ lobbyists to fend off the "consequences teachers and principals (and superintendents and school-board members) do.

Market-style accountability faces considerable political obstacles because it menaces the entrenched interests and power bases of public education. It also raises intense constitutional and philosophical issues, and requires more technocratic tuning than is commonly realized. Few favor an unfettered marketplace with no other mechanism to look after children's and taxpayers' interests. But the restraints are challenging to get right. Should children from wealthy families get the same vouchers as youngsters from poor families?

What about those with disabilities? Or those already enrolled in private schools? Should charter schools be funded on exactly the same basis as regular public schools? What rules should govern their sponsoring bodies? In what ways are they accountable, and to whom?

Standards-based and market-based reform strategies have additional drawbacks. The public is less familiar with them than old-fashioned bureaucratic compliance or reliance on the "experts." Because they both stress outside-the-system accountability, they are objectionable to the system's many potent insider factions. The marketplace strategy bears the added burden of seeming to cater to "private" interests. For standards-based reform to succeed, poorly performing educators must be sanctioned, but most of these are protected by tenure and by muscular unions. On the other hand, experts bring their own problems, notably the fact that governors and business leaders suspect that they have little interest in true reform.

Mixed Results

None of these reform strategies has so thoroughly proven itself as to be fit for national adoption. Evidence of success is spotty and ambiguous, partly because the versions tried so far have been limited in size or scope and because the simultaneous use of more than one method has muddied the water and confounded the data.

The approach with the longest history—traditional bureaucratic control by the public education system—is so discredited that it does not even deserve consideration. We have plentiful evidence showing that, while that system sometimes runs good schools, it cannot fix the bad ones. It just keeps them going.

Professionalism has had the second longest run, but public schools almost never cede full authority to their paid professionals. The professional educators don't wield complete control nor are they held to account for the system's performance. As for "guru-led" school designs, there have been many over the past two decades—consider the influence of Gardner, Sizer, Christopher Whittle, E. D. Hirsch, and Robert Slavin—but their teachings rarely are implemented in pure form, never in properly controlled experiments, and they hardly ever yield clear data as to their effectiveness.

Standards-based reform has been the favorite of policy makers since at least 1989, when President George H. W. Bush and the state governors set national education goals. But only a few states have successfully implemented these reforms, and there is much dispute about the effectiveness, unintended consequences, and long-term costs of this approach. The new federal education law rests on the dubious assumption that Washington can make every state follow the Texas example. In Texas, attention from state authorities usually has prompted local leaders to make improvements in faltering schools. But the political culture in the Lone Star State may be unique. In Ohio, Maryland, and New York, for example, schools linger for years on state-generated lists of poor performers, yet nobody lifts a finger to change them. In Massachusetts, when it began to look as if test-based sanctions were imminent, an anti-testing backlash set in, fanned by the teachers union. (Massachusetts authorities have persevered, however, and mo re students are passing the state high school graduation test in successive administrations.) Nor does the federal government have any record of success in imposing this kind of change in resistant states and communities. It provides too little of the public school budget to influence curriculum or standards, and federal officials have not had the stomach to withhold even their paltry grants from poorly performing locales.

As for market-style education reform, it's not a new idea—Milton Friedman first proposed it in 1962—but it has been so controversial that experiments have been small and short-lived. The average charter school is less than three years old, and we have little national data on these schools' effectiveness. Only three publicly financed voucher programs have been put into place, and their constitutionality remains in doubt. Privately funded "scholarships" are more numerous, thanks to generous donors like John Walton and Theodore Forstmann, but their per-pupil amounts are too small to trigger a "supply-side" response from potential school builders. Such scholarships have served primarily to fill empty seats in existing private schools, hardly a fair test of the education marketplace.

If happiness were the ultimate criterion of success, we would embrace market-style reform to yield happier parents, standards-based reform to produce happier business leaders and governors, and professional-style reform to deliver happier educators. But that's the wrong measure. The right measure is the academic gains that these reform strategies produce among children. And on this question, the evidence remains incomplete.

Charter School Lessons

Charter schools provide a close-up of all three accountability systems operating simultaneously. These independent public schools of choice must answer to the parents or they cannot survive. But because they are public schools, they are also answerable to government for fulfilling the terms of their charters. These charters are typically issued by some public authority (usually a state or local school board, sometimes a university), and nearly always incorporate the state's academic standards and tests as part of the school's accountability terms. Thus charter schools are accountable in two directions: to their sponsoring body for meeting academic standards, and to their "clients," the parents, whose support insures their existence.

Many charter schools also display professional accountability at work. Roughly one-third of the nation's 2,400 charter schools were founded by educators, often the sort of teachers who enjoy running their own school and designing curricula and methods of instruction. Hundreds of charter schools have embraced the "Gore Knowledge" program developed by E. D. Hirsch. Others include Edison Schools, "National Heritage Academies," and "accelerated" schools (following the design of education economist Henry Levin).

The best charter schools are those that harmonize the three reform strategies. They embrace a proven educational idea or school design, employ educators who believe in it, and give them considerable freedom to implement it as they think best. At the same time, the schools satisfy their clients on many fronts: accessible staff, plenty of feedback, parental involvement, and small classes. And they work out a modus vivendi with their governmental sponsor such that they are freed from much red tape in return for delivering the results set forth in their charter. Moreover, they do so without going broke or misspending public dollars.

Alas, such schools are rare and, at this point in the evolution of the charter movement, it is not clear how many more of them we can reasonably expect. Schools turn out to be exceedingly complex organizations that must juggle myriad competing pressures. Starting such an institution from scratch is truly daunting. The political compromises that nearly every state has made in its charter law mean that founding a successful charter school entails finding or building a facility, making do with partial funding, and enduring a lot of red tape. Leaders with the inclination, talent, and stomach to do this are rare in primary and secondary education. It seems likely that large, franchise-style corporate charter operators such as Edison will predominate, not "mom and pop" charter schools with a few hundred pupils apiece.

What we really learn from the charter-school experience is the precariousness of accountability in education. Standards-based reform is only as good as the quality of a state's standards and tests and the wisdom and toughness of a school's sponsor. The fecklessness of many charter sponsors adds another layer of uncertainty. Many charter schools adopt trendy curricula, silly fads, and ideologically driven practices. As for the marketplace, that works fine when its clients are well informed, demanding, and reasonably sophisticated, and when enough decent school alternatives are available.

Now we have reached the central dilemma of school accountability. None of these approaches is immune to bad ideas, distorted priorities, inept management, or laziness. Every one of them hinges on the sagacity, competence, integrity, and determination of those running it, whether that be governors, education experts, or parents. Each also depends for its success upon the creation of a consistent and even-handed system—the school-accountability equivalent of the "rule of law"— rather than one that is quixotic, unpredictable, and prey to favoritism and politics. Yet the ground rules of all such systems depend in turn upon the wisdom, steadfastness, and deftness of the policy makers who determine how they operate.

Public Policy Pluralism

American education is today involved in a wide-ranging experiment with education accountability. We now have, in effect, three kinds of schools: conventional public, charter, and private. We also have three different versions of school accountability that are simultaneously working alongside—and often at odds with—the traditional "compliance style" governance of the unreformed public education system. The combinations and emphases vary greatly from state to state, sometimes even school to school. With 50 separate state systems, some 15,000 districts, and about 100,000 schools employing 5 million people and enrolling 50 million youngsters, the system is too large—and the country is too varied—for any one theory of education or education reform to gain universal support or prove equally satisfactory everywhere. Viewed from afar, the education system is certainly unsettled. It does not lend itself to clear conclusions or sure prescriptions. That being so, it is less risky to live with the variety of reform s trategies and accountability schemes than to impose a single regimen. It may be that the crosscurrents of education politics and the competing priorities of different interests destine this enterprise to permanent untidiness.

Questions

1. What drives the demand for accountability in public education?
2. Briefly explain each of the three ideas of accountability.
3. In your opinion, who is accountable for the "failure" of American public schools? Explain.
4. What is (are) the greatest drawback(s) to each reform approach? Which seems to face the greatest hurdles?
5. What elements or programs in your local public school system correspond with the approaches described here? What does this say about your community's perception of who is accountable for the success (or failure) of your local schools?

Let Them Eat Fat

The Heavy Truths about American Obesity

GREG CRITSER

Have you ever supersized your meal at a fast-food outlet? Many people do; why not get more food for just a few additional cents? While supersizing might make sense economically, author Greg Critser argues that your decision to do so has potential dangers—especially if you supersize regularly. Critser examines the effects of poor eating habits, particularly consumption of high-fat meals that are a staple of fast-food chains, on the health of Americans. He highlights the often ignored relationship between fast-food consumption and race, socioeconomic status, sedentary lifestyle, and health problems. After reading this article, you may never look at the golden arches (or any other fast-food outlet) the same way.

Not long ago, a group of doctors, nurses, and medical technicians wheeled a young man into the intensive care unit of Los Angeles County-USC Medical Center, hooked him to a ganglia of life-support systems—pulse and respiration monitors, a breathing apparatus, and an IV line—then stood back and collectively stared. I was there visiting an ailing relative, and I stared, too.

Here, in the ghastly white light of modern American medicine, writhed a real-life epidemiological specter: a 500-pound twenty-two-year-old. The man, whom I'll call Carl, was propped up at a 45-degree angle, the better to be fed air through a tube, and lay there nude, save for a small patch of blood-spotted gauze stuck to his lower abdomen, where surgeons had just labored to save his life. His eyes darted about in abject fear. "Second time in three months," his mother blurted out to me as she stood watching in horror. "He had two stomach staplings, and they both came apart. Oh my God, my boy . . ." Her boy was suffocating in his own fat.

I was struck not just by the spectacle but by the truth of the mother's comment. This *was* a boy—one buried in years of bad health, relative poverty, a sedentary lifestyle, and a high-fat diet, to be sure, but a boy

---

nonetheless. Yet how surprised should I have been? That obesity, particularly among the young and the poor, is spinning out of control is hardly a secret. It is, in face, something that most Americans can agree upon. Along with depression, heart disease, and cancer, obesity is yet another chew in our daily rumination about health and fitness, morbidity and mortality. Still, even in dot-com America, where statistics fly like arrows, the numbers are astonishing. Consider:

- Today, one fifth of all Americans are obese, meaning that they have a body mass index, or BMI, of more than 30. (BMI is a universally recognized cross-measure of weight for height and stature.) The epidemiological figures on chronic corpulence are so unequivocal that even the normally reticent dean of American obesity studies, the University of Colorado's James O. Hill, says that if obesity is left unchecked almost all Americans will be overweight within a few generations. "Becoming obese," he told the *Arizona Republic,* "is a normal response to the American environment."
- Children are most at risk. At least 25 percent of all Americans now under age nineteen are overweight or obese. In 1998, Dr. David Satcher, the new U.S. surgeon general, was moved to declare childhood obesity to be epidemic. "Today," he told a group of federal bureaucrats and policymakers, "we see a nation of young people seriously at risk of starting out obese and dooming themselves to the difficult task of overcoming a tough illness."
- Even among the most careful researchers these days, "epidemic" is the term of choice when it comes to talk of fat, particularly fat children. As William Dietz, the director of nutrition at the Centers for Disease Control, said last year, "This is an epidemic in the U.S. the likes of which we have not had before in chronic disease." The cost to the general public health budget by 2020 will run into the hundreds of billions, making HIV look, economically, like a bad case of the flu.

Yet standing that day in the intensive care unit, among the beepers and buzzers and pumps, epidemic was the last thing on my mind. Instead I felt heartbreak, revulsion, fear, sadness—and then curiosity: Where did this boy come from? Who and what had made him? How is it that we Americans, perhaps the most health-conscious of any people in the history of the world, and certainly the richest, have come to preside over the deadly fattening of our youth?

The beginning of an answer came one day last fall, in the same week that the Spanish language newspaper *La Opinión* ran a story headlined "Diabetes epidemia en latinos," when I attended the opening of the newest Krispy Kreme doughnut store in Los Angeles. It was, as they say in marketing circles, a "resonant" event, replete with around-the-block lines, celebrity news anchors, and stern cops directing traffic. The store, located in the heart of the San Fernando Valley's burgeoning Latino population, pulsed with excitement. In one corner stood the new store's manager, a young Anglo fellow, accompanied by a Krispy Kreme publicity director. Why had Krispy Kreme decided to locate here? I asked.

"See," the manager said, brushing a crumb of choco-glaze from his fingers, "the idea is simple—accessible but not convenient. The idea is to make the store accessible—easy to get into and out of from the street—but just a tad away from the—eh, mainstream so as to make sure that the customers are presold and very intent before they get here," he said, betraying no doubts about the company's marketing formula. "We want them intent to get at least a dozen before they even think of coming in."

But why this slightly non-mainstream place?

"Because it's obvious . . ." He gestured to the stout Mayan doñas queuing around the building. "We're looking for all the bigger families."

Bigger in size?

"Yeah." His eyes rolled, like little glazed crullers. "*Bigger in size.*"

Of course, fast-food and national restaurant chains like Krispy Kreme that serve it have long been the object of criticism by nutritionists and dietitians. Despite the attention, however, fast-food companies, most of them publicly owned and sprinkled into the stock portfolios of many striving Americans (including mine and perhaps yours), have grown more aggressive in their targeting of poor inner-city communities. One of every four hamburgers sold by the good folks at McDonald's, for example, is now purchased by inner-city consumers who, disproportionately, are young black men.

In fact, it was the poor, and their increasing need for cheap meals consumed outside the home, that fueled the development of what may well be the most important fast-food innovation of the past twenty years, the sales gimmick known as "supersizing." At my local McDonald's, located in a lower-middle-income area of Pasadena, California, the supersize bacchanal goes into high gear at about five P.M., when the various urban caballeros, drywalleros, and jardineros get off work and head for a quick bite. Mixed in is a sizable element of young black kids traveling between school and home, their economic status apparent by the fact that they've walked instead of driven. Customers are cheerfully encouraged to "supersize your meal!" by signs saying, "If we don't recommend a supersize, the supersize is free!" For an extra seventy-nine cents, a kid ordering a cheeseburger, small fries, and a small Coke will get said cheeseburger plus a supersize Coke (42 fluid ounces versus 16, with free refills) and a supersize order of french fries (more than double the weight of a regular order). Suffice it to say that consumption of said meals is fast and, in almost every instance I observed, very complete.

But what, metabolically speaking, has taken place? The total caloric content of the meal has been jacked up from 680 calories to more than 1,340 calories. According to the very generous U.S. dietary guidelines, 1,340 calories represent more than half of a teenager's recommended daily caloric consumption, and the added calories themselves are protein-poor but fat- and carbohydrate-rich. Completing this jumbo dietetic horror is the fact that the easy availability of such huge meals arrives in the same years in which physical activity among teenage boys and girls drops by about half.

Now consider the endocrine warfare that follows. The constant bombing of the pancreas by such a huge hit of sugars and fats can eventually wear out the organ's insulin-producing "islets," leading to diabetes and its inevitable dirge of woes: kidney, eye, and nerve damage; increased risk of heart disease; even stroke. The resulting sugar-induced hyperglycemia in many of the obese wreaks its own havoc in the form of glucose toxicity, further debilitating nerve endings and arterial walls. For the obese and soon to be obese, it is no overstatement to say that after supersized teen years the pancreas may never be the same. Some 16 million Americans suffer from Type 2 diabetes, a third of them unaware of their condition. Today's giggly teen burp may well be tomorrow's aching neuropathic limb.

Diabetes, by the way, is just the beginning of what's possible. If childhood obesity truly is "an epidemic in the U.S. the likes of which we have not had before in chronic disease," then places like McDonald's and Winchell's Donut stores, with their endless racks of glazed and creamy goodies, are the San Francisco bathhouses of said epidemic, the places where the high-risk population indulges in high-risk behavior. Although open around the clock, the Winchell's near my house doesn't get rolling until seven in the morning, the Spanish-language talk shows frothing in the background while an ambulance light whirls atop the Coke dispenser. Inside, Mami placates Miguelito with a giant apple fritter. Papi tells a joke and pours ounce upon ounce of sugar and cream into his 20-ounce coffee. Viewed through the lens of obesity, as I am inclined to do, the scene is not so *feliz*. The obesity rate for Mexican-American children is shocking. Between the ages of five and eleven, the rate for girls is 27 percent; for boys, 23 percent. By fourth grade the rate for girls peaks at 32 percent, while boys top out at 43 percent. Not surprisingly, obesity-related disorders are everywhere on display at Winchell's, right before my eyes—including fat kids who limp, which can be a symptom of Blount's disease (a deformity of the tibia) or a sign of slipped capital femoral epiphysis (an orthopedic abnormality brought about by weight-induced dislocation of the femur bone). Both conditions are progressive, often requiring surgery.

The chubby boy nodding in the corner, waiting for his Papi to finish his *café,* is likely suffering from some form of sleep apnea; a recent study of forty-one children with severe obesity revealed that a third had the condition and that another third presented with clinically abnormal sleep patterns. Another recent study indicated that "obese children with obstructive sleep apnea demonstrate clinically significant decrements in learning and memory function." And the lovely but very chubby little girl tending to her schoolbooks? Chances are she will begin puberty before the age of ten, launching her into a lifetime of endocrine bizarreness that not only will be costly to treat but will be emotionally devastating as well. Research also suggests that weight gain can lead to the development of pseudotumor cerebri, a brain tumor most common in females. A recent review of 57 patients with the tumor revealed that 90 percent were obese. This little girl's chances of developing other neurological illnesses are profound as well. And she may already have gallstones: obesity accounts for up to 33 percent of all gallstones observed in children. She is ten times more likely than her non-obese peers to develop high blood pressure, and she is increasingly likely to contract Type 2 diabetes, obesity being that disease's number-one risk factor.

Of course, if she is really lucky, that little girl could just be having a choco-sprinkles doughnut on her way to school.

What about poor rural whites? Studying children in an elementary school in a low-income town in eastern Kentucky, the anthropologist Deborah Crooks was astonished to find stunting and obesity not just present but prevalent. Among her subjects, 13 percent of girls exhibited notable stunting; 33 percent of all kids were significantly overweight; and 13 percent of the children were obese—21 percent of boys and 9 percent of girls. A sensitive, elegant writer, Crooks drew from her work three important conclusions: One, that poor kids in the United States often face the same evolutionary nutritional pressures as those in newly industrializing nations, where traditional diets are replaced by high-fat diets and where labor-saving technology reduces physical activity. Second, Crooks found that "height and weight are cumulative measures of growth . . . reflecting a sum total of environmental experience over time." Last, and perhaps most important, Crooks concluded that while stunting can be partially explained by individual household conditions—income, illness, education, and marital status—obesity "may be more of a community-related phenomenon." Here the economic infrastructure—safe playgrounds, access to high-quality, low-cost food, and transportation to play areas—was the key determinant of physical-activity levels.

Awareness of these national patterns of destruction, of course, is a key reason why Eli Lilly &. Co., the $75 billion pharmaceutical company, is now building the largest factory dedicated to the production of a single drug in industry history. That drug is insulin. Lilly's sales of insulin products totaled $357 million in the third quarter of 1999, a 24 percent increase over the previous third quarter. Almost every leading pharmaceutical conglomerate has like-minded ventures under way, with special emphasis on pill-form treatments for non-insulin-dependent forms of the disease. Pharmaceutical companies that are not seeking to capture some portion of the burgeoning market are bordering on fiduciary mismanagement. Said James Kappel of Eli Lilly, "You've got to be in diabetes."

Wandering home from my outing, the wondrous smells of frying foods wafting in the air, I wondered why, given affluent America's outright fetishism about diet and health, those whose business it is to care—the media, the academy, public-health workers, and the government—do almost nothing. The answer, I suggest, is that in almost every public-health arena, the need to address obesity as a class issue—one that transcends the inevitable divisiveness of race and gender—has been blunted by bad logic, vested interests, academic cant, and ideological chauvinism.

Consider a story last year in the *New York Times* detailing the rise in delivery-room mortality among young African-American mothers. The increases were attributed to a number of factors—diabetes, hypertension, drug and alcohol abuse—but the primary factor of obesity, which can foster both diabetes and hypertension, was mentioned only in passing. Moreover, efforts to understand and publicize the socioeconomic factors of the deaths have been thwarted. When Dr. Janet Mitchell, a New York obstetrician charged with reviewing several recent maternal mortality studies, insisted that socioeconomics were the issue in understanding the "racial gap" in maternal mortality, she was unable to get government funding for the work. "We need to back away from the medical causes," she told the *Times*, clearly exasperated, "and begin to take a much more ethnographic, anthropological approach to this tragic outcome."

In another example, a 1995 University of Arizona study reported that young black girls, who are more inclined toward obesity than white girls, were also far less likely to hold "bad body images" about themselves. The slew of news articles and TV reports that followed were nothing short of jubilant, proclaiming the "good news." As one commentator I watched late one evening announced, "Here is one group of girls who couldn't care less about looking like Kate Moss!" Yet no one mentioned the long-term effects of unchecked weight gain. Apparently, when it comes to poor black girls the media would rather that they risk diabetes than try to look like models.

"That's the big conundrum, as they always say," Richard MacKenzie, a physician who treats overweight and obese girls in downtown L.A., told me recently. "No one wants to overemphasize the problems of being fat to these girls, for fear of creating body-image problems that might lead to anorexia and bulimia." Speaking anecdotally, he said that "the problem is that for every one affluent white anorexic you create by 'overemphasizing' obesity, you foster ten obese poor girls by downplaying the severity of the issue." Judith Stern, a professor of nutrition and internal medicine at UC Davis, is more blunt. "The number of kids with eating disorders is positively dwarfed by the number with obesity. It sidesteps the whole class issue. We've got to stop that and get on with the real problem."

Moreover, such sidestepping denies poor minority girls a principal, if sometimes unpleasant, psychological incentive to lose weight: that of social stigma. Only recently has the academy come to grapple with this. Writing in a recent issue of the *International Journal of Obesity,* the scholar Susan Averett looked at the hard numbers: 44 percent of African-American women weigh more than 120 percent of their recommended body weight yet are less likely than whites to perceive themselves as overweight.[1] Anglo women, poor and otherwise, registered higher anxiety about fatness and experienced far fewer cases of chronic obesity. "Social stigma may serve to control obesity among white women," Averett reluctantly concluded. "If so, physical and emotional effects of greater pressure to be thin must be weighed against reduced health risks associated with overweight and obesity." In other words, maybe a few more black Kate Mosses might not be such a bad thing.

While the so-called fat acceptance movement, a very vocal minority of super-obese female activists, has certainly played a role in the tendency to deny the need to promote healthy thinness, the real culprits have been those with true cultural power, those in the academy and the publishing industry who have the ability to shape public opinion. Behind much of their reluctance to face facts is the lingering influence of the 1978 bestseller, *Fat Is a Feminist Issue,* in which Susie Orbach presented a nuanced, passionate look at female compulsive eating and its roots in patriarchal culture. But although Orbach's observations were keen, her conclusions were often wishful, narcissistic, and sometimes just wrong. "Fat is a social disease, and fat is a feminist issue," Orbach wrote. "Fat is not about self-control or lack of will power. . . . It is a response to the inequality of the sexes."

Perhaps so, if one is a feminist, and if one is struggling with an eating disorder, and if one is, for the most part, affluent, well-educated, and politically aware. But obesity itself is preeminently an issue of class, not of ethnicity, and certainly not of gender. True, the disease may be refracted though its concentrations in various demographic subgroupings—in Native Americans, in Latinos, in African Americans, and even in some Pacific Island Americans—but in study after study, the key adjective is *poor:* poor African Americans, poor Latinos, poor whites, poor women, poor children, poor Latino children, etc. From the definitive *Handbook of Obesity:* "In heterogeneous and affluent societies like the United States, there is a strong inverse correlation of social class and obesity, particularly for females." From *Annals of Epidemiology:* "In white girls . . . both TV viewing and obesity were strongly inversely associated with household income as well as with parental education."

Yet class seems to be the last thing on the minds of some of our better social thinkers. Instead, the tendency of many in the academy is to fetishize or "postmodernize" the problem. Cornell University professor Richard Klein, for example, proposed in his 1996 book, *Eat Fat,* "Try this for six weeks: Eat fat." (Klein's mother did and almost died from sleep apnea, causing Klein to reverse himself in his epilogue, advising readers: "Eat rice.") The identity politics of fat, incidentally, can cut the other way. To the French, the childhood diet has long been understood as a serious medical issue directly affecting the future of the nation. The concern grew directly from late-nineteenth-century health issues in French cities and the countryside, where tuberculosis had winnowed the nation's birth rate below that of the other European powers. To deal with the problem, a new science known as puériculture emerged to educate young mothers about basic health and nutrition practices. Long before Americans and the British roused themselves from the torpor of Victorian chub, the French undertook research into proper dietary and weight controls for the entire birth-to-adolescence growth period. By the early 1900s, with birth rates (and birth weights) picking up, the puériculture movement turned its attention to childhood obesity. Feeding times were to be strictly maintained; random snacks were unhealthy for the child, regardless of how "natural" it felt for a mother to indulge her young. Kids were weighed once a week. All meals were to be supervised by an adult. As a result, portion control—perhaps the one thing that modern obesity experts can agree upon as a reasonable way to prevent the condition—very early became institutionalized in modern France. The message that too much food is bad still resounds in French child rearing, and as a result France has a largely lean populace.

What about the so-called Obesity Establishment, that web of researchers, clinicians, academics, and government health officials charged with finding ways to prevent the disease? Although there are many committed individuals in this group, one wonders just how independently minded they are. Among the sponsors for the 1997 annual conference of the North American Association for the Study of Obesity, the premier medical think tank on the subject, were the following: the Coca-Cola Company, Hershey Foods, Kraft Foods, and, never to be left out, Slim Fast Foods. Another sponsor was Knoll Pharmaceuticals, maker of the new diet drug Meridia. Of course, in a society where until recently tobacco companies sponsored fitness pageants and Olympic games, sponsorship hardly denotes corruption in the most traditional sense. One would be hard-pressed to prove any kind of censorship, but such underwriting effectively defines the parameters of public discussion. Everybody winks or blinks at the proper moment, then goes on his or her way.

Once upon a time, however, the United States possessed visionary leadership in the realm of childhood fitness. Founded in 1956, the President's Council on Youth Fitness successfully laid down broad-based fitness goals for all youth and established a series of awards for those who excelled in the effort. The council spoke about obesity with a forthrightness that would be political suicide today, with such pointed slogans as "There's no such thing as stylishly stout" and "Hey kid, if you see yourself in this picture, you need help."

By the late 1980s and early 1990s, however, new trends converged to undercut the council's powers of moral and cultural suasion. The ascendancy of cultural relativism led to a growing reluctance to be blunt about fatness, and, aided and abetted by the fashion industry's focus on baggy, hip-hop-style clothes, it became possible to be "stylishly stout." Fatness, as celebrated on rap videos, was now equated with wealth and power, with identity and agency, not with clogging the heart or being unable to reach one's toes. But fat inner-city black kids and the suburban kids copying them are even more disabled by their obesity. The only people who benefit from kids being "fat" are the ones running and owning the clothing, media, food, and drug companies. In upscale corporate America, meanwhile, being fat is taboo, a surefire career-killer. If you can't control your own contours, goes the logic, how can you control a budget or a staff? Look at the glossy business and money magazines with their cooing profiles of the latest genius entrepreneurs: to the man, and the occasional woman, no one, I mean *no one*, is fat.

Related to the coolification of homeboyish fat—perhaps forcing its new status—is the simple fact that it's hard for poor children to find opportunities to exercise. Despite our obsession with professional sports, many of today's disadvantaged youth have fewer opportunities than ever to simply shoot baskets or kick a soccer ball. Various measures to limit state spending and taxing, among them California's debilitating Proposition 13, have gutted school-based physical-education classes. Currently, only one state, Illinois, requires daily physical education for all grades K–12, and only 19 percent of high school students nationwide are active for twenty minutes a day, five days a week, in physical education. Add to this the fact that, among the poor, television, the workingman's baby sitter, is now viewed at least thirty-two hours a week. Participation in sports has always required an investment, but with the children of the affluent tucked away either in private schools or green suburbias, buying basketballs for the poor is not on the public agenda.

Human nature and its lazy inclinations aside, what do America's affluent *get* out of keeping the poor so fat? The reasons, I'd suggest, are many. An unreconstructed Marxist might invoke simple class warfare, exploitation fought through stock ownership in giant fast-food firms. The affluent know that the stuff will kill them but need someone (else) to eat it so as to keep growing that retirement portfolio. A practitioner of vulgar social psychology might argue for "our" need for the "identifiable outsider." An economist would say that in a society as overly competitive as our own, the affluent have found a way to slow down the striving poor from inevitable nipping at their heels. A French semiotician might even say that with the poor the affluent have erected their own walking and talking "empire of signs." This last notion is perhaps not so far-fetched. For what do the fat, darker, exploited poor, with their unbridled primal appetites, have to offer us but a chance for we diet- and shape-conscious folk to live vicariously? Call it boundary envy. Or, rather, boundary-free envy. And yet, by living outside their boundaries, the poor live within ours; fat people do not threaten our way of life; their angers entombed in flesh, they are slowed, they are softened, they are *fed*.

Meanwhile, in the City of Fat Angels, we lounge through a slow-motion epidemic. Mami buys another apple fritter. Papi slams his second sugar and cream. Another young Carl supersizes and double supersizes, then supersizes again. Waistlines surge. Any minute now, the belt will run out of holes.

Endnote

[1]Certainly culture plays a role in the behavior of any subpopulation. Among black women, for example, obesity rates persist despite increases in income. A recent study by the National Heart, Lung, and Blood Institute concludes that obesity in black girls may be "a reflection of a differential social development in our society, wherein a certain lag period may need to elapse between an era when food availability is a concern to an era of affluence with no such concern." Other observers might assert that black women find affirmation for being heavy from black men, or believe themselves to be "naturally" heavier. Such assertions do not change mortality statistics.

Questions

1. Describe some health problems that can result from poor eating habits. Who is most likely to suffer from these problems? Why?
2. According to the author, why have public health officials done so little to change the way many Americans eat?
3. Does Critser convince you that there is a link between socioeconomic status and health problems? Why, or why not?
4. Survey 10 students, and find out how often they eat fast food in a typical week. Do they supersize their meals? Also collect data on their race, class, age, and gender. Bring your data to class so it can be collated with the data collected by your classmates. What did you learn from this activity?
5. Use the Internet to find information about the last fast-food meal you ate. (Search for "fast food chains," and links for most major fast-food

chains will appear; most of their homepages provide nutrition information.) Did you know how many calories and how much fat you consumed in that meal? Did you see nutritional information displayed in the restaurant? If not, why do you think this was the case? If so, was it easy to read?

Panic: Myth or Reality?

LEE CLARKE

What would you do if you were in a crowded movie theater and someone yelled "Fire!" Would you push past slower people to ensure your own safety, or would you stop to help them get to safety? While "common sense" might suggest that people are more likely to take care of themselves, research shows that they are actually more likely to take care of each other. In this article, Lee Clarke differentiates between the myths and realities of human behavior in disaster situations.

It was like a disaster movie, only more unreal. The smoke and debris chased would-be survivors of the World Trade Center disaster through the glass and steel canyons of New York City. It was "chaos," the media told us. The description seemed viscerally correct, for how could such an unforeseen disaster generate anything but panic? A construction worker who was on the 34th floor of the North Tower recounted, "The whole building shook. We saw debris flying and then there was an explosion. We hit the stairwell; it was a mass panic."

Such a story represents a common tale about panic, which the Oxford English Dictionary defines as an "excessive feeling of alarm or fear . . . leading to extravagant or injudicious efforts to secure safety." We often see self-interest added to the common tale, the idea that people react so strongly that they will sacrifice others to save themselves. In other words, people become overly frightened and then overreact in ways that hurt themselves and others. However, this image of panic makes a necessary link between fear and reckless action, sometimes with a measure of selfishness thrown in. In fact, such behavior doesn't happen as often as one might think.

Nonetheless, Hollywood producers tell tales of panic-stricken chaos in movie and television depictions of catastrophes. The media are quick to report panic after building fires or mass transit crashes. Leaders seem to believe that the general population is prone to irrational panic, as witnessed by Washington's reluctance to fully inform the public about anthrax.

However, we have nearly 50 years of evidence on panic, and the conclusion is clear: people rarely panic, at least in the usual sense that word is used. Even when people feel "excessive fear"—a sense of overwhelming doom—they usually avoid "injudicious efforts" and "chaos." In particular, they are unlikely to cause harm to others as they reach for safety and may even put their own lives at risk to help others.

Panic Myths

Movies fuel the idea that people are quick to panic. *Independence Day, Armageddon* and *Earthquake in New York* are typical: people climb over friends, family and strangers to save themselves. The films suggest a tipping point beyond which people are so overcome with fear that they put self-interest over regard for others. After all, the reason we think it's wrong to yell "fire" in a crowded theater—even if the theater is on fire—is our assumption that the ensuing panic would cause more death than the fire itself. In Hollywood's depictions, panic strips away people's veneer of social responsibility to reveal raw selfishness.

Officials also perpetuate such images. Before the Y2K rollover, for example, politicians and business managers urged people not to overreact, not to panic, if there were software failures. Alan Greenspan, chair of the Federal Reserve Board, worried that people would rush to take their money out of banks. As the critical moment approached, John Koskinen, chair of the President's Commission on Year 2000 Conversion, became concerned less about failing machines than about panic: "As it becomes clear our national infrastructure will hold, overreaction becomes one of the biggest remaining problems."

Decision makers sometimes withhold information because they believe that panic will ensue. For example, during the nuclear incident at Three Mile Island, utility representatives failed to tell people and even government officials how serious the situation was because they were trying to "ease the level of panic and concern."

The general public probably holds this notion of panic, too. It is not unusual to read quotes from survivors of catastrophes—recall the World Trade Center survivor—in which people interpret the behavior of others, or even themselves, in terms of panic. What they are usually reporting, though, are feelings of fear and not panic-stricken behavior.

Panic Facts

Panicky behavior is rare. It was rare even among residents of German and Japanese cities that were bombed during World War II. The U.S. Strategic Bombing Survey, established in 1944 to study the effects of aerial attacks, chronicled the unspeakable horrors, terror and anguish of people in cities devastated by firestorms and nuclear attacks. Researchers found that, excepting some uncontrolled flight from the Tokyo firestorm, little chaos occurred.

An enormous amount of research on how people respond to extreme events has been done by the Disaster Research Center, now at the University of Delaware. After five decades studying scores of disasters such as floods, earthquakes and tornadoes, one of the strongest findings is that people rarely lose control. When the ground shakes, sometimes dwellings crumble, fires rage, and people are crushed. Yet people do not run screaming through the streets in a wild attempt to escape the terror, even though they are undoubtedly feeling terror. Earthquakes and tornadoes wreak havoc on entire communities. Yet people do not usually turn against their neighbors or suddenly forget personal ties and moral commitments. Instead the more consistent pattern is that people bind together in the aftermath of disasters, working together to restore their physical environment and their culture to recognize shapes.

Consider a few cases where we might have expected people to panic. The first, investigated by Norris Johnson, happened during Memorial Day weekend in 1977, when 165 people perished trying to escape a fire at the Beverly Hills Supper Club in Southgate, Kentucky. The supper club case recalls the fire-in-the-theater concept in which panic supposedly causes more deaths than the failure to escape in time.

Roughly 1,200 people were in the club's Cabaret Room, which had three exits. Two exits were to the side and led outdoors, and one was in the front and led to another part of the club. When the club's personnel, having discovered fire in the building, started telling customers to leave, a handful of people went to the front entrance while the others started filing calmly out of the other exits. However, the people who tried to get out of the front entrance soon ran into smoke and fire, so they returned to the Cabaret Room.

Survivors reported feeling frightened, but few acted out their fear. People were initially calm as they lined up at the two side exits, near which all of the deaths occurred. When smoke and fire started pouring into the Cabaret Room, some began screaming and others began pushing. As fire entered the room, some people jumped over tables and chairs to get out.

Notice what they did not do. They did not pick up those chairs and use them to strike people queued up in front of them. They did not grab their hair and shove them aside in a desperate rush to get out. They did not overpower those more helpless than themselves. They did not act blindly in their own self-interest. In Kentucky, few people acted out a panic. Indeed, had people developed a sense of urgency sooner, more would have gotten out and fewer would have died. Panic was probably not the the cause of any of the deaths. It is more accurate to say that the building layout was inadequate for emergencies. The second case, also researched by Johnson, happened in December 1979 at the Riverfront Coliseum (as it was then called) in Cincinnati, where 11 people were killed at a rock concert by The Who. The concertgoers were killed in a crush that was popularly perceived as a panic. The reality was far different. Approximately 8,000 people were waiting for the concert, but the building was not built to accommodate that many people waiting at once. After the doors opened, about 25 people fell. Witnesses say there was little panic. In fact, people tried to protect those who had fallen by creating a human cordon around them. But the push of the people behind was too strong. The crowd trampled the 25 people out of ignorance rather than panic. Like the Beverly Hills Club, Cincinnati's Riverfront Coliseum was not designed to fail gracefully. Users would be safe as long as they arrived in anticipated numbers and behaved in ways designers had anticipated.

Consider, also, the tragic flight of American Airlines 1420. In Little Rock, Arkansas, on June 1, 1999, Flight 1420 tried to land in a severe thunderstorm. As the pilots approached, they couldn't line the plane up with the runway and by the time they righted the craft they were coming in too fast and too hard. Seconds after the plane touched down, it started sliding and didn't stop until after lights at the end of the runway tore it open. The plane burst into flames, and 11 of the 145 aboard were killed.

The National Transportation Safety Board's "Survival Factors Factual Report" has more than 30 pages of survivor testimony. Most survivors who were asked about panic said there was none. Instead there were stories of people helping their spouses, flight attendants helping passengers, and strangers saving each other's lives. One fellow said that after the plane came to rest "panic set in." But his description of subsequent events doesn't look much like panic. Having discovered the back exit blocked, he found a hole in the fuselage. Then, "he and several men," says the report, "tried to pull the exit open further." He then allowed a flight attendant and "six to eight people" to get out before he did. Another passenger said that people panicked somewhat. But in his telling, too, people worked together to push an exit door open. He himself helped pick up a row of seats that had fallen atop a woman. As "smoke completely filled the cabin from floor to ceiling," people could barely see or breathe; yet they "were in a single file [and] there was no pushing and shoving." We would not expect that much order if everyone was panicking.

The same message rises from the rubble of the World Trade Center. Television showed images of people running away from the falling towers, apparently panic-stricken. But surely no one would describe their flight as evincing "excessive fear" or "injudicious effort." Some survivors told of people being trampled in the mass exodus, but those reports are unusual. More common are stories such as the one from an information architect whose subway was arriving underneath the Trade Center just as the first plane crashed. He found himself on the north side of the complex, toward the Hudson River: "I'm looking around and studying the people watching. I would say that 95 percent are completely calm. A few are grieving heavily and a few are running, but the rest were very calm. Walking. No shoving and no panic." We now know that almost everyone in the Trade Center Towers survived if they were below the floors where the airplanes struck. That is in large measure because people did not become hysterical but instead created a successful evacuation.

Absent a full survey of disasters, we do not have statistical evidence that chaotic panic is rare, but consider the views of E. L. Quarantelli, co-founder of the Disaster Research Center and a don of disaster research. He recently concluded (in correspondence to me) that "I no longer believe the term 'panic' should be treated as a social science concept. It is a label taken from popular discourse. . . . During the whole history of [our] research involving nearly 700 different field studies, I would be hard pressed to cite . . . but a very few marginal instances of anything that could be called panic behavior."

Panic Rules

That people in great peril usually help others, even strangers, seems to contradict common sense. It also contradicts the idea that people are naturally self-interested. If people are so self-regarding, why do they act altruistically when their very lives are at stake? One answer is that people sometimes act irrationally by going against what is in their best interests. From this view, the men on American Airlines Flight 1420 were not exercising sound judgment when they helped free the woman whose legs were pinned. They could have used the time to save themselves.

If cases like this were rare, it might be reasonable to call such behavior irrational. But they're not rare, and there is a better explanation of them than irrationality. When the World Trade Center started to burn, the standards of civility that people carried around with them every day did not suddenly dissipate. The rules of behavior in extreme situations are not much different from rules of ordinary life. People die the same way they live, with friends, loved ones and colleagues—in communities. When danger arises, the rule—as in normal situations—is for people to help those next to them before they help themselves. At the Supper Club fire and The Who concert, people first helped their friends and family. As we have seen, people help strangers. That's one of the big lessons from the World Trade Center. Such behavior seems odd only if we're all naturally selfish. Instead, an external threat can create a sense of 'we-ness' among those who are similarly threatened.

Disasters, like other social situations, have rules, and people generally follow them. They are not special rules, even though disasters are special situations. The rules are the same ones at work when the theater is not on fire. Human nature is social, not individually egoistic. People are naturally social, and calamities often strengthen social bonds.

Failing Gracefully

All of this is not to say that the stereotypic panic reactions never happen. Individuals do experience feelings of uncontrollable dread. The American Psychological Association says. 1 out of every 75 people might suffer a "panic attack," an overwhelming sense of fear that's out of proportion to a perceived threat or to no threat at all. We've all heard the post-September 11 stories about powdered milk being mistaken for anthrax. There are also occasional soccer stampedes and bona fide cases of uncontrolled flight. It would be folly to say that people are always sensible. There are overreactions to scares about witches, drugs and sex. Scholars dub such phenomena "moral panics," or overreactions that are governed by people's moral sensibilities rather than actual threat. Nonetheless, the panic of popular imagery is rare.

The myth of panic endures because it provides an easy explanation for complex things. For example, attributing the deaths at The Who concert to panic detracts the attention from an engineering failure (the building could not accommodate so many people waiting at once), a management failure (not forecasting the demand for entry into the concert) and an organizational failure (once the disaster began it could not be stopped). Or consider a soccer "stampede" in Ghana in 2001 in which 130 people were killed. Calling that event a panic would deflect attention away from the police who fired tear gas into a crowd of about 30,000 and from the fact that the exits were locked. The idea of panic works to blame the victims of a disaster, deflecting attention from the larger contexts of people's behavior.

An alternative to panic as an explanation of how people respond to disasters is the idea of failing ungracefully. In software engineering a system that fails "gracefully" can take discrete breakdowns without crashing the whole computer program. In the present context social relationships and artifacts (walls, machines, exits, etc.) no longer function as they were designed. Such conditions make collective panic more likely. U.S. air traffic control fails gracefully. A new procedure begun in 2000 tracks data so that if one component fails, another is immediately available; controllers do not panic because their monitoring systems are highly reliable. Modern elevator systems are designed to fail with grace. In January 2000, a cable on one of the Empire State Building's elevators broke, sending its occupant on a quick 40-story drop; but other safety systems kicked in to control the elevator's stop. An example of ungracefulness was the system of building football rally bonfires at Texas A&M University. When, in November 1999, that system started to fail, there was little to prevent loss of life and 12 were killed.

Not Panicking about Panic

Dispelling the myth of public panic highlights the sociality rather than the individuality of human nature. It leads to optimism about people. If people generally act well under the most trying circumstances—precisely when it would be easiest to turn their backs on others—it gives us reason to look for the good and the sensible in them at other times as well. Jettisoning the myth of public panic could also increase elites' trust of people. Politicians and corporate managers have a litany of responses after some mishap:

"There was never any danger to the public."

"Everything is under control."

"There is no reason for concern."

Behind such public pacifiers is the presumption that people cannot be trusted with bad news.

Communications based on that presumption generate distrust and suspicion. The U.S. Army is headed down that road. The Army is destroying America's stockpile of chemical weapons. Army representatives have asserted that none of the chemicals could be released into the environment. The Army has been wrong. There have been releases of mustard gas and of Sarin gas.

After the accidents Army representatives assured everyone that "there was no danger to the surrounding communities or to the environment." University of Arizona researchers found that a lot of people do not trust the U.S. Army's promises. The Army's attitude is one of public pacification; it assumes that people are prone to irrational panic. The problem is that in the event of a real hazardous mustard gas release, people may not trust what Army personnel have to say.

Before, during and after disasters, the "general public" warrants trust and respect. Panic is often used as a justification by high-level decision makers to deny knowledge and access to the public, on the presumption that people cannot handle bad news. Research on how people respond to life-threatening disasters and the stories from the World Trade Center show that people handle even the most terrifying news civilly and cooperatively. Our leaders would do well to see us a partners in recovery rather than as a "constituency" to be handled.

◎ ◎ ◎

Questions:

1. What does research reveal about how people usually behave in disasters? Do these findings surprise you? Why, or why not?
2. If so little evidence supports the belief that people panic during disasters, why do panic myths endure?
3. How do officials and decision makers inadvertently perpetuate panic myths?
4. Illustrate what Clarke means when he says, "Disasters, like other social situations, have rules, and people generally follow them."
5. Have you ever been in a disaster situation? If so, were your observations consistent with those described by Clarke?

How Will the Internet Change Society?

CONRAD L. KANAGY, Elizabethtown College

DONALD B. KRAYBILL, Messiah College

In this selection, Conrad Kanagy and Donald Kraybill ask us to ponder the Internet's impact on society. They not only reveal the Internet's effect on our culture through the emergence of virtual communities, but they argue that our participation in virtual communities is creating unique norms, rituals, and values. This article sheds light on the world of new possibilities offered by the Internet—and the potential problems that it may bring as well.

. . .

The first Internet exchanges occurred in November 1969 under the authority of the U.S. Department of Defense. The Internet was born as ARPANET, a worldwide network of computers linking a few university scientists, military personnel, and computer experts. ARPANET's purpose was to enhance U.S. military prowess in the Cold War against communism. Initial communication was formal and official, some users worried that personal e-mail messages might violate U.S. postal laws. But by the mid-1980s, ARPANET was linked to other networks. The change created near chaos, a "full-scale Mardi Gras parade." By 1990 ARPANET had been shut down, and private companies were overseeing activity in cyberspace.[1]

To many college students today, the Internet is a taken-for-granted part of the objective social world, just like cable TV and Nintendo.

"How Will the Internet Change Society?" by Conrad L. Kanagy and Donald B. Kraybill, reprinted from *The Riddles of Human Society*, 1999. Copyright © by Pine Forge Press. pp. 260–268.

They've grown up in a digital world. They've internalized expectations for high-speed communication on the Internet. They watch less television than their parents did, finding its old-fashioned pace too slow. They want technology they can interact with and control. The world has shrunk for these students; it lies at their fingertips.

Clearly, use of the Internet is changing our world. In fact, its effects might parallel the transformations brought about by the invention of the printing press. Both technologies expand exponentially the access of ordinary persons to information once held by experts and elites. Sociologists are beginning to develop a sociology of the Internet to study these social changes, and this subfield is likely to grow rapidly in the next several years.

Culture and the Internet

We already know a few things about the beliefs, norms, and values of Internet culture. For instance, social scientists have been debating for some time the reality of Internet communities, or virtual communities.*[2] Some have argued that such communities are little more than social networks, because they lack the typical characteristics of communities—things like residential proximity and economic dependence. However, digital technology has been pressing us to renovate some standard definitions, and the concept of community may be one of them. . . .

In the age of television, many bemoaned the loss of written text as a form of communication. Interestingly, text-based communication has returned on the Internet. The need for writing, reading, and critical expression are as great as, or greater than, ever. But electronic text is extemporaneous, transitory, and soon trashed, unlike the enduring works of Shakespeare and other classic writers.

---

*Eds. Note–Virtual communities are networks of relationships in which people identify with one another and share feelings for one another but don't share their physical selves or physical space. They share cyberselves and cyberspace.

A problem with text-based communication is the difficulty of expressing emotions and feelings. To counter this difficulty, many Internet users resort to "smileys," combinations of characters that symbolize emotional responses. (Examples . . . are presented in Figure 1.) Besides smileys, people communicating on the Internet are using some new forms of abbreviation and spelling, such as *jc* for "just curious," *bmf* for "biting my fingernails," *brb* for "be right back," *imho* for "in my humble opinion," and *lol* for "laughing out loud."

Internet norms, sometimes referred to as netiquette, are in the process of being defined.[3] Because of the rapid growth and fluidity of the Internet, ambiguity abounds about how people should behave in cyberspace. However, threats of censorship have hastened the development of some norms. Internet users are particularly concerned that outrageous behavior by some will prompt government agencies to censor the Internet. Certain legal norms probably will be defined

<table>
<tr><td>:-)</td><td>Smiling</td><td>;-(</td><td>Feel like crying</td></tr>
<tr><td>:-D</td><td>Laughing</td><td>:'-(</td><td>Crying</td></tr>
<tr><td>:-}</td><td>Grin</td><td>:-\</td><td>Undecided</td></tr>
<tr><td>:-(</td><td>Sad</td><td>}:(</td><td>Mad</td></tr>
<tr><td>:-||</td><td>Angry</td><td>;-)</td><td>Wink</td></tr>
<tr><td>:-P</td><td>Sticking tongue out</td><td>}}}}}}} :-)</td><td>Big hair</td></tr>
<tr><td>;-0</td><td>Flirt</td><td>d:-D</td><td>Baseball hat on</td></tr>
<tr><td>:-0</td><td>Astonished</td><td>&: (</td><td>Bad hair day</td></tr>
<tr><td>8-)</td><td>Wide-eyed or glasses</td><td>@@@:)</td><td>Marge Simpson</td></tr>
<tr><td>:-o</td><td>Shocked or amazed</td><td>*<{:O})</td><td>Santa Claus</td></tr>
</table>

Note: Turn page 90° to view smileys.

SOURCE: *Tapscott, 1998*

FIGURE 1 *Some "smileys" used in cyberspace to express feelings*

eventually. In addition, subcultural groups will undoubtedly develop their own particular norms, just as subcultures do in the real world.

What are the values of Internet users that will shape these norms? Don Tapscott, in *Growing Up Digital*, identifies several themes that are important to this subculture. For example, independence, free expression, and inclusion, which are core American values as well. These values are undoubtedly reinforced for Internet users by the freedom and diversity of Internet communication. Other cyberspace values, however, have been socially constructed and reinforced through electronic interaction.

- Openness characterizes Internet communication.
- Innovation created the Internet and continues to shape it.
- An investigative spirit is encouraged by the vast scope of the Internet wilderness.
- Immediacy is driven by the speed of Internet processing.
- Internet users, particularly the younger ones, are skeptical of corporate interests and the greed driving some efforts to shape Internet technology.
- Authenticity and trust are expected in the open environment of the Internet, where the cooperation of the parts (individuals) is needed to preserve the whole.[4]

Although several of these cyberculture values intersect with more traditional American values, others are relatively new and are likely to influence the cultural values of the larger society in years to come.

Social Structure and the Internet

The changes brought about by the Internet will accelerate as the number of youth who have been socialized into cyberculture grows. Some refer to this generation as the "net generation." These are the children of the baby boomers, the cohort born between 1945 and 1964, who now represent 29% of the U.S. population. The net generation, or "N-geners," born since 1977, comprise 30% of the U.S. population. The baby boomers represent the television generation, their children the digital generation. In their youth, many baby boomers sat staring at programs like "M*A*S*H," "The Brady Bunch," and "The Jeffersons." But N-geners controlled a host of interactive devices, such as Nintendo games and computers. For people who grew up with these technologies, their operation is second nature. The Internet will develop and become more influential as the people who grew up with it become a larger part of the population.

Two cohorts—baby boomers and N-geners—have unique intergenerational problems. In place of a generation gap, where the growing-up experiences of children and parents are simply different, we may have a "generation lap," as children outpace their parents in the race for technological knowledge. Young children often know much more than their parents about the computer. In one study by researchers at Carnegie Mellon University, children were the heaviest computer users in a large majority of families. Two-thirds of children in another survey said they are more proficient on the computer than their parents. In Finland, 5,000 N-geners teach computing to the country's teachers.[5] The "generation lap" turns typical patterns of socialization upside down: The parents, who typically teach their children, are now learning from them. As a result, children and youth have become the gatekeepers of technology and information for their families, teachers, and supervisors. This generational shift means that some entry-level employees will have greater skills and knowledge in some areas than their supervisors, managers, and administrators.

The new generation gap has four themes:

- Older people are anxious about the new technology being embraced by youth.
- Older people are uneasy about the new media, such as the Internet, which are part of everyday life among youth.
- Older media (newspapers, radio, television) are apprehensive about the newer media.

- The digital revolution, unlike previous revolutions, is not completely controlled by adults.[6]

Reconciliation between baby boomers and N-geners may lie in the willingness of N-geners to share their knowledge and the humility of baby boomers to receive it.

The digital revolution may create other structural fault lines as well. Some fear that computer technology will exacerbate the existing divide between rich and poor. In fact, only 7% of low-income households have a computer, while among those making more than $50,000 a year, 53% have a computer. Thus economic poverty leads to information poverty, which leads to even greater economic poverty. In addition, racial discrimination in society leads to racial discrimination in media and technology access.[7] Blacks are two-thirds less likely to have a computer than whites, and two-thirds of white students have used the Web as opposed to fewer than half of black students.[8] On the brighter side, the Internet has the potential to equalize without regard to race, sex, or economics. Students in poor, inner-city schools could have access equal to those in wealthy, suburban schools. The challenge for the government and for educators is to ensure such equality. Whether in the final analysis the Internet will increase or diminish social inequality remains to be seen.

Structural differences in technology use also occur in the global arena. . . . Developed and developing countries differ substantially in their resources. Information technology will probably heighten those differences. In 1996, 66% of households connected to the Internet were in North America. Even developed countries in Western Europe fall behind the United States in Internet access and use. At the same time, the Internet has the potential to democratize political systems around the world, by giving everyone equal access to information, regardless of cultural or political boundaries. The Internet makes possible the development of a truly global culture, where children in Hong Kong can learn the same information as children in Papua New Guinea. They can also learn about each other.

Ritual and the Internet

Although some social divisions are sharpened by digital technology, the Internet levels the playing field for individuals communicating through e-mail, chat rooms, bulletin boards, and discussion lists. The only symbols of communication are written words; facial expressions, voice intonations, hand gestures, and physical appearance are gone. The context of each individual's social world—family life, occupation, income, residence—is minimized. Such decontextualization* is quite different from the high context of face-to-face interaction, where we can see the person. The decontextualized nature of Internet culture is the opposite of, say, Amish life, which is a high-context culture that values face-to-face interaction and knowledge of everyone in the community. In a high context culture, social actors know many background details of each other—home, habits, lifestyle, friends, and work. Conversation is embedded in this rich social context.

On the Internet, everyone is alike. The decontextualized space of the Internet brings a new openness in communication and weakens the features that often lead to discrimination and prejudice. People with disabilities, who usually face discrimination can interact without the scorn of prejudice. Age, beauty, size, body odor, color of hair and eyes, and facial hair lose their power. Labels, stereotypes, and stigmas disappear.

In Goffman's terms, on the Internet the frontstage is the same for everyone, without the typical props, signals, sounds, and appearances of social life. Individuals can create any frontstage that they wish. It may not be real, but who will ever know? Said one 14-year-old: "I'd have to say I'm very shy unless I know a person very well. This doesn't happen though in cyberspace. On the Net, I am one of

---

*Decontextualization is the loss of identifiable social landmarks in human interaction. In a decontextualized social world like the Internet, we don't have the contextual knowledge—the other person's facial expressions and gestures, a physical setting such as a home or office, and the other person's friends or family—that we usually use to interpret our interaction.

the most outgoing people I know. Probably why I spend so much time there."[9]

In general, we all have greater control over disclosure and our presentation of self on the Internet than in other social contexts. If we dislike someone, we can break off the communication without serious consequences, especially if we have kept our identity disguised. We'll likely never see the other person, and if we do, we won't recognize each other.

Relationships on the Internet are often disposable, fragile, and superficial. At the same time, however, they can be deeply intimate and personal, because so much contextual baggage is left behind. Some of the values of N-geners arise from these characteristics of ritual interaction on the internet.[10]

Decontextualized interaction on the Internet poses some interesting dilemmas, which some voice as concerns:

- Individuals can enter chat rooms or post messages on bulletin boards using multiple identities. Some deliberately create artificial identities to deceive unsuspecting individuals. On-line romances have occasionally resulted in fraud or homicide. Children can be manipulated and harmed by menacing adults.[11]
- Another danger is Internet addiction, sometime called "netomania" or "on-lineaholism." Some view this condition as a symptom of a psychiatric disorder; others see it as a disorder in its own right.[12] One analyst, Kimberly Young, has written a self-help guide called *Caught in the Net* to aid those who abandon family, friends, and work to be on-line. She believes up to 5 million Internet users may be addicted.[13] Examples of those with symptoms of Internet addiction include a 31-year-old man who spent more than 100 hours a week on-line, ignoring others and stopping only for sleep. In another case, a 21-year-old college student disappeared, only to be found in the computer lab hooked on seven consecutive days of on-line chat. Some individuals with Internet addiction have reported an average of five psychiatric disorders, including manic-depressive disorder, social phobia,

bulimia or binge eating, impulse-control problems, and substance abuse.[14]

- Some experts fear that N-geners are losing their social skills. Others are concerned about the short attention span that N-geners may develop through overexposure to interactive communication. Some fear the Internet is stressing children and spreading them too thin. Others worry about the cruelty that children may experience on the Internet. Some argue that the opportunity to create one's own homepage leads to vanity—an artificially heightened self-esteem.[15]

All these issues raise a host of ethical questions for an Internet society. How much freedom should Internet users have? How much control should the government and other social institutions exert? Is it ethical to change one's identity on-line? When is on-line deception potentially harmful to individuals and society? Is Internet addiction harmful? Should we have Internet police to regulate activity in chat rooms and discussion groups? Should individuals be held accountable for everything they write on the Internet? How much further will the Internet renovate social relations?

Summary: Internet

Because the development of the Internet is relatively new, we can't really consider its renovation yet. But the recent development of the Internet provides a fascinating opportunity to watch a culture being constructed from scratch.

The construction of the Internet reflects to some extent the cultural norms and structural division of the larger society. The Internet has the potential, however, to make the same information available to everyone, regardless of race, class, education, occupation, or residence.

The rituals of interaction on the Internet are still being shaped. It is a decontextualized environment where we can minimize everyday prejudices by carefully controlling the presentation of self. We can remain relatively anonymous while still being intimate. We can create relationships with few obligations but with high levels of authenticity.

It remains to be seen whether the Internet will remain a communication medium of the middle and upper classes or whether, like television, it will override class lines and serve the masses.

. . .

Endnotes

[1]Diamond, E., & Bates, S. (1995). The ancient history of the Internet, *American Heritage, 46*, 34–41.

[2]Reingold, H. (1993). *Virtual communities: Homesteading on the electronic frontier.* New York: Harper Perennial, p. 5.

[3]For an on-line description of netiquette, see <http://rs6000.adm.fau.edu/rinaldi/netiquette.html>. Another valuable resource, titled "A Primer on How to Work with the Usenet Community," is available through the news group news.announce.newusers, with the archive name usernet/primer/part1.

[4]A substantial part of our discussion of the Internet is based on Tapscott, D. (1998). *Growing up digital.* New York: McGraw-Hill.

[5]Tapscott, D. (1998). *Growing up digital.* New York: McGraw-Hill.

[6]Tapscott, D. (1998). *Growing up digital.* New York: McGraw-Hill.

[7]Tapscott, D. (1998). *Growing up digital.* New York: McGraw-Hill.

[8]World White Web. (1998, April 27). *Time.*

[9]Tapscott, D. (1998). *Growing up digital.* New York: McGraw-Hill.

[10]Tapscott, D. (1998). *Growing up digital.* New York: McGraw-Hill.

[11]Tapscott, D. (1998). *Growing up digital.* New York: McGraw-Hill.

[12]Tapscott, D. (1998). *Growing up digital.* New York: McGraw-Hill.

[13]Kiernan, V. (1998, May 29) Some scholars question research methods of expert on Internet addiction. *The Chronicle of Higher Education.*

[14]Ritter, M. (1998, June 2). *Associated Press.*

[15]Tapscott, D. (1998). *Growing up digital.* New York: McGraw-Hill.

References

Diamond, E., & Bates, S. (1995). *American Heritage, 4,* 34–41.

Reingold, H. *Virtual communities: Homesteading on the electronic frontier.* New York: Harper Perennial.

Tapscott, D. (1998). *Growing up digital: The rise of the net generation.* New York: McGraw-Hill.

Questions

1. What is a virtual community? What are some norms and values of virtual communities?
2. What is the "generation lap"? How does it affect our social interactions?
3. In what ways does the Internet "level the playing field" for those who have access to it? Give an example of how this leveling effect is relevant in your own life.
4. Why can we say that what occurs on the Internet occurs "front stage"?
5. Compare your knowledge and use of the Internet to that of your parents. What factors have influenced your use of the Internet?